IMAGES
of America

LOWER COAST OF ALGIERS

On the Cover: This image of the Second Baptist Church male chorus was taken after a groundbreaking service for the Baptist Faith Home in the 1950s. This talented group of men was invited to join in a service with Reverend Earl and Lillian Green, who accompany them in the photograph. (Courtesy of Leroy "Royal" Phoenix.)

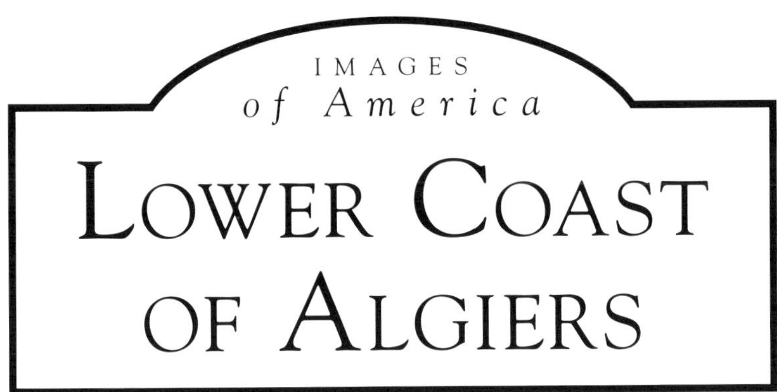

Dari L. Green, PhD, and Robin Crawford
Foreword by Coach Frank Wilson III

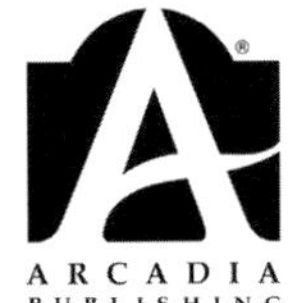

ISBN 978-1-4671-2837-7

Published by Arcadia Publishing
Charleston, South Carolina

Printed in the United States of America

Library of Congress Control Number: 2017957380

For all general information, please contact Arcadia Publishing:
Telephone 843-853-2070
Fax 843-853-0044
E-mail sales@arcadiapublishing.com
For customer service and orders:
Toll-Free 1-888-313-2665

Visit us on the Internet at www.arcadiapublishing.com

In memory of Caesar Ruffin Sr., Herbert Sullen Sr., and Taza Green Sr.

Contents

Foreword

Of the many parts of Louisiana that are written about, New Orleans's Westbank, the Cut-Off in particular, holds a very special place in my heart. I am the product of several generations of proud, prayerful, hardworking people who rank God, family, and community as the cornerstones of their daily life.

My mother's family, the Sullens, are bedrocks of this great community. My grandfather Herbert Sullen, upon his return from the war, helped establish basic necessities like running water and electricity for this newly developing neighborhood. He and his wife, Rebecca, provided a real source of stability and honor within the families of our small but strong community. Growing up, living, and learning on a street named after our family was a source of huge pride. My generation, our peers, and our children are of the best and brightest that this small town has produced. The coauthor of this book, Dari Green, is part of that rich lineage. She's the first grandchild of Gail Sullen and Frank Wilson Jr. She's my first niece, a doctor, a mother, a scholar, and a product of this place we affectionately call the Cut-Off.

Our stories have been passed down through at least four generations and have provided us a foundation that has sustained most of us in the toughest of times. We're from a people that are considered the salt of the earth. This holy ground and the unique spirit that dwells here are part of our core, and we can't escape it. This essence has instilled a measure of immense pride and esteem that is not lost on us. It was this area of land where free blacks lived during the turbulent times of segregation. Those ancestors were not sharecroppers or slaves, but free! We honor them and remember their love for education, community building, and family.

I know you will enjoy this pictorial view of our birthplace. I'm happy to be the person to open this book with you. In all that I do, in all of my life's successes, I take the lessons from the Cut-Off with me. It is one of my greatest sources of inspiration and self-worth. This is a place where truly everyone is family. With this book, my hope is that you, too, will enjoy a glimpse of our joy and the values we treasure most. We are, after all, naturally New Orleans!

—Coach Frank Wilson III

Acknowledgments

This publication was made possible as a result of the contributions made by members of the Lower Coast of Algiers community. Many members of the community shared their photograph collections, time, and memories with us, and for that, we are grateful. We would like to give special thanks to Charlie Benn Jr., Catherine Brickley, Altar Butler, Mabel Jones, Gail Langford, Bevelyn Manuel, Doris Phoenix, Royal Phoenix, Schelander Phoenix, Henry Price Jr., Kathleen Robertson, Enola Rose, Wesley Ruffin Jr., Evelyn Waters, Dena Watkins, and Gregory Wilson for their valuable contributions.

We would also like to extend a special thank-you to Dr. Lori Martin of the African and African American Studies program at Louisiana State University for her initial endorsement of this project.

Finally, we thank our families, friends, and community for their support. While this single book is incapable of telling each member of the community's story in its entirety, we are hopeful that this is an accurate, positive, and comprehensive representation of the Cut-Off. We tried our best to reach as many residents in the community as possible and apologize to anyone that we may have missed who desired to contribute to this collection of photographs.

INTRODUCTION

The Algiers neighborhood is the second-oldest neighborhood in Orleans Parish. It is the only community that is considered to be a part of New Orleans that is located on the west bank of the Mississippi River. The Cut-Off community, located in the Lower Coast of Algiers, has been in existence for more than a century. This book is the first formally published pictorial history with text about the area. Historically isolated by the natural barrier of the Mississippi River and the swamp and forestlands that once separated it from the rest of "civilization," the Cut-Off, once called the Puissant subdivision by locals, was a community affectionately named so by members of the community for both its seclusion and inclusion.

Originally made up of only five streets, the area known as the Cut-Off community is still served by its churches, schools, and neighborhood businesses—as it has been for decades. The story of the Cut-Off is like that of many African American communities: it has seen the best of times and the worst of times. Presented through themes of historic faith-based institutions, community leaders, businesses and landmarks, schools, and residential development, Images of America: *Lower Coast of Algiers* focuses on the people who shaped the Cut-Off community spiritually, culturally, politically, economically, and socially.

African slaves were imported to Algiers, which had many slave pens during the 18th century, to allow for their recovery after a long trek across the Atlantic Ocean. Before slaves were shipped and sold off in the French Quarter, they were often housed in the Algiers neighborhood. Sometimes, slaves were sold to plantations in the local area as well. Some slaves served at Aurora plantation, which at one time had over 1,400 acres of sugarcane and cotton. Others served on Stanton plantation, which was the largest sugar mill in Orleans Parish, with a daily capacity of 500 tons. The Civil War brought great change for populations of enslaved people in the area, as warehouses and goods were set afire by Confederate troops.

After the Civil War ended in 1865, slaves were freed and moved from local plantations such as Stanton, Aurora, Ganascheau, Norman, and Point Beka and established many different communities of their own. Some settled in portions of Algiers known as Freetown and McDonoughville. Others moved down into a more secluded area in the lower coast, which came to be known as the Cut-Off. Even after being emancipated, some members of the community continued to participate in sharecropping on plantations. On Stanton plantation, in particular, individuals would still pick tomatoes, mulch, rice, and sugarcane even into the 1900s. After a category 4 hurricane hit the area on September 25, 1915, flooding the plantation, there was another huge migration of people into different areas of town. This led more people and institutions to move into the Lower Coast of Algiers.

From its origin until the late 1950s, residents in the Cut Off community struggled to have streets paved, running water, and electricity. Individuals in the neighborhood walked along gravel roads to get wood to make fires and often walked to the river to draw water. For many years, there was no heating systems or indoor plumbing. Round, steel basin tubs and scrub boards were used to wash clothes; kerosene lamps were used for lighting; and iceboxes were used to refrigerate their food for a long time after modern amenities had been introduced to other parts of the area. Outsiders often mocked residents' dialect and language, a patois of sorts that many outsiders were unfamiliar with. The locals' distance from other parts of town and deep desire for self-sufficiency made them a mysterious people in the eyes of many.

The Cut-Off has undergone many changes from its humble beginnings as a small village until now. This collection of photographs tells the story of the people and places of the Lower Coast of Algiers from the 19th to 21st centuries. The photographs that are displayed in this work were taken by amateurs and professionals alike, with the majority of the images being provided by members of the community. The people who are portrayed in this collection often invested their lives into seeing the community become a better place. For that, we remember them by presenting photographs once shared only in the privacy of family homes and relating their stories to a much broader audience.

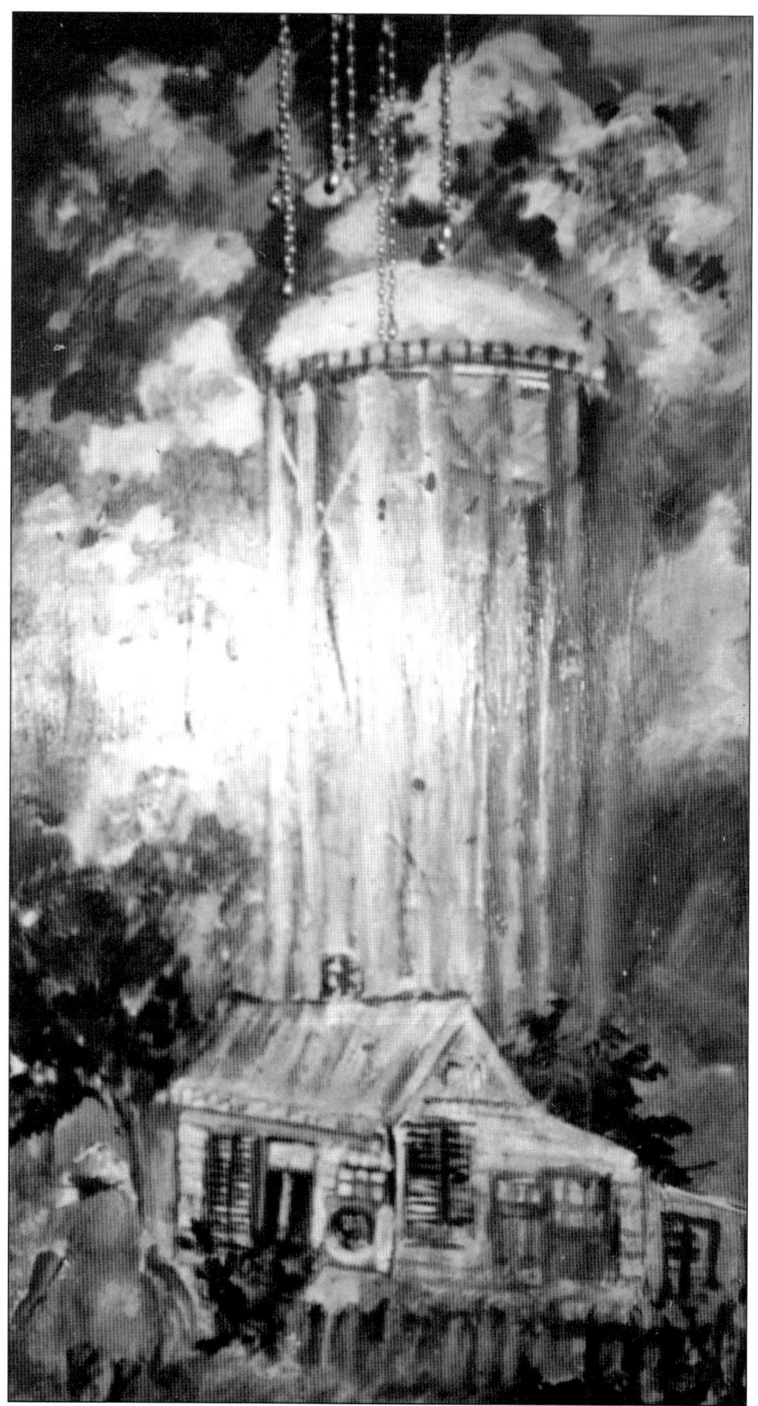

This painting is of Etienne Brooks Jr.'s home, which sat just beneath the water tower in the Lower Coast of Algiers. This image is a great representation of the community and its heritage, as it depicts the central landmark of the area: the water tower. It also offers a great representation of an original Cut-Off home, which people in the area pride themselves on having always owned outright. The artist is unknown. (Courtesy of Robin Crawford.)

One

Pioneering Families and Community Leaders

Sticks in a Bundle are Unbreakable

Prior to Reconstruction, the Lower Coast of Algiers was an area made up predominantly of farms, dairies, and citrus groves that were worked by slaves and sharecroppers. The farmland and pastures in the area changed drastically after the conclusion of the Civil War when newly freed slaves moved from these plantations and began to create communities of their own. This chapter examines those pioneering families and community leaders in the area. By pioneering families, the authors mean those individuals of African descent who developed the Cut-Off community.

Prior to its development as the Cut-Off, the Lower Coast of Algiers was a subdivision that sat beside what was known as Public Road. Judah P. Benjamin, a Jewish Confederate lawyer, politician, and owner of several plantations in the area, had difficulty moving quickly from one plantation to the next without having to travel around the River Road. He later had the Public Road cleared to create a shorter distance. The area that eventually became the Cut-Off, located along Public Road, was owned at the time by an Italian family whom many in the area called "the Puissants." In the French language, *puissant* literally means "powerful" or "strong," but many Africans also used it as a family name for the white landowners.

As the story goes, the Puissant family, particularly the woman of the household, was very empathetic towards people of African descent. This angered many Europeans in the area. Mrs. Puissant began to sell off small plots of land to blacks for $25 and $30. Some folks attempted to attack her because of this, but somehow Rev. Reason Boyd was able to intervene, which she believed saved her life. As a result, she rewarded him with land from one end of Common Street to the other. From there, the population continued to grow in number.

Eventually, the area was made up of a majority of African Americans who brought a new culture to the space, making it one of their very own. The original settlers in the small village that were of African descent included the Benn, Boyd, Green, Ross, and Rose families. From these families grew most of the population that resided in the area. Filled with faith and determination, the descendants of these people went on to be leaders of the community, enacting change within the community and fighting for systemic change on a much broader scale.

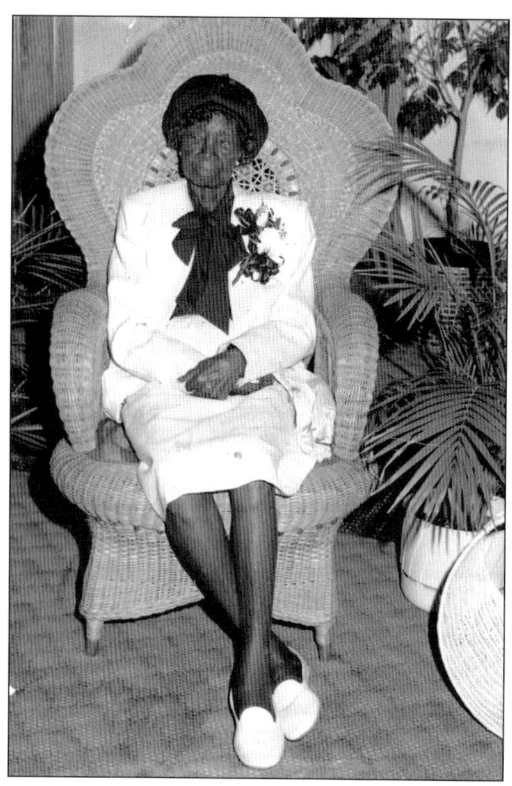

Orelia "Mama Felo" Johnson was born May 15, 1889. Orelia, a matriarch in the community, was known as the "Gumbo Queen." After baptism services, Mama Felo was known to cook a huge pot of gumbo for the community. She became so well known for her talents, disc jockeys on the radio would even recognize her. She died at the age of 100 on April 26, 1990. (Courtesy of Robin Crawford.)

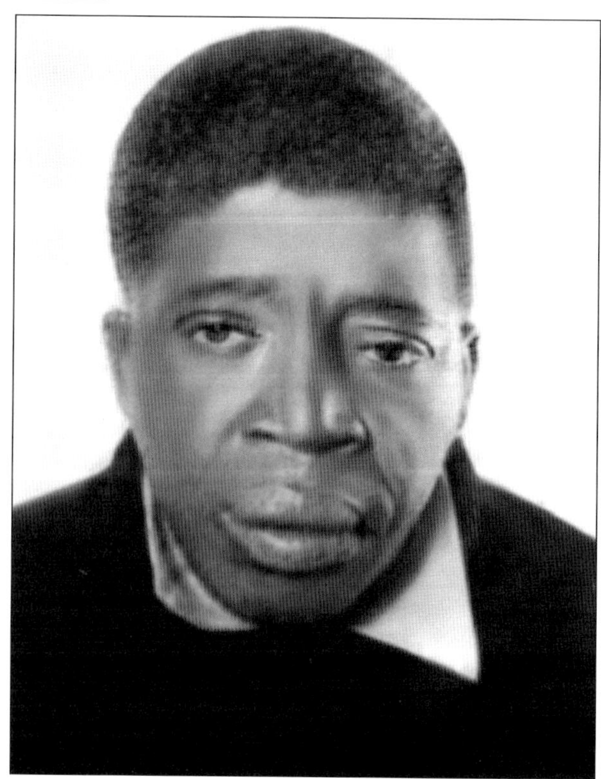

Lawrence Johnson was born in 1896. Lawrence was the husband of Orelia Johnson. He worked as a longshoreman on the riverfront. (Courtesy of Robin Crawford.)

Stella Young-Henry was born August 18, 1912. She was reared by her aunt Estelle and uncle William Johnson. Stella married Robert Henry Sr. and 18 children (9 boys and 9 girls) were added to their union. (Courtesy of Robin Crawford.)

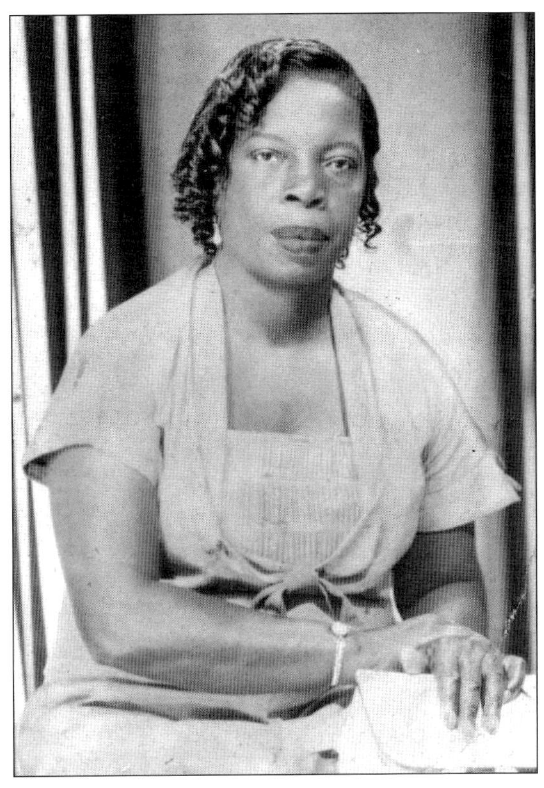

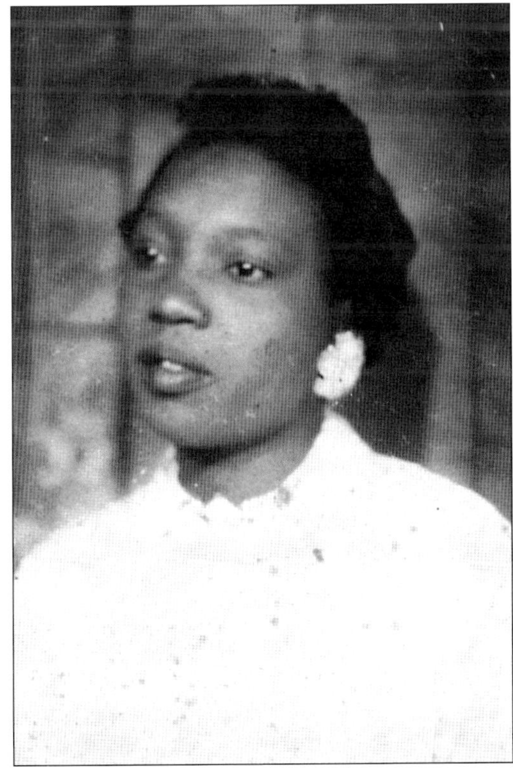

Evelina Johnson was born September 17, 1927, to Orelia and Lawrence Johnson Sr. A resident of the Lower Coast of Algiers, Evelina was very well known in the area for her talent as a beautician. (Courtesy of Robin Crawford.)

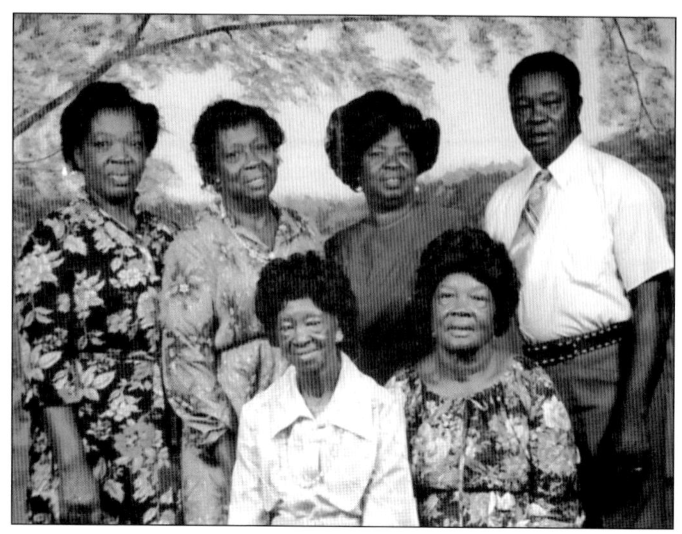

Orelia "Mama Felo" Johnson is pictured with her family. She is seated with her daughter Olivia L. Ruffin. Standing are, from left to right, Alberta J. Franklin, Sophie Y. Charles, Mary J. Johnson, and Dood Johnson Sr. She instilled in her children "to always to show love and love will return back to you." Though they are all now deceased, her legacy and motto are still remembered in the community. (Courtesy of Robin Crawford.)

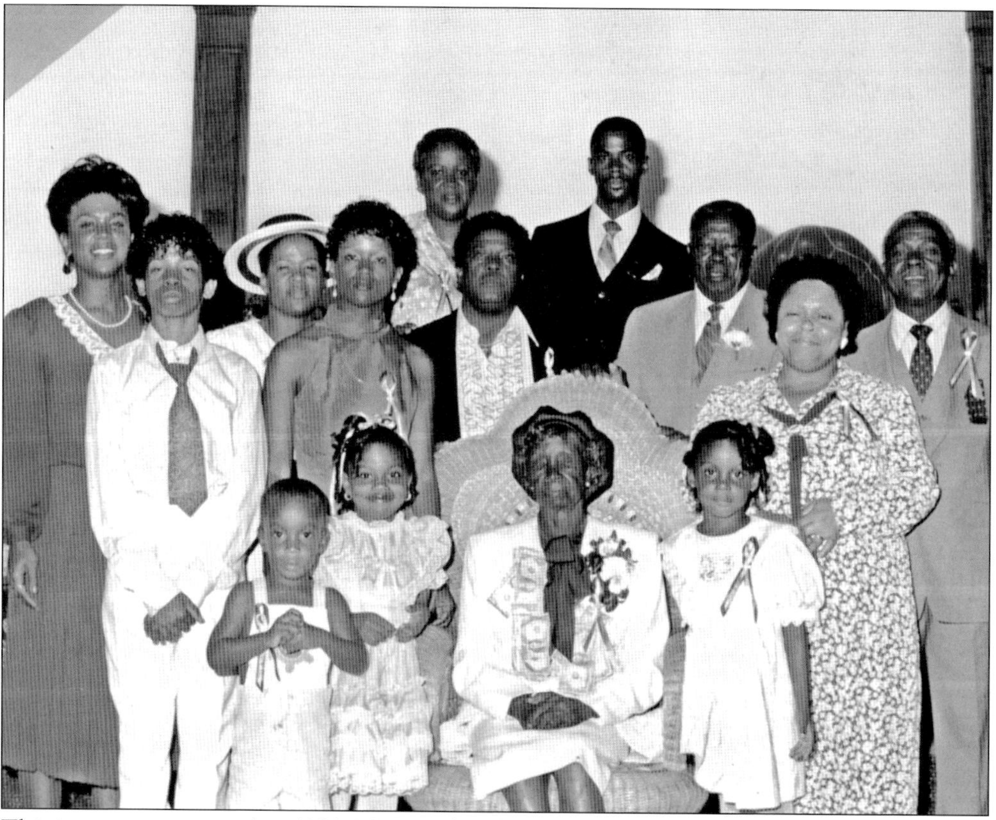

This image was captured in 1989. Mama Felo Johnson is joined by her family during her 100th birthday celebration at the Four Columns. Pictured are, from left to right, (first row) DeShaun Johnson, Shontrell Johnson, Mama Felo and Danyell Johnson; (second row) Shawn Johnson, Wanda J. Jackson, Dood Johnson Jr., Dood Johnson Sr., Barbara C. Johnson, and Lawrence Johnson Sr. (third row): Debra J. Young, Robin J. Crawford, Ernestine H. Johnson, and Dood Johnson III. (Courtesy of Robin Crawford.)

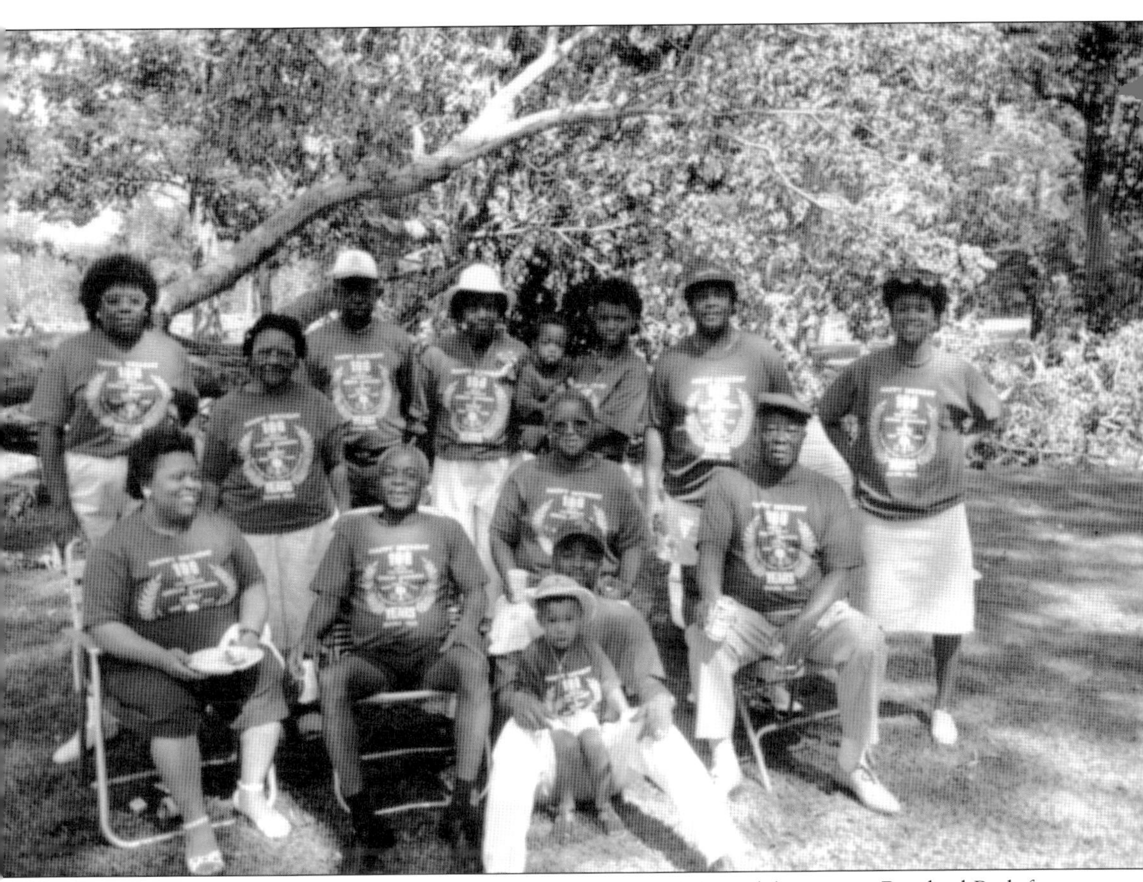

Dood Johnson Sr. is pictured during an informal 100th birthday celebration at Brechtel Park for his mother, Orelia. He is pictured with several members of her family. They are, from left to right, (first row) Perry Johnson Jr., Perry Johnson Sr.; (second row) Barbara Cook, Lawrence Johnson Sr., Ernestine Johnson, Dood Johnson Sr., Debra J. Young, Dood Johnson Jr., Tracy Ford (holding his son Desmond Johnson), Mathilda B. Cook, and three other unidentified persons. (Courtesy of Robin Crawford.)

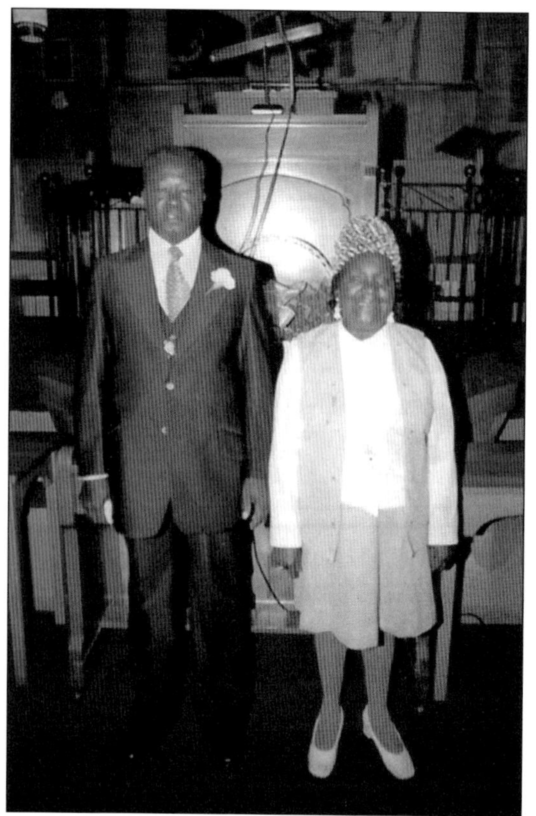

Dolly and Dood Johnson Sr. were natives of the Lower Coast of Algiers community. Dolly attended Second Nazarene Baptist Church, where she was active in the senior choir. Dolly was a quiet woman but never minded sharing what she had with others, especially if this meant her grandchildren over for a visit. (Courtesy of Robin Crawford.)

Dood Johnson Sr. was born December 16, 1918. He is pictured in this image with his sons Lawrence and Dood Johnson Jr. Dood Sr. worked as a longshoreman for much of his life. Dood's first marriage was to Della Johnson-Johnson, who served as an usher at Second Baptist Church. Della passed away in 1958, leaving Dood a widower. (Courtesy of Robin Crawford.)

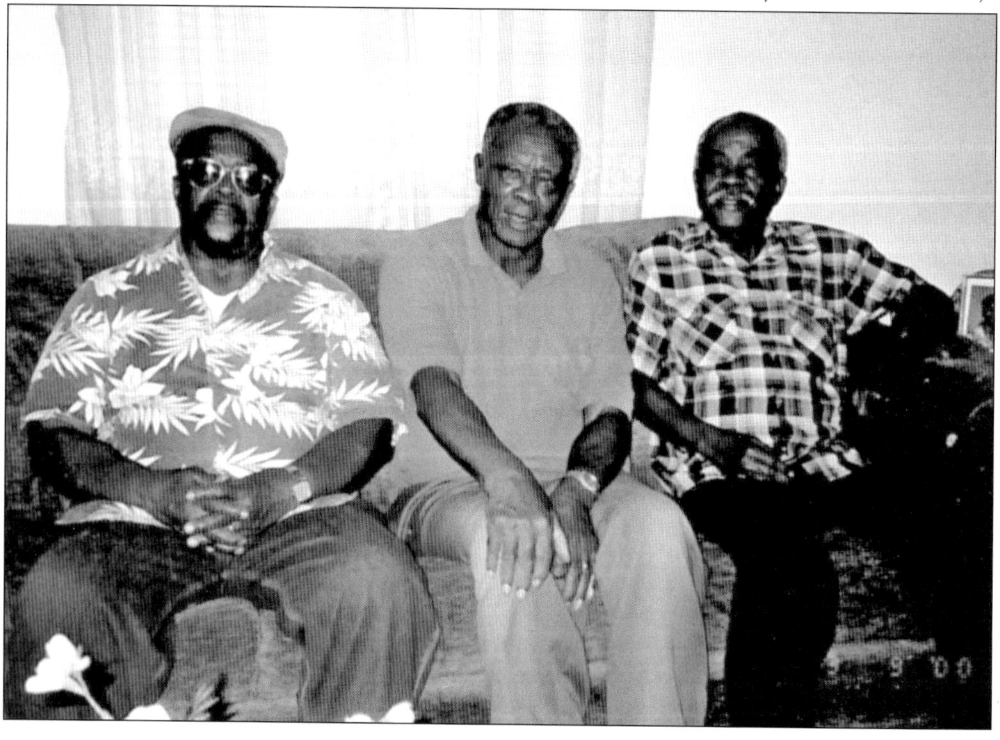

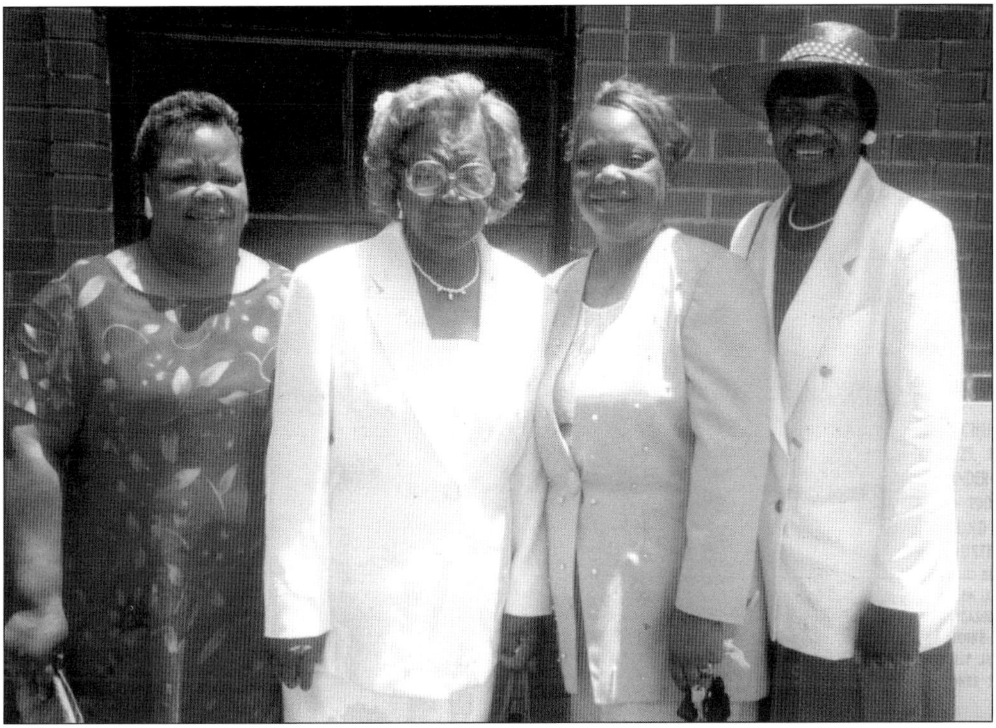

Alberta Johnson-Franklin (second from left) was born September 1, 1921. Franklin is pictured here with her daughters—from left to right, Carolyn Ross, Joel Stemley, and Alberta Taylor—after church services. Franklin was a founding member of the Lower Coast of Algiers Senior Citizen Center that began on April 13, 1973. She was a deaconess in the church who loved to cook and welcomed everyone to her home, much like her mother, Mama Felo. (Courtesy of Robin Crawford.)

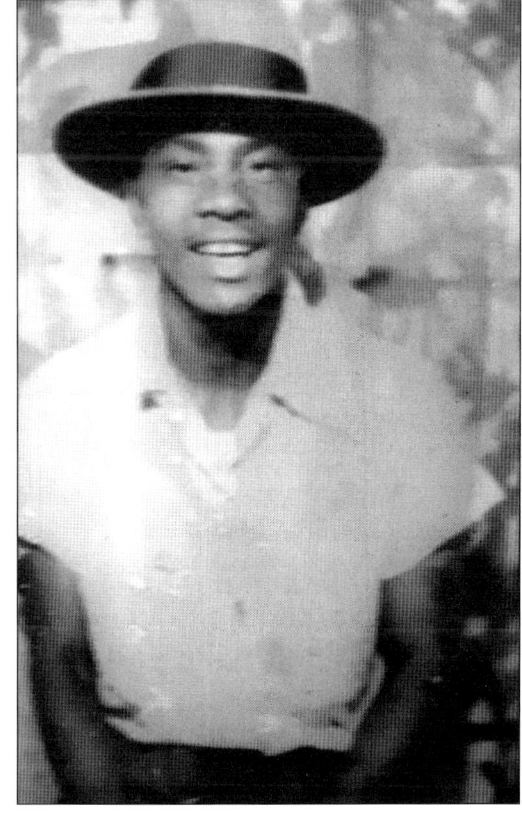

Dood Johnson Jr. was born April 3, 1937. Dood is pictured in attire typical of the fashion styles of the late 1940s. (Courtesy of Robin Crawford.)

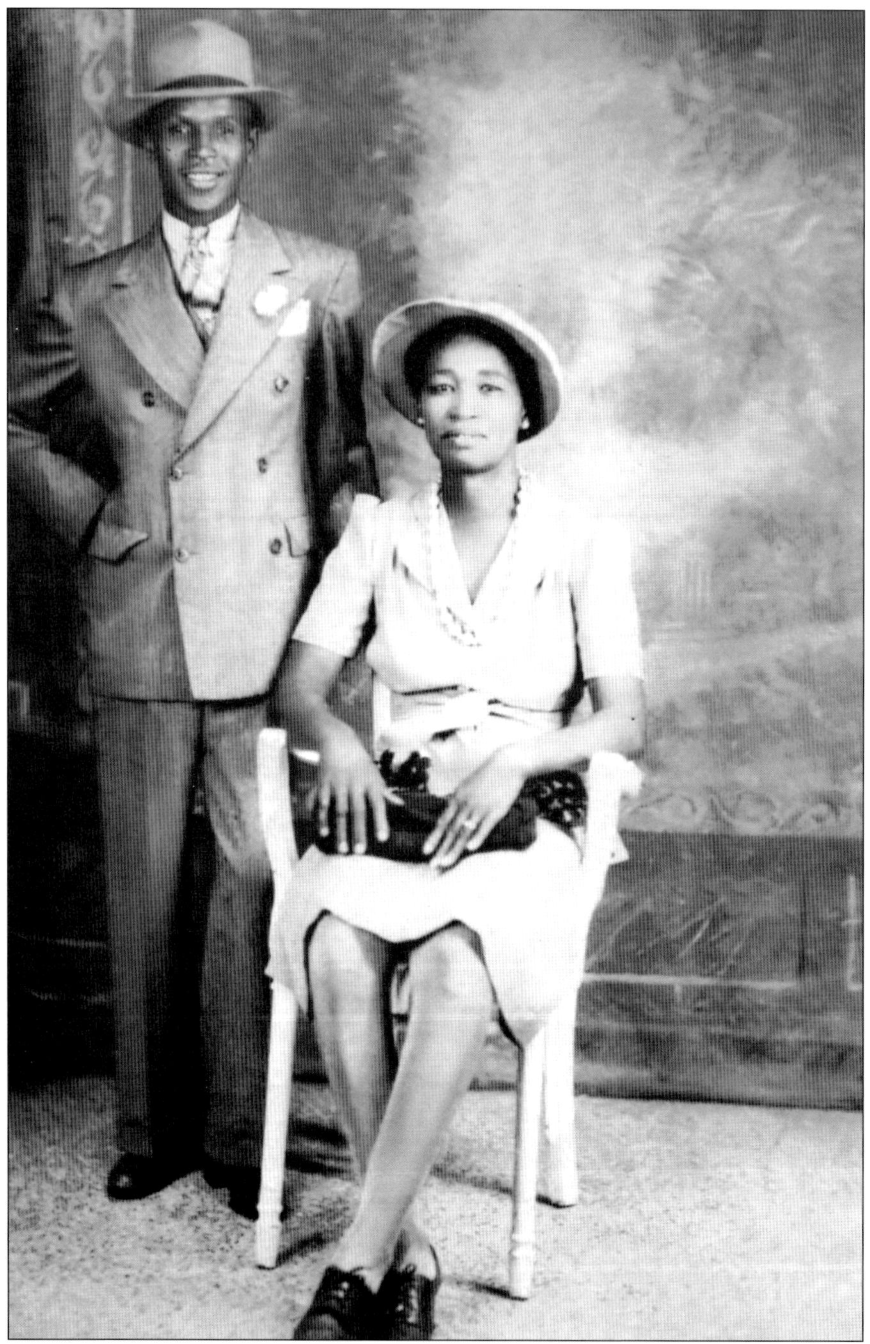

Ernestine and Clarence Henry Sr., both natives of the Lower Coast of Algiers, moved to the east bank in the 1930s and resided at the intersection of Conti and Liberty Streets. Clarence worked for the Pullman Brothers and Ernestine was a homemaker. Clarence also pursued entrepreneurship, owning his own snowball stand and roasting peanuts to sell to the crowds gathered on Canal Street during Mardi Gras. Clarence had a knack for music and could play any stringed instrument. In 1947, they returned to the Lower Coast of Algiers, where they raised each of their children. (Courtesy of Robin Crawford.)

Debra J. Young (left), Robin J. Crawford (center), and Wanda J. Jackson are pictured in front of the home of their parents on April 24, 1984. The family gathered together after church service on this Resurrection Sunday. They, like many members in the community, took great pride in maintaining close family bonds and still share in many of these activities. Crawford and Jackson remain deeply connected to the community. Young passed from this life in September 1996. (Courtesy of Robin Crawford.)

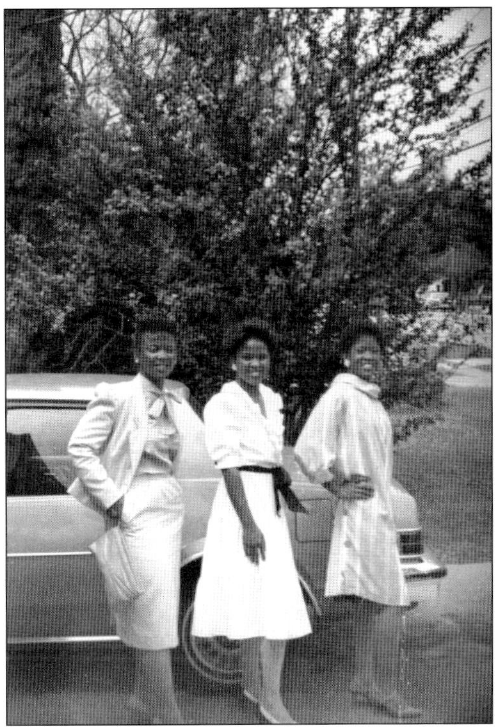

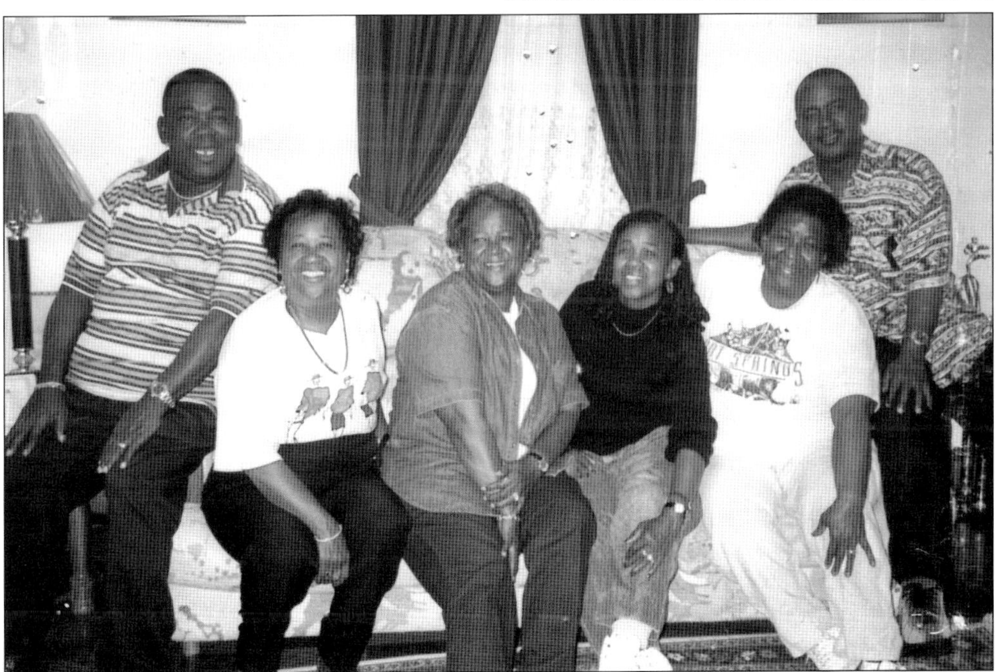

This photograph includes the children of Ernestine and Clarence Henry. Pictured are, from left to right, Clarence Jr., Lizzie, Ernestine, Corinne, Doris, and John Henry. On January 1, 1947, their parents moved back to the Lower Coast of Algiers community. Each of the children has maintained ties to the community, with most remaining residents for over 70 years. (Courtesy of Robin Crawford.)

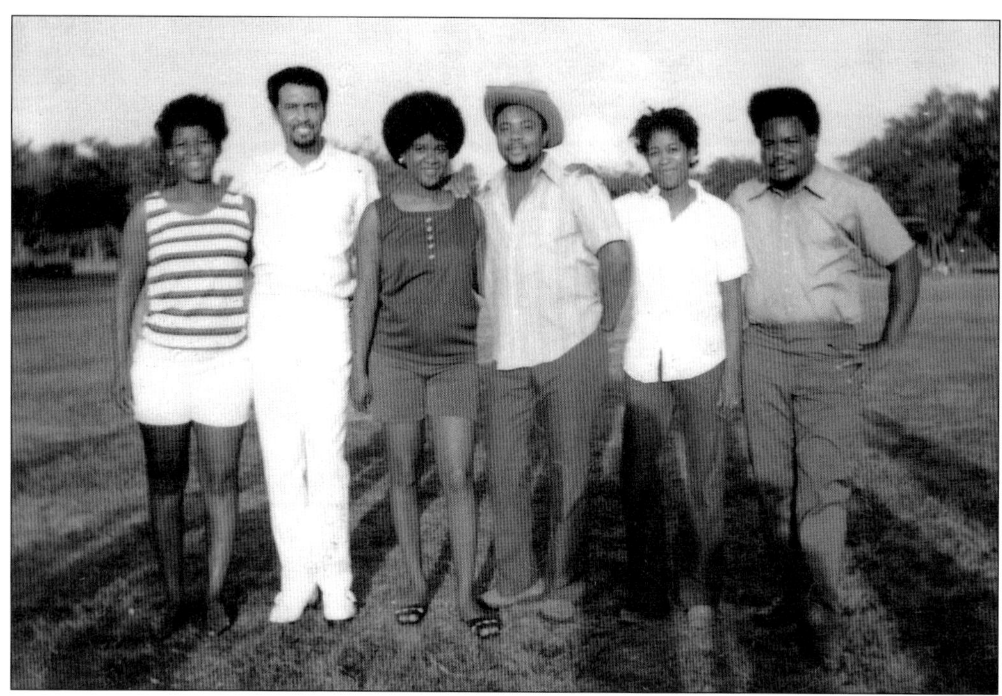

Pictured are, from left to right, Doris and Huey Madison Sr., Ernestine and Dood Johnson Jr., Lizzie Charles, and Lewis Jackson at Ponderosa Park in 1971. (Courtesy of Robin Crawford.)

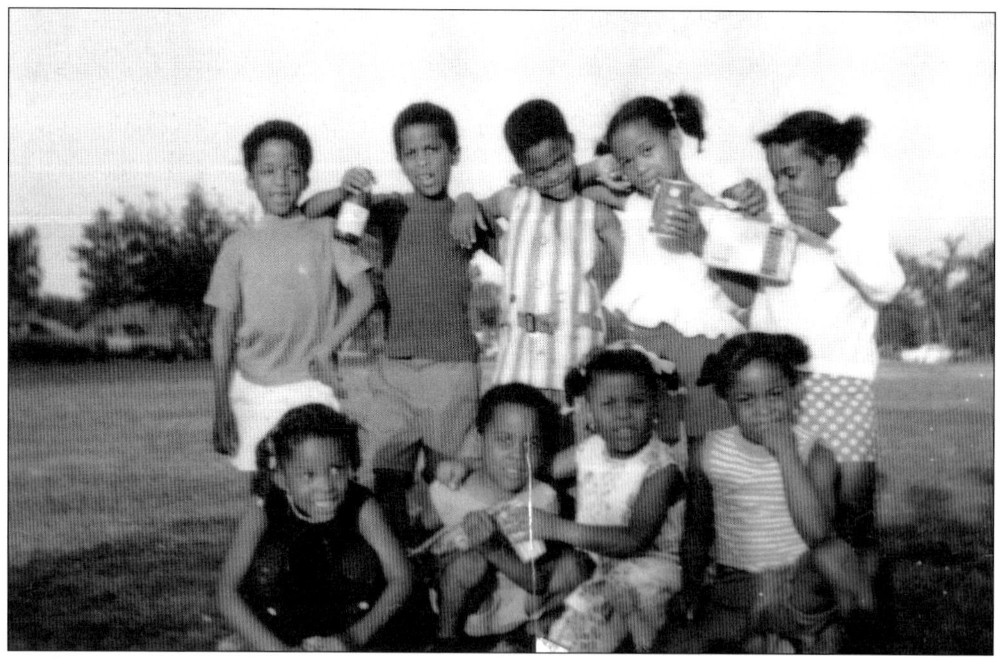

Panderosa Park is a staple in the community, as it provides an open space for family gatherings. Pictured in the park in 1971 are, from left to right, cousins (first row) April M. Anderson, Muchell Charles Sr., Andrea M. Opara, and Precious Charles; (second row) Huey Madison Jr., Brian Charles, Perry Johnson Sr., Robin J. Crawford, and Roxanne Charles. (Courtesy of Robin Crawford.)

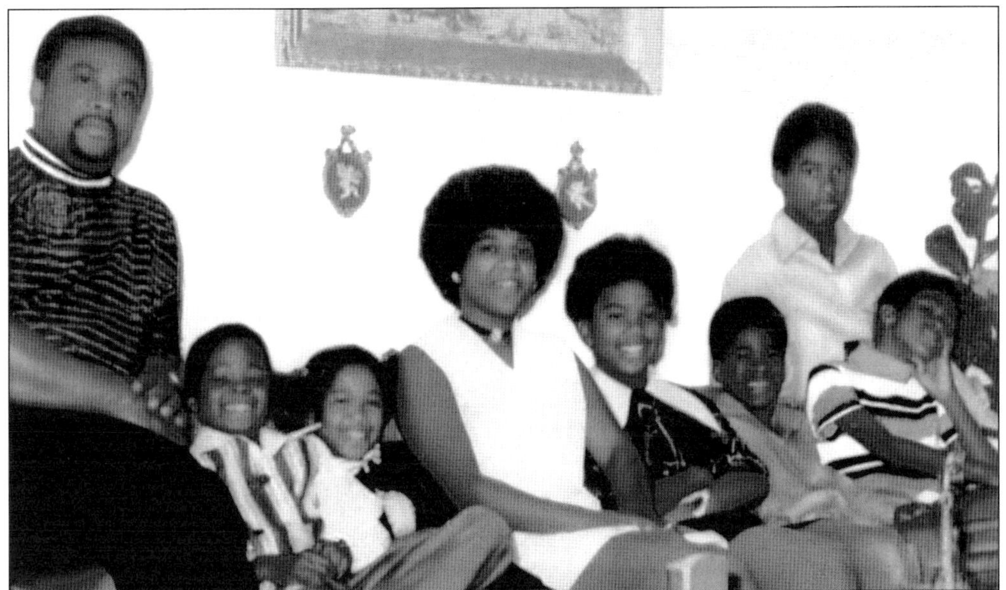

In this 1970s image of the Johnson family are, from left to right, Dood Sr., Perry, Robin, Ernestine, Debra, Dood III, Wanda, and Stanley. The family is gathered here in celebration of Resurrection Sunday. Ernestine, Dood, and all of their children are natives of the community. Dood Jr. was employed with the Mississippi Grain Elevator, and Ernestine was employed with the Orleans Parish public schools for many years. Ernestine and Dood Jr. were married for over 62 years—until Dood's passing on January 19, 2017. (Courtesy of Robin Crawford.)

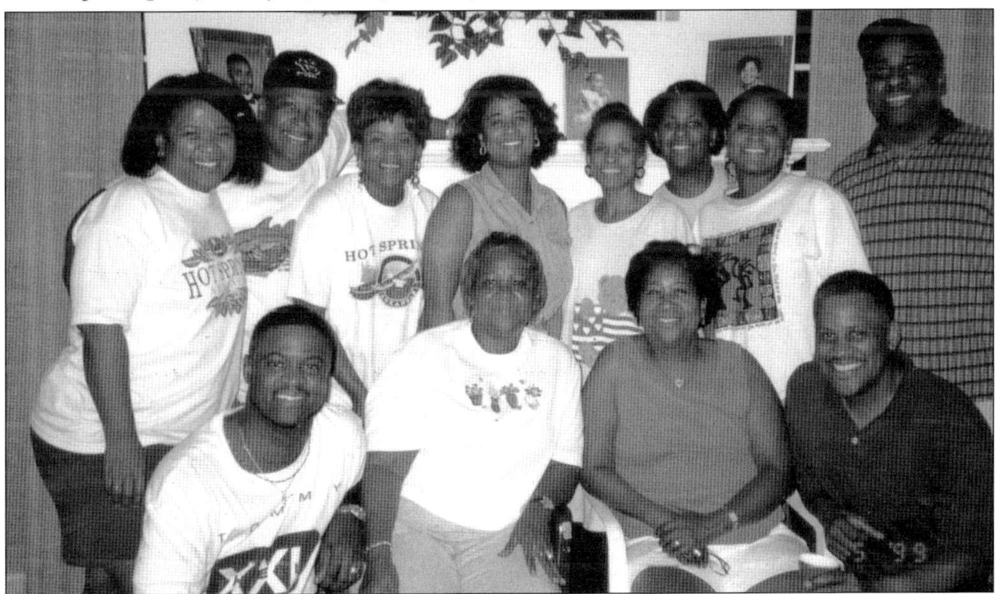

Ernestine H. Johnson and Lizzie H. Charles pose with their children in Houston, Texas. Although some have migrated away from the Cut-Off community, families still travel in large numbers to maintain a bond of unity. Pictured are, from left to right, (first row) Perry Johnson Sr., Ernestine, Lizzie, and Hammond Charles Jr.; (second row) Robin J. Crawford, Liroy Charles Sr., Wanda J. Jackson, Trudy C. Kent, Cubie Charles, Roxanne Charles, Precious Charles, and Muchell Charles Sr. (Courtesy of Robin Crawford.)

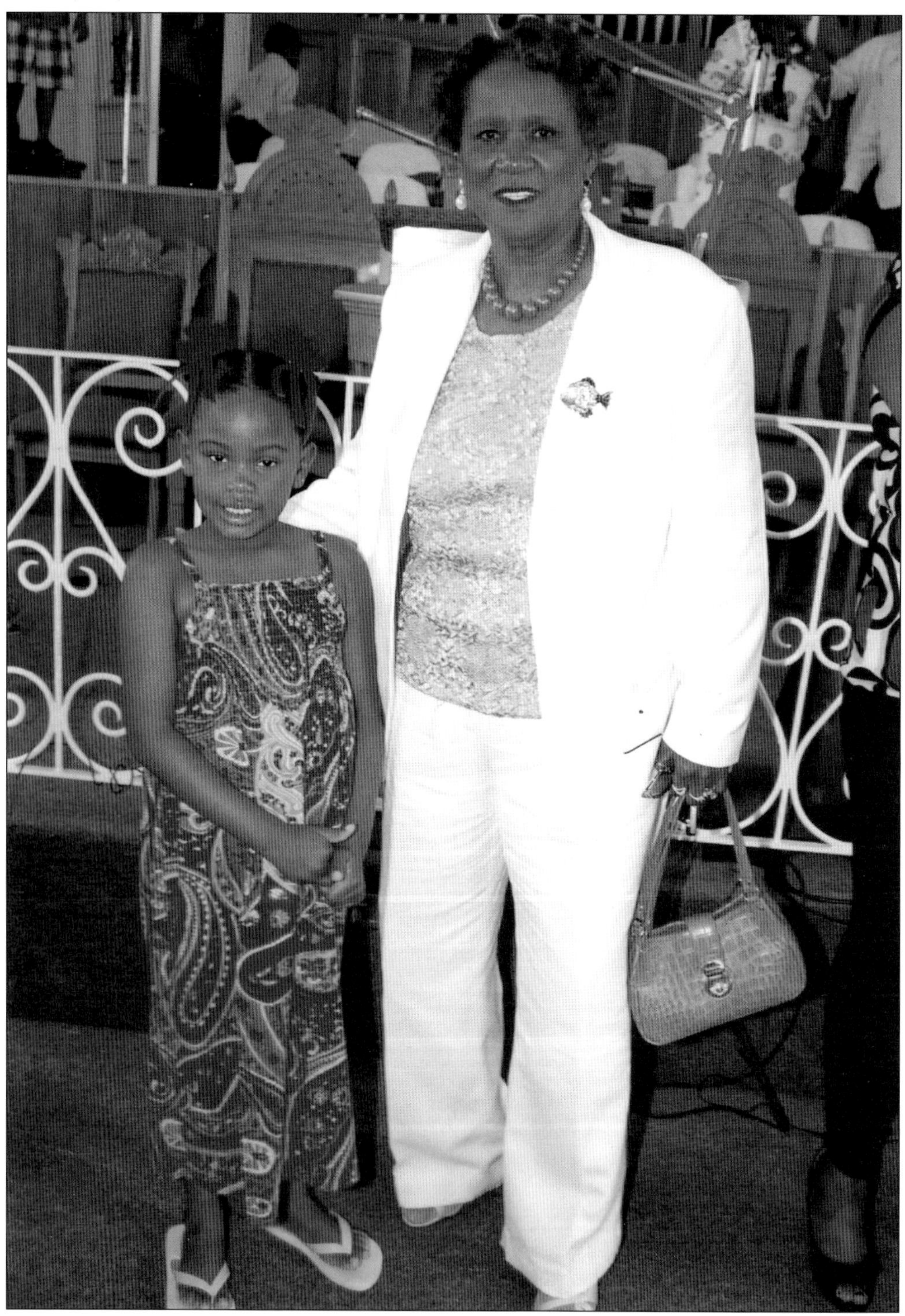

Ernestine Henry-Johnson was born December 16, 1938. She is pictured here with her great-granddaughter Yasmin Miller for her baptism. (Courtesy of Robin Crawford.)

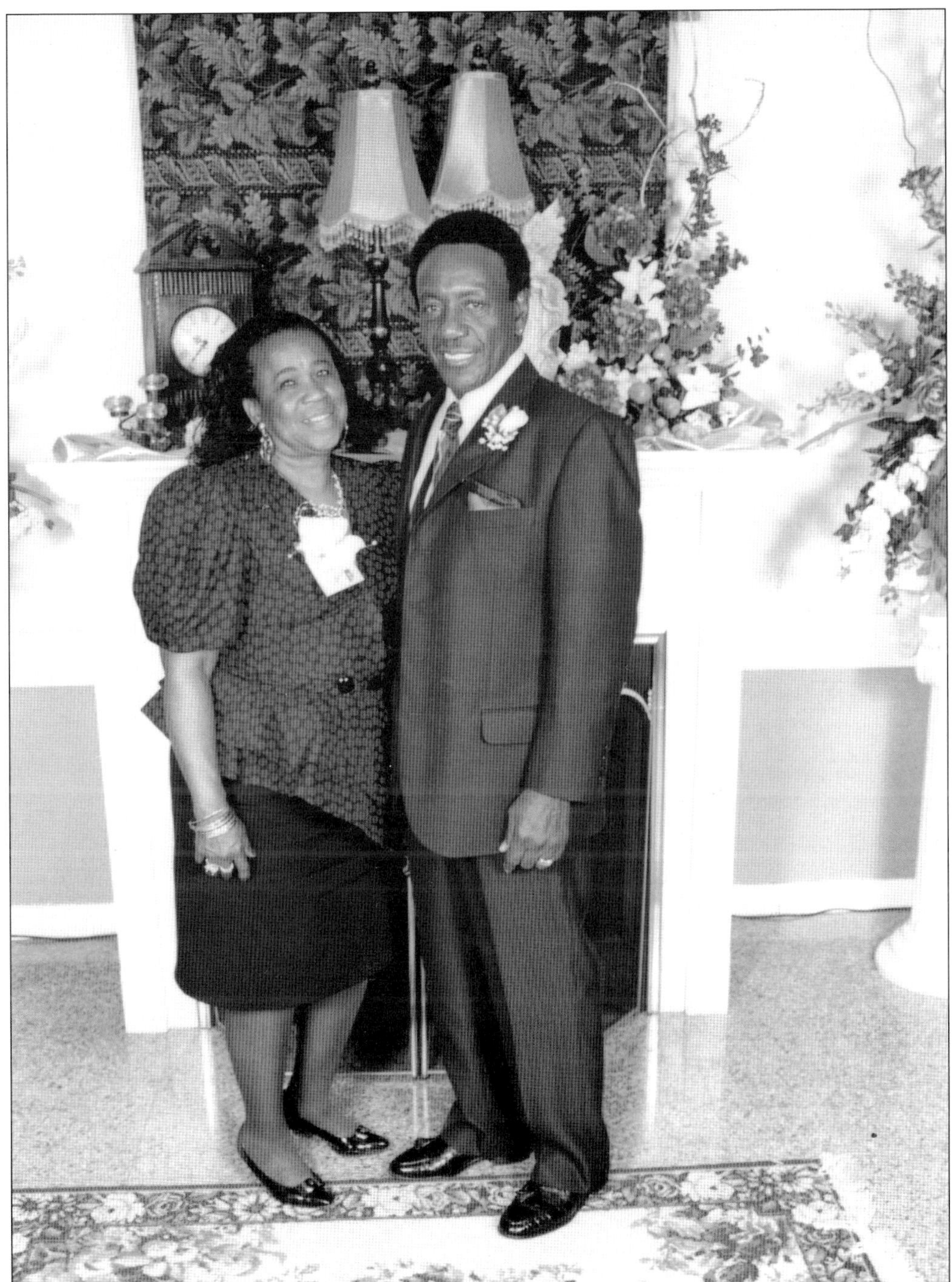

Corinne Henry-Noel Broussard was born on July 20, 1939. Corinne was a resident of the Lower Coast of Algiers from the age of 8. After her marriage to Percy Noel, she sought greater life opportunities in California and never returned. She passed on November 30, 2015, and her funeral was held at Asbury United Methodist Church in the Lower Coast of Algiers. (Courtesy of Robin Crawford.)

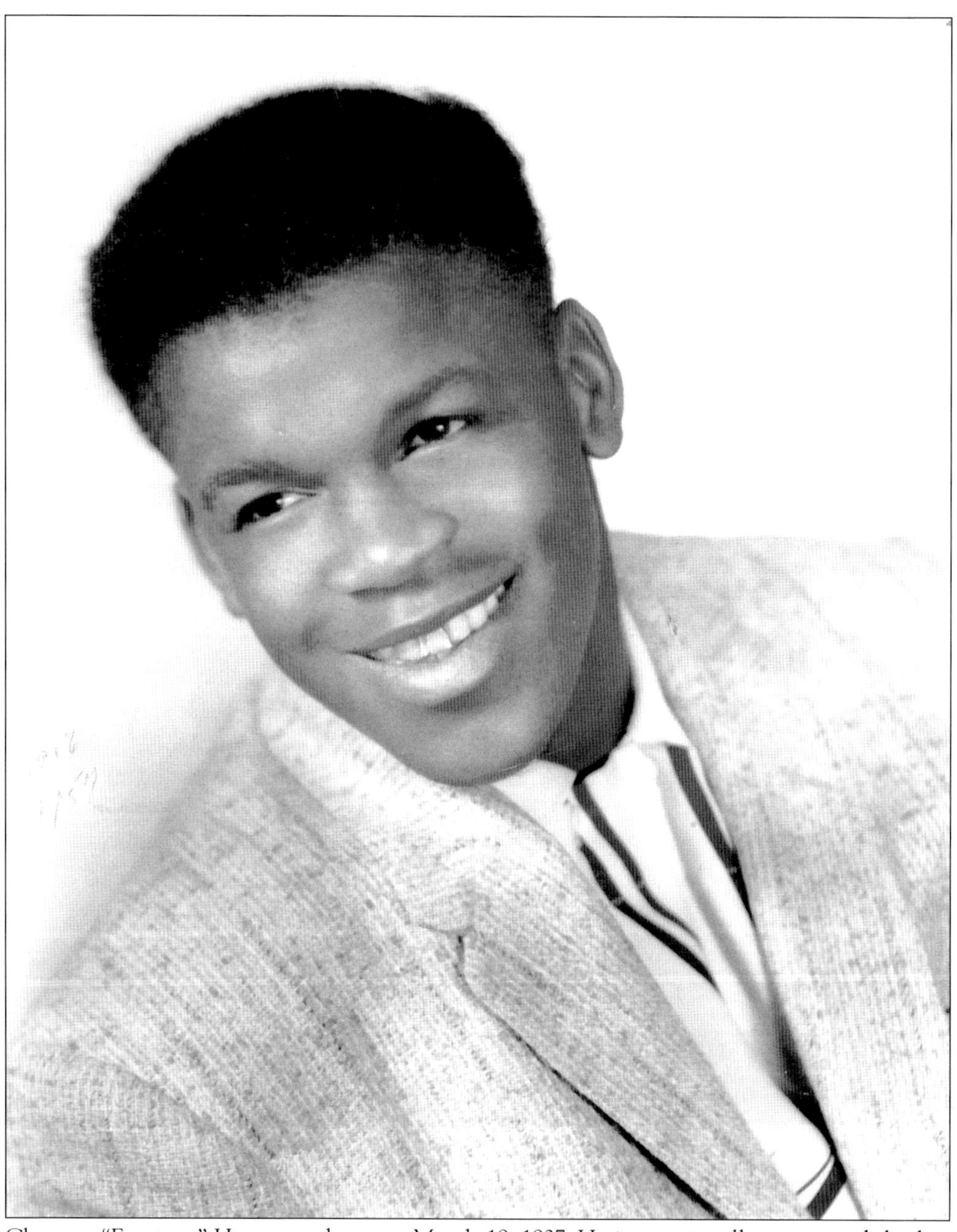

Clarence "Frogman" Henry was born on March 19, 1937. He is a nationally recognized rhythm and blues singer who found fame in the 1950s and 1960s with hits like "Ain't Got No Home" and "But I Do." Though he has traveled the world, touring with bands as popular as the Beatles, he affectionately calls Algiers home. (Courtesy of Clarence Henry Jr.)

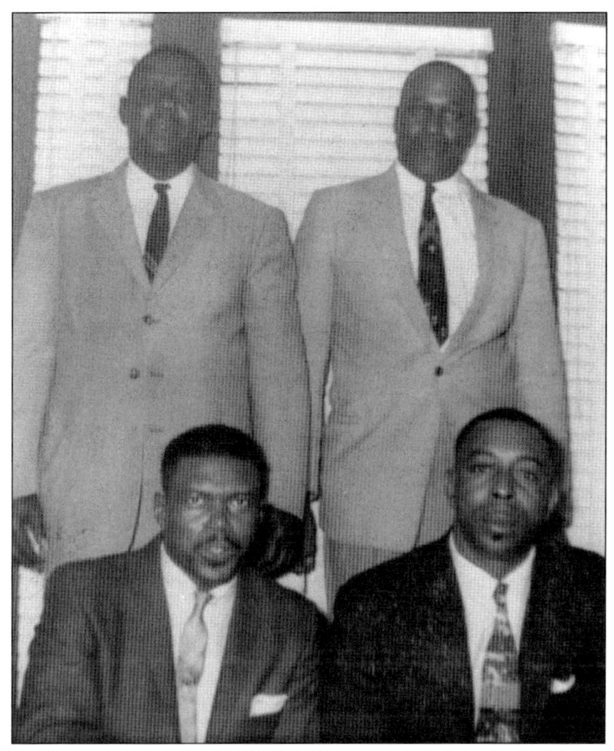

Pictured are the Brooks brothers, from left to right, (seated) Charles "Freddie Brooks" Victor Jr. and Wilmer Brooks; (standing) Edward Brooks and Lloyd Henry. Wilmer was the owner of Brooks Grocery & Deli, LLC located at 2434 Allen Street in Greater New Orleans. (Courtesy of Robin Crawford.)

Clarence Henry Sr. was born June 1, 1912. He is pictured in this 1950s photograph with his siblings and daughter Corinne. The family had a tradition of gathering together on Sunday evenings after church service for fun and fellowship. Pictured during this particular Sunday's gathering are, from left to right, (standing) Wilmer, Corrinne, Clarence Sr., and Charles Victor Jr.; (sitting) Lloyd, Elizabeth, and her husband, Howard Queen. (Courtesy of Robin Crawford.)

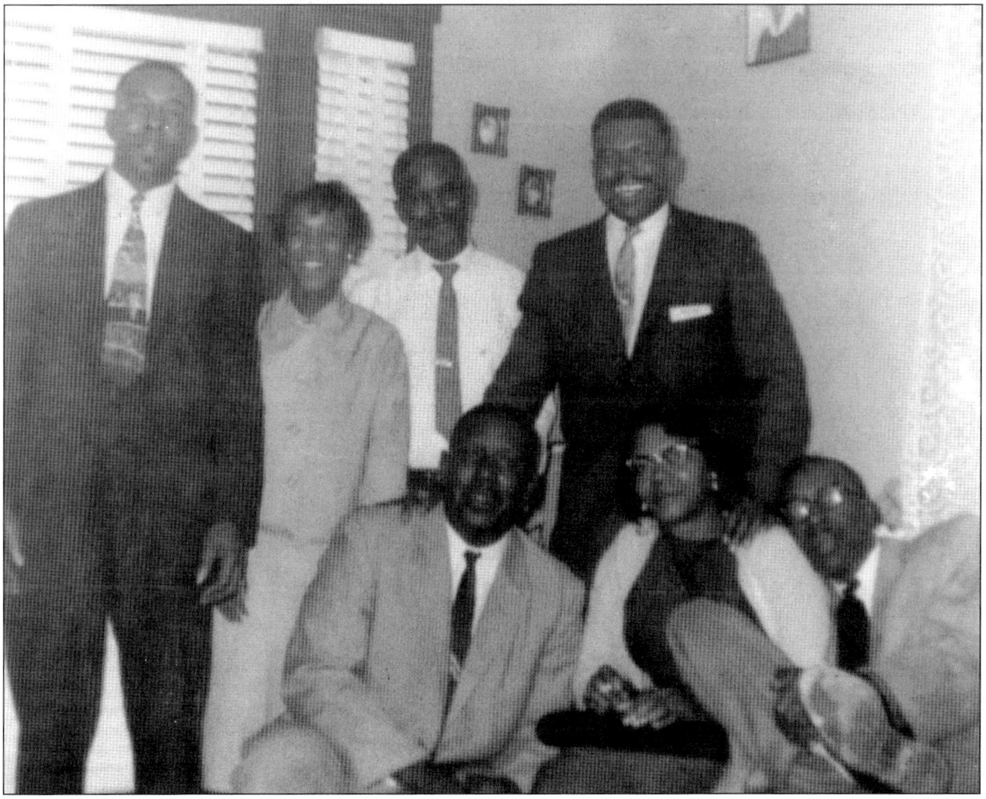

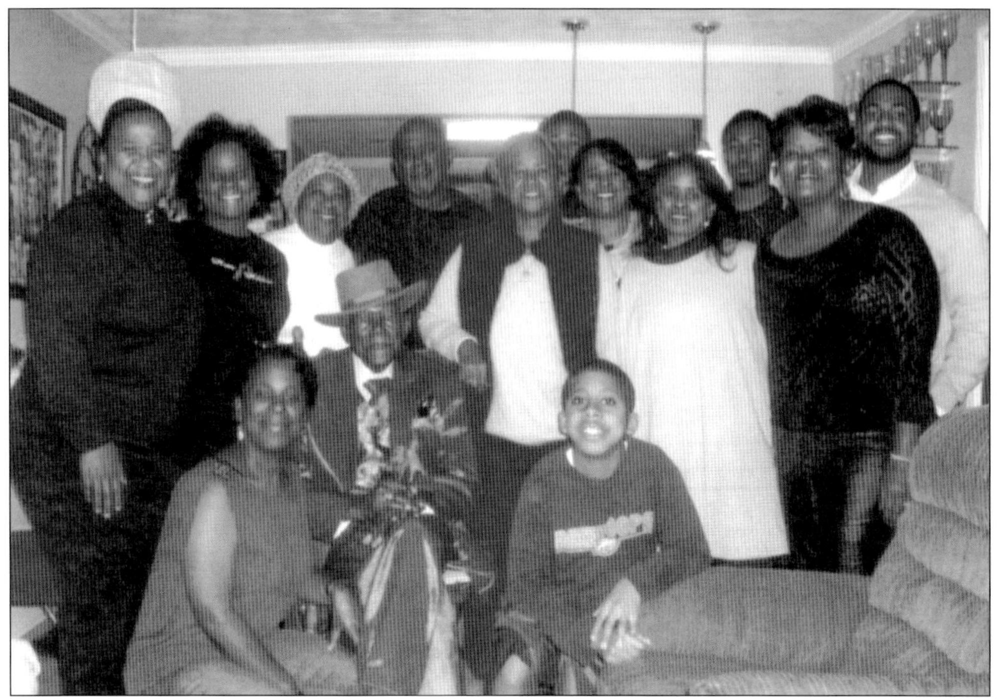

The Henry family surrounds Charles "Freddie Brooks" Victor Jr. Pictured are, from left to right, Roxanne Charles, Logan Simeon, Robin J. Crawford, Precious Charles, Liz Charles, John Henry, Ernestine Johnson, Tyler Richardson, Trudy Kent, Cubie Charles, Cedric Charles, Campanell Kent Jr., and Wanda J. Jackson. "Freddie Brooks" passed away in 2015 at the age of 91. (Courtesy of Robin Crawford.)

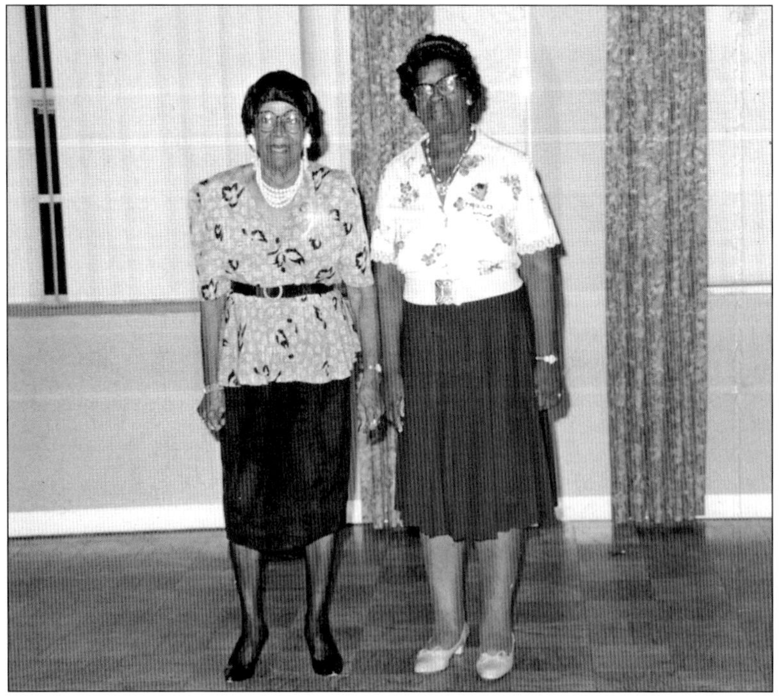

Pictured to the left is Lillian Perrymon, who was born on February 18, 1915. She stands beside her sister Ethel Knight, who was born on April 14, 1923. Both women were known in the area for their selfless service to Second Baptist Church. (Courtesy of Robin Crawford.)

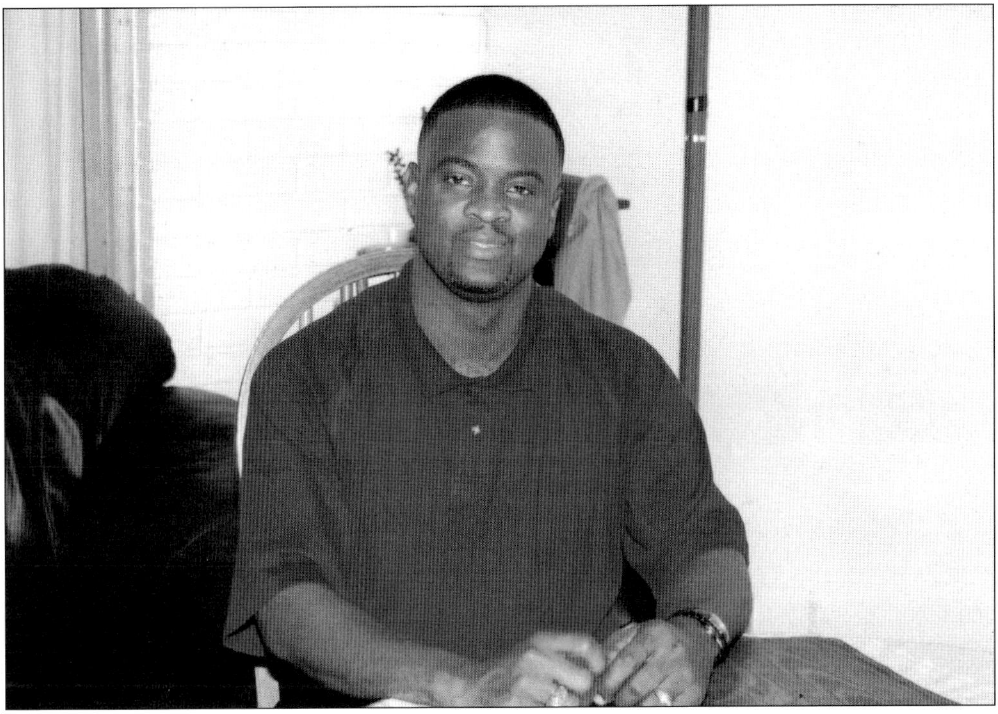

Perry Johnson Sr. was born July 22, 1963, to the union of Ernestine and Dood Johnson. Perry moved from the Lower Coast of Algiers to Houston, Texas, in 1989 because of the failing economic infrastructure in New Orleans. His acts of kindness and dedication to both the Lower Coast of Algiers and Houston are a result of the God-given strength and character that was first instilled in him during his upbringing in the Cut-Off. (Courtesy of Robin Crawford.)

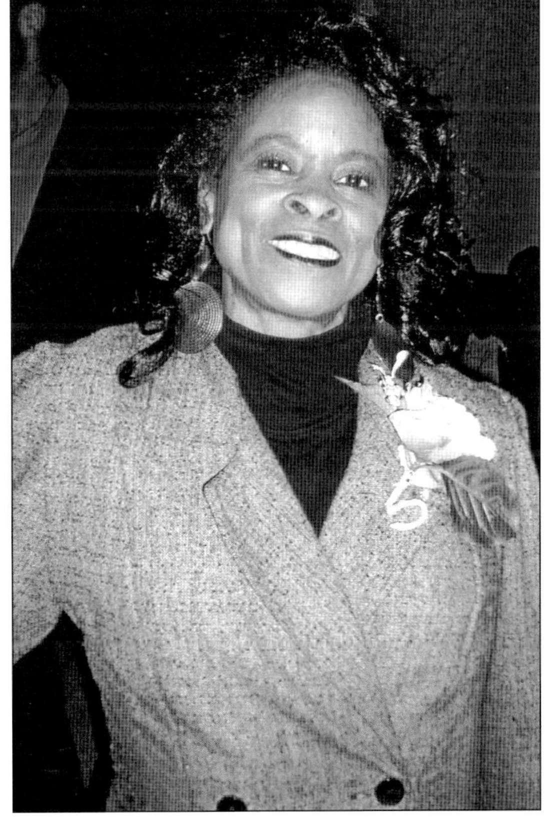

Cubie Doll Charles was born September 1, 1954, to the union of Lizzie and the late Hammond Charles Sr. Cubie has worked since the 1980s to stay active in local politics, particularly in the fight for children's rights. She has served as president of the Cut-Off booster club for many years and took part in the ground-breaking ceremony for the opening of the Cut-Off Recreation Center. (Courtesy of Robin Crawford.)

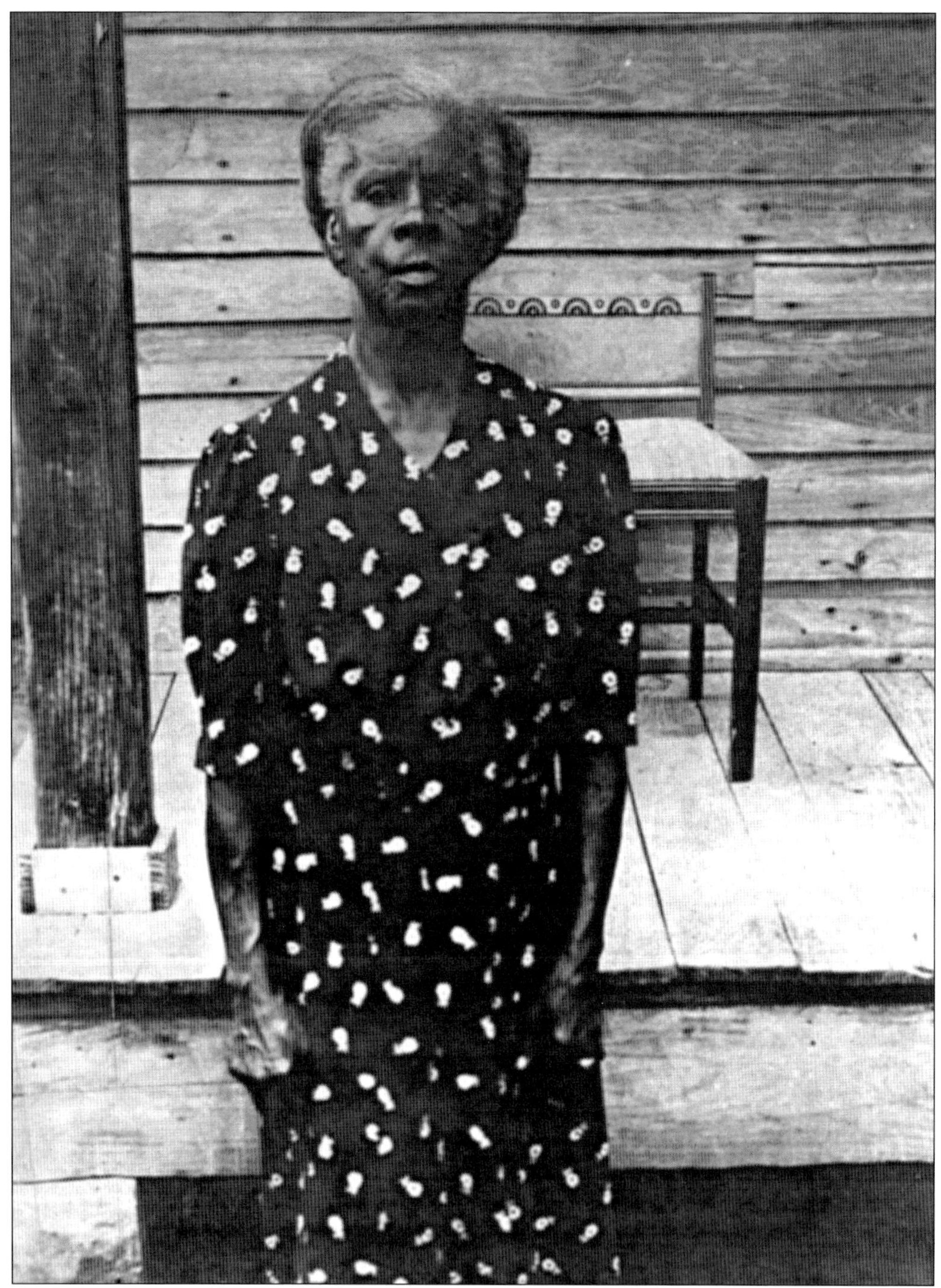

Marguerite "Ma-Polly" Bailey-Charles was born September 11, 1879, in Braithwaite, Louisiana. In the early 1900s, she and her husband, Norah Charles, relocated to the Lower Coast of Algiers. Marguerite and Norah were the parents of 12 children. Marguerite was a housewife for the majority of her life. Norah passed away in 1937, and Marguerite never remarried. She continued to care for her family until she lost her sight. She later became ill and passed away on April 18, 1962. (Courtesy of Robin Crawford.)

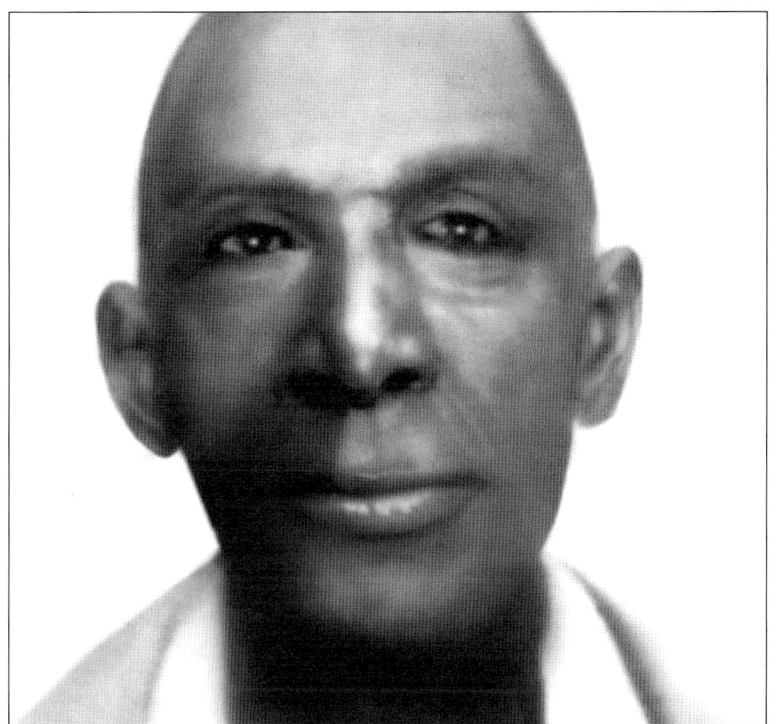

Ather Johnson Sr. was born on June 2, 1893. He was a native of the Lower Coast of Algiers who suffered an untimely death. Ather's death remains a mystery, as he was found unconscious near his outhouse after an encounter with local police. He died on August 28, 1945. (Courtesy of Robin Crawford.)

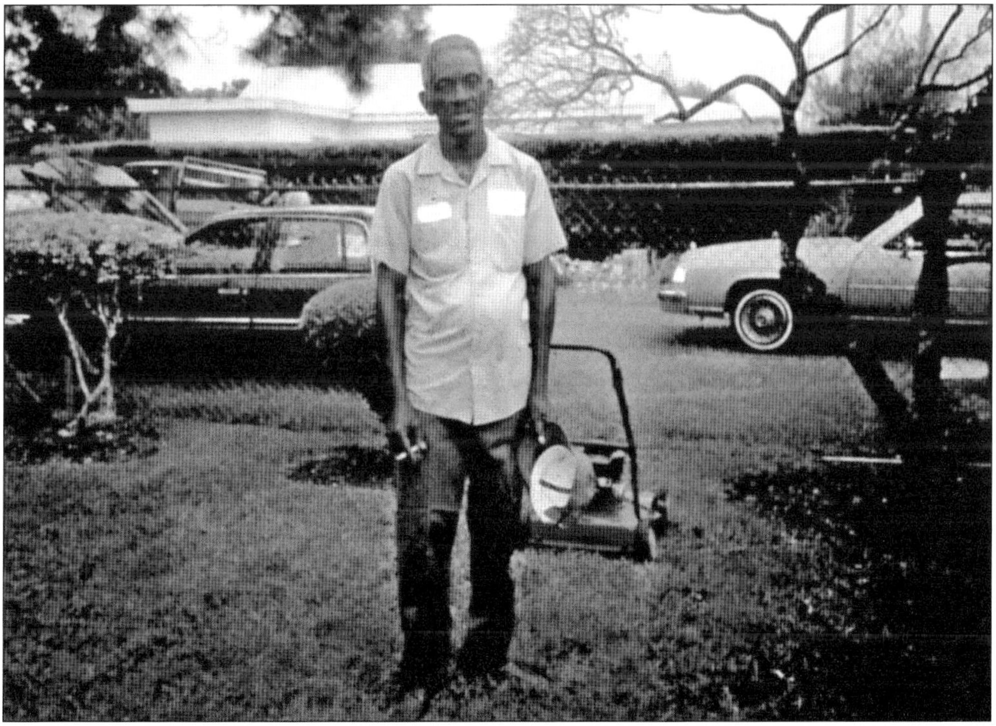

Lawrence "Archie" Johnson was born on July 9, 1935, to the union of Leanna and Ather Johnson Sr. Lawrence was highly praised in the community for his well-kept yard. (Courtesy of Robin Crawford.)

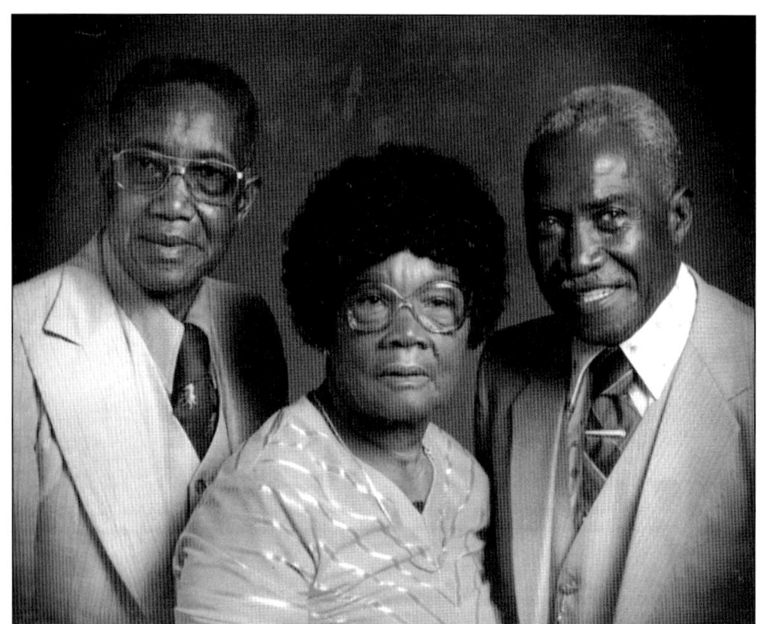

Olivia Landry-Ruffin is pictured with John and Wesley Ruffin Sr. Olivia and Wesley were the proud parents of 13 children. Wesley was born on May 3, 1905, and passed on June 24, 1992. Olivia was born on December 20, 1908, and passed on March 23, 1989. Wesley's brother John Ruffin was born on September 18, 1920, and died in May 1980. (Courtesy of Wesley Ruffin Jr.)

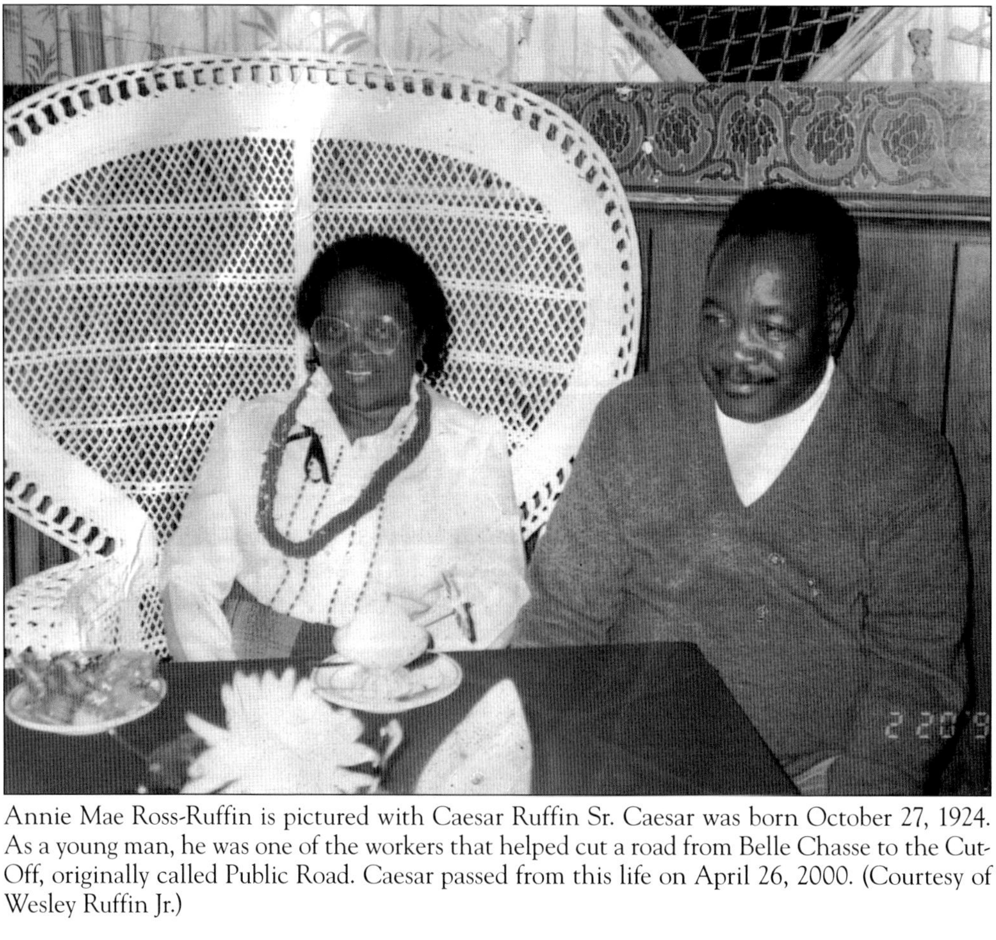

Annie Mae Ross-Ruffin is pictured with Caesar Ruffin Sr. Caesar was born October 27, 1924. As a young man, he was one of the workers that helped cut a road from Belle Chasse to the Cut-Off, originally called Public Road. Caesar passed from this life on April 26, 2000. (Courtesy of Wesley Ruffin Jr.)

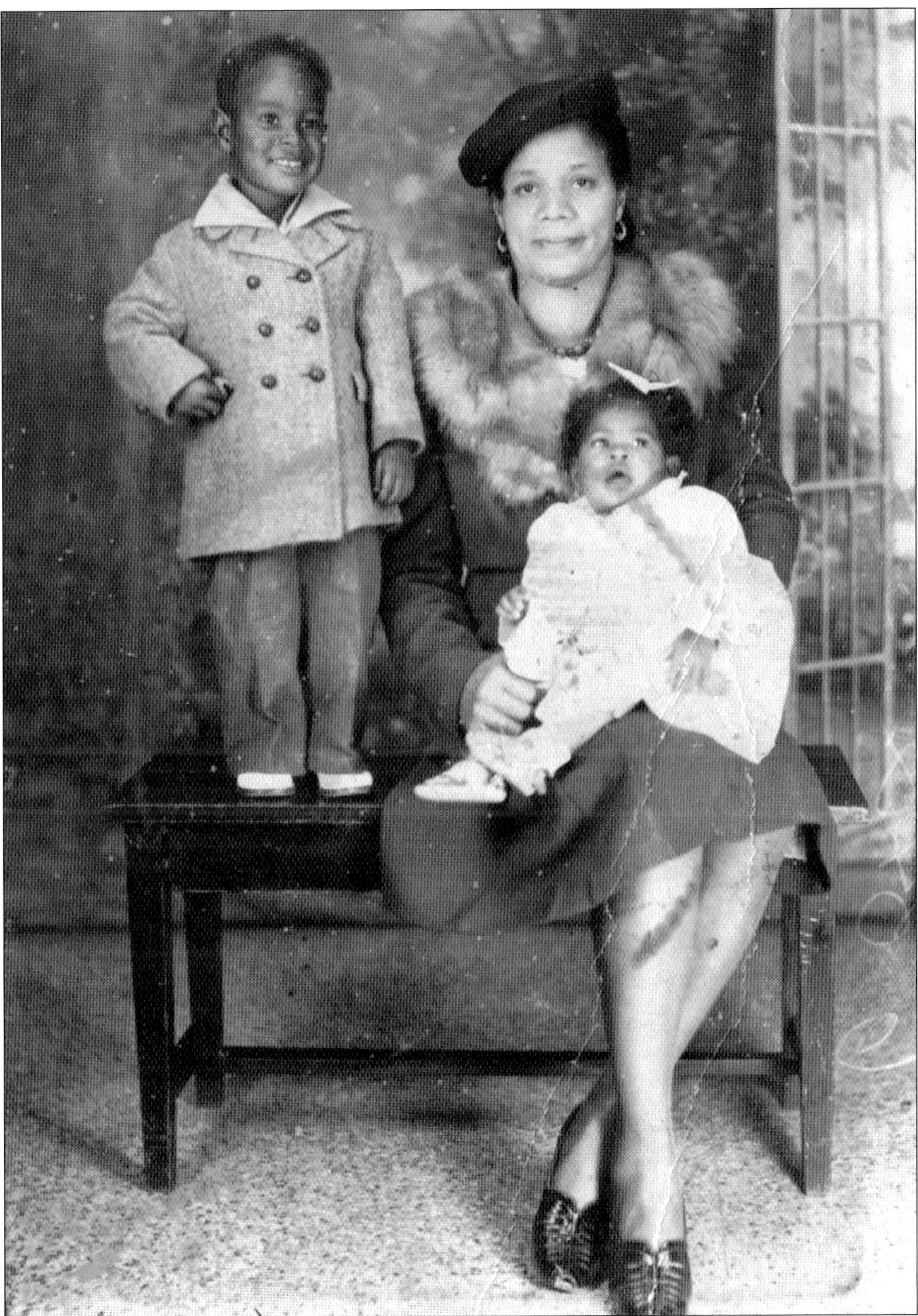

Louise Wright is pictured with her grandchildren Herbert Sullen Jr. and Bevelyn Sullen in a professional photograph taken in 1944. Louise, affectionately known as "Ma-Mi" to those whom she loved, lived through Jim Crow, World War II, the civil rights era, and much more until she passed from this life on November 10, 1995. (Courtesy of Bevelyn Manuel.)

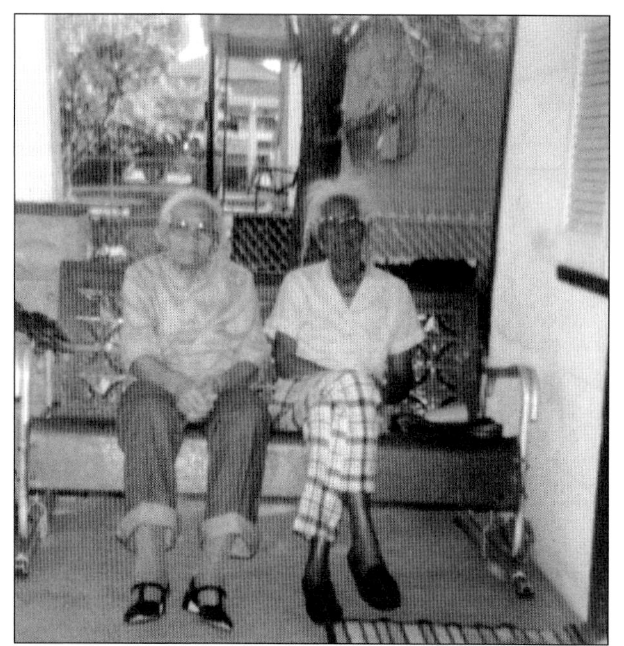

Seated on the left is Louise Wright and seated on the right is her sister Beulah Correct. Louise was born on September 15, 1893, and passed away on November 10, 1995. Beulah was born on January 7, 1891, and passed away on November 23, 1980. Daughters of Amelia Crawford-Price and Henry Laddus, these sisters are pictured on the front porch of Louise's home in the 1980s. (Courtesy of Cheryl Jackson.)

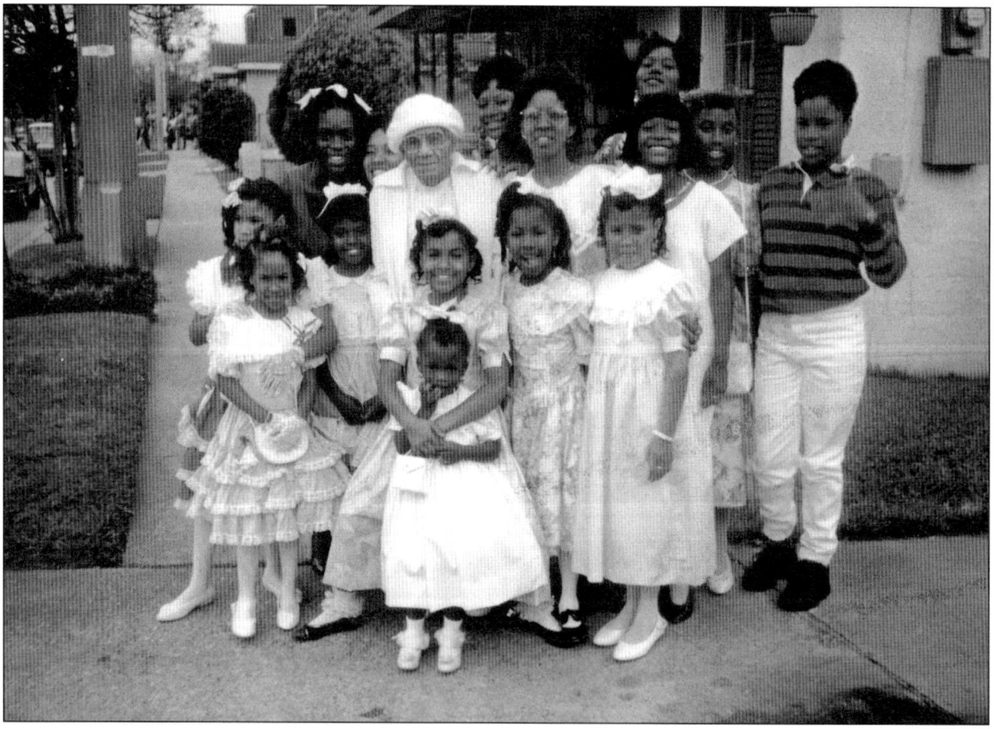

Louise "Mami" Wright is pictured with several generations of grandchildren after a Resurrection service in 1993. Pictured are (first row) Dari Green; and, from left to right, (second row) Daranika Nicholas, Arieal LaSalle, Tawanya Rivers, and Alicia McDonald; (third row) Ariante Nicholas, Chandra Sullen, Louise Wright, Bevelyn Manuel, and Quran Wilson; (fourth row) Yashica Wilson, Dena Manuel, Schabandol Wilson, Bashama Wilson, Shante Sullen, and Shakita Johnson. (Courtesy of Gail Langford.)

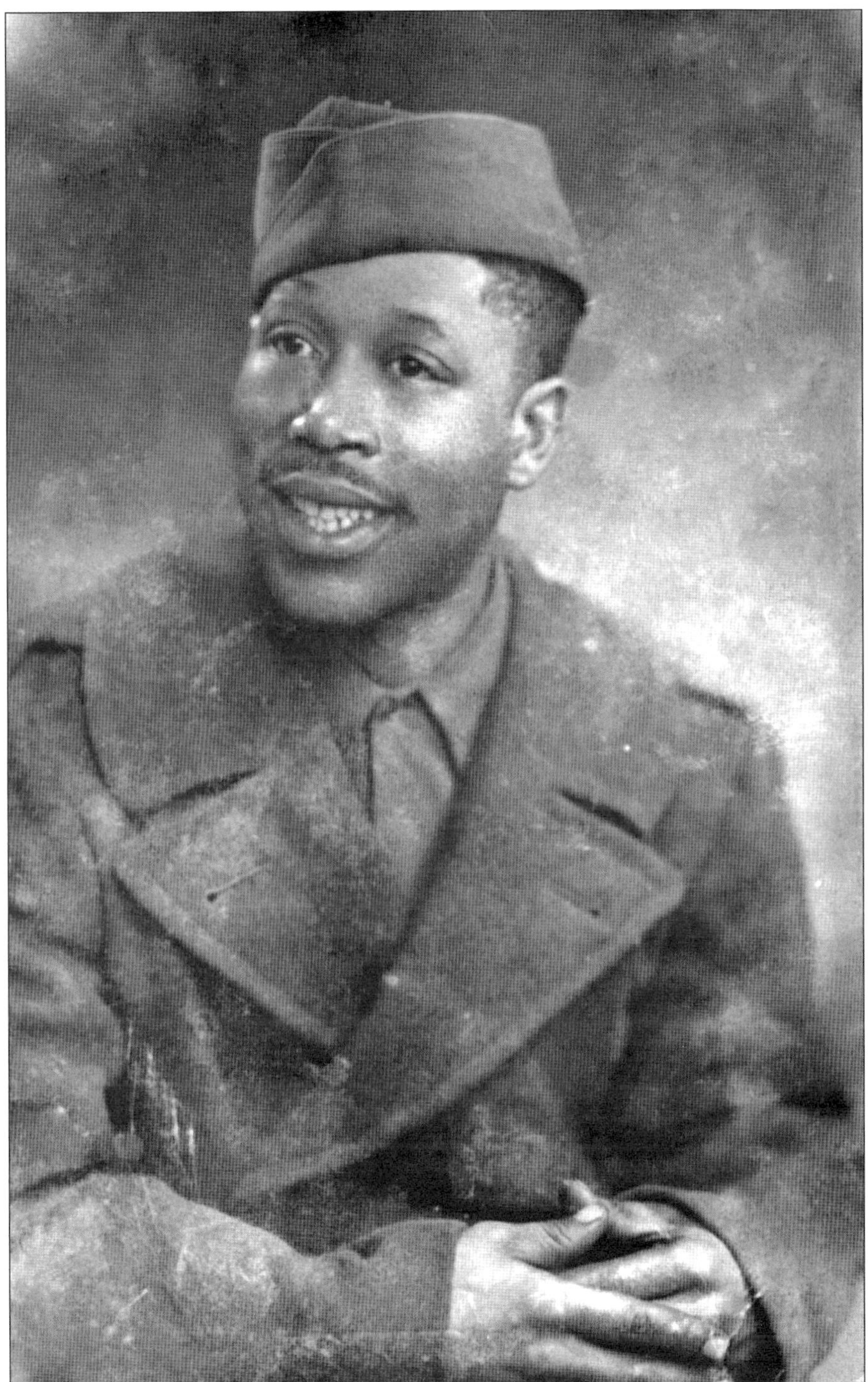

Herbert Sullen Sr. was a great leader who fought tirelessly for paved streets, sewerage, and draining systems to be placed in the Cut-Off community. At the expiration of his tour of duty in the US Army during World War II, Sullen returned to his home in the Cut-Off to find deplorable conditions. He camped out at city hall to have gravel roads paved and pleaded for streetlights—both requests were eventually honored. (Courtesy of Enola Rose.)

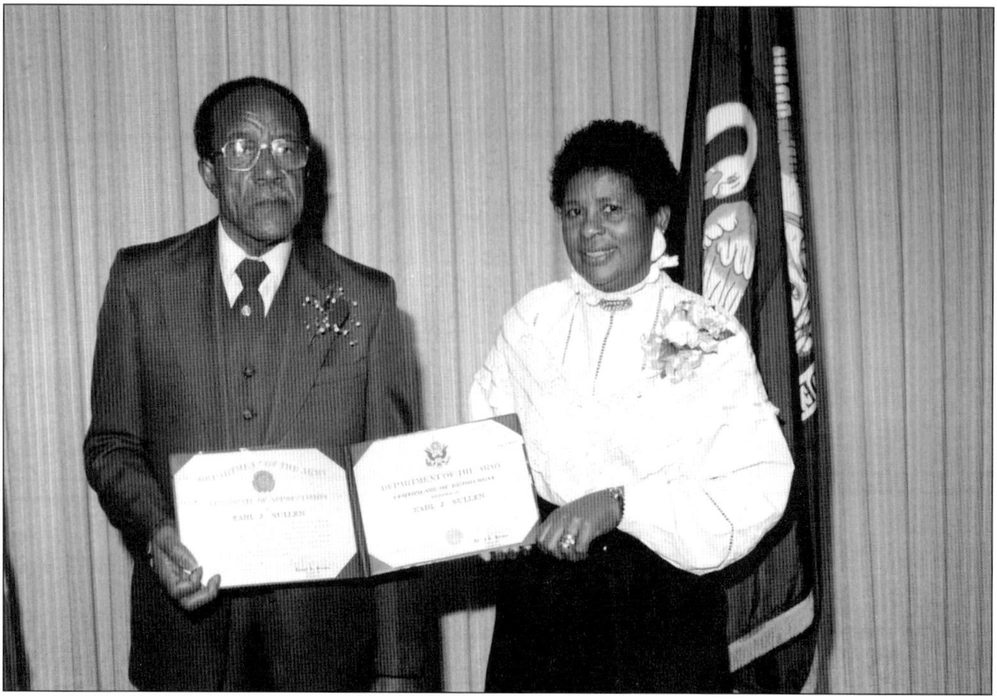

Earl John Sullen Sr. was born on November 22, 1920, to Louise Wright and Herbert Sullen. Earl was employed by the US Army Corps of Engineers for over 45 years. He was a lifelong resident of the Lower Coast of Algiers and is pictured here with his wife, Mary Foley Sullen. They had three daughters and five sons: Mary, Spencena, Sondia, Earl Jr., George, Arthur, Donald, and David. (Courtesy of Enola Rose.)

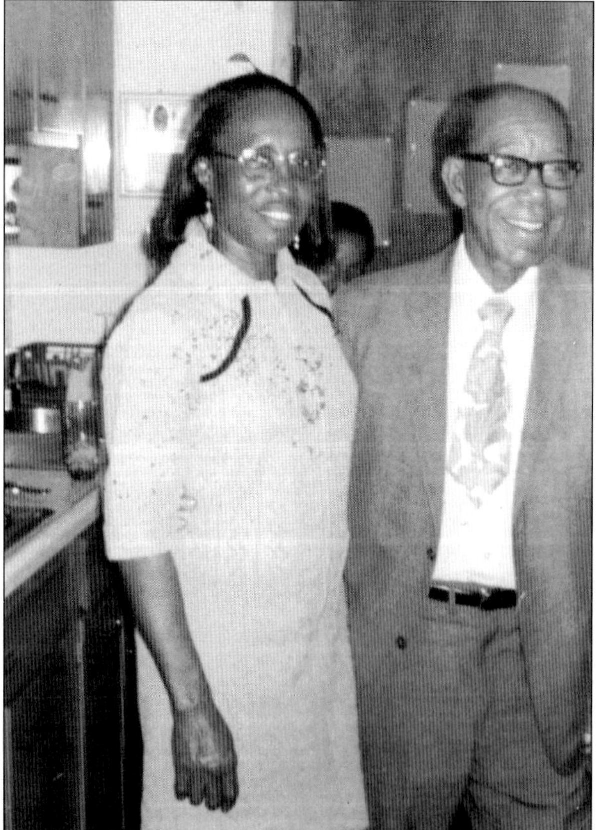

Herbert Sullen Sr. was born on May 20, 1915, four years before the birth of his wife, Rebecca, in 1919. The two were united in marriage in September 1938. They remained united until the passing of Rebecca in 1976. Herbert lived until October 1982. (Courtesy of Schelander Phoenix.)

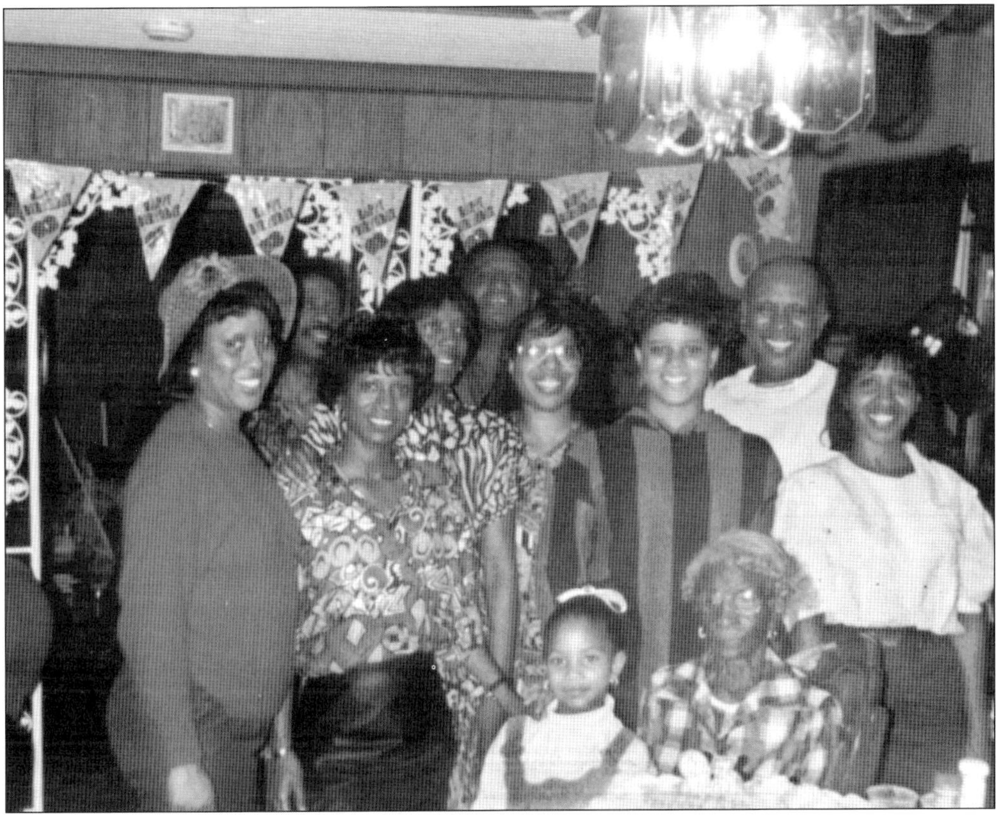

Herbert and Rebecca Sullen had eight children who were able to extend their lineage. Their children, from left to right to right, are Enola, Condell, Bernadette, Gail, Kermit, Schelander, Herbert Jr., and Bevelyn. They are accompanied by their cousins Shannon (standing behind) and Alicia McDonald (sitting in the lap) during their grandmother Minerva Lewis's 97th birthday celebration. (Courtesy of Marylee McDonald.)

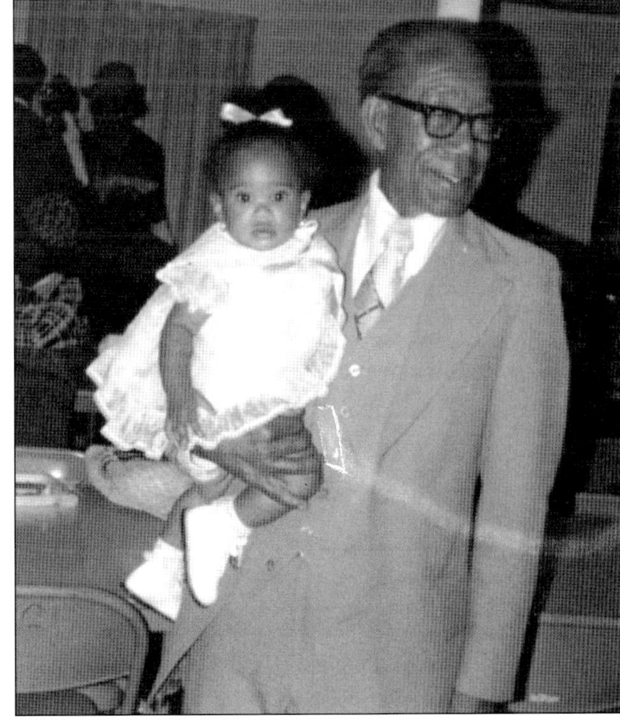

Herbert Sullen Sr. is pictured with his granddaughter Krishuan Phoenix in this 1970s photograph. This picture, among a few others that exist of Herbert, are highly treasured by his family, as he is known to have been camera-shy. (Courtesy of Schelander Phoenix.)

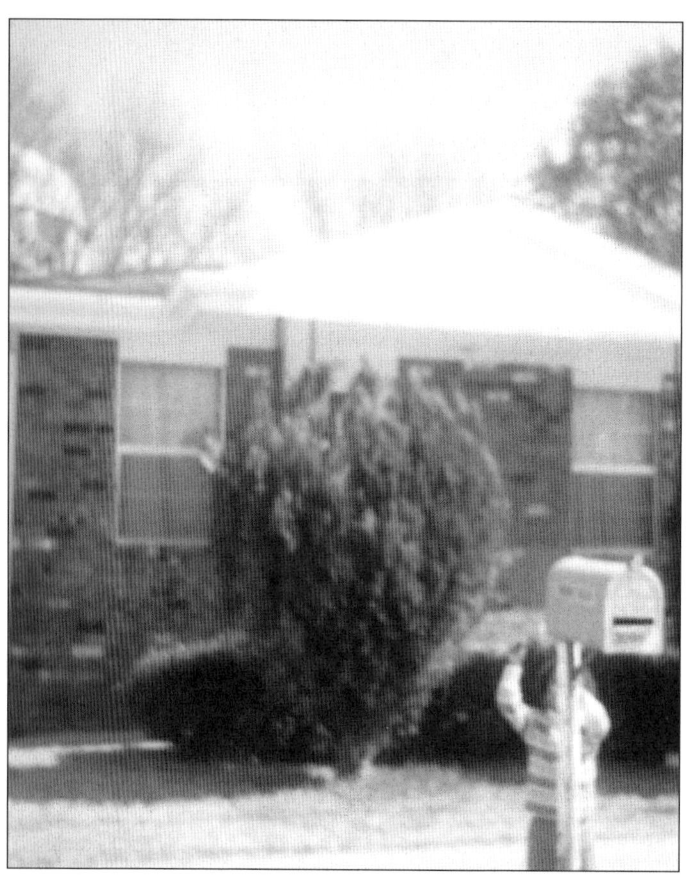

The family home of Herbert and Rebecca Sullen stands at 3000 Sullen Place in the Lower Coast of Algiers. Once known as Simpson Place, this street was renamed in honor of Herbert Sullen Sr. after a petition was sent out by Rev. Earl Green, Percy Rose, and Charles M. Green on behalf of the citizens of the Lower Coast of Algiers. The team wrote to Councilman Mike Early in September 1985, and after a review of the many accomplishments that Herbert had achieved, particularly during points in time when the system had been very hostile toward people of color, the request was honored. Herbert and Rebecca's home still stands in its original place. (Left, courtesy of Gail Langford; below, courtesy of Frederick Weil.)

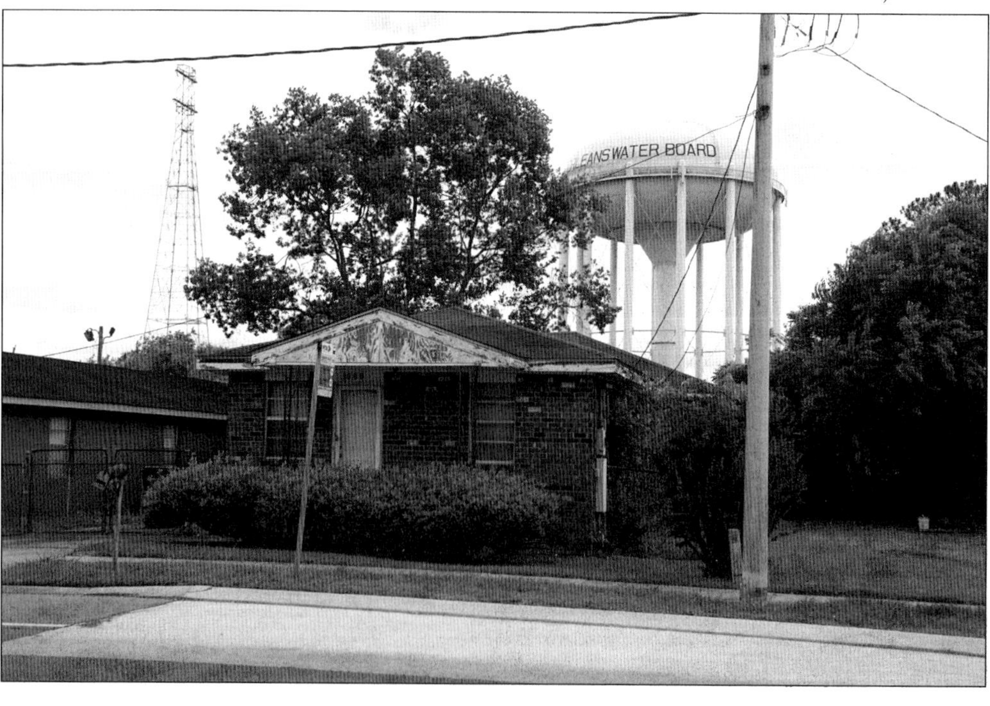

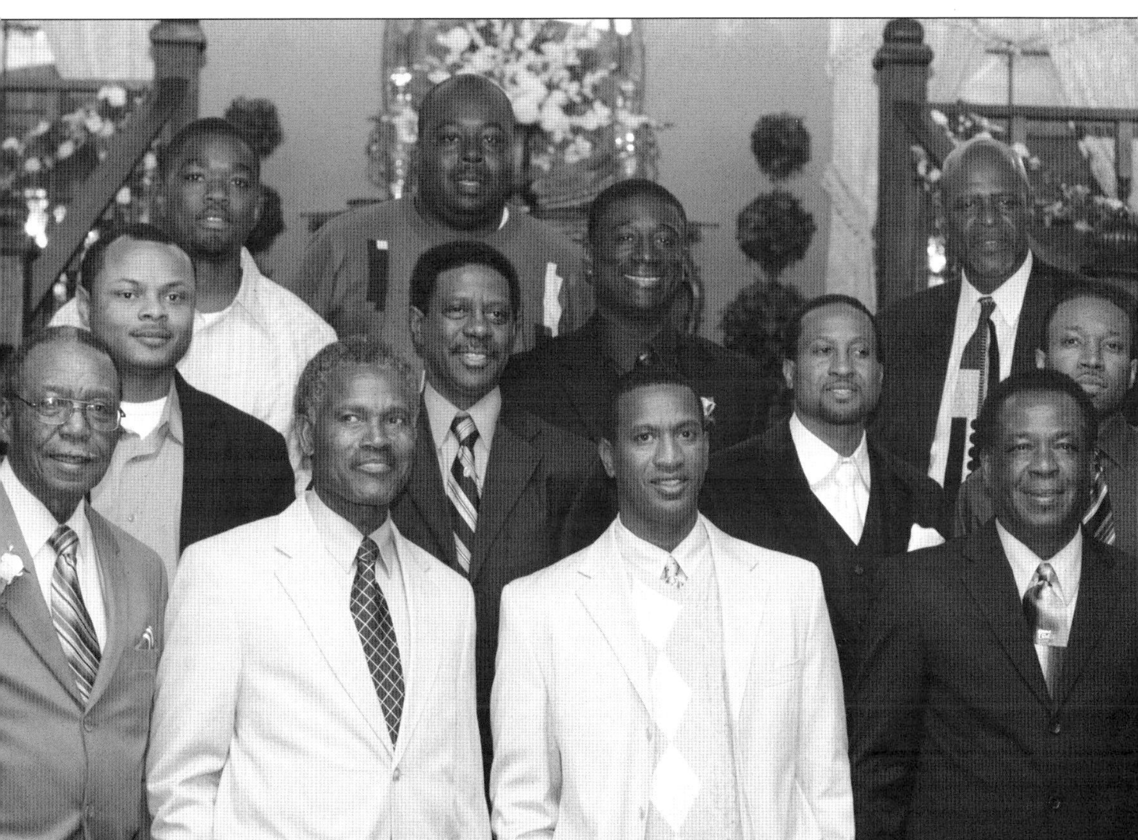

Pictured, from left to right, are (first row) Willie Langford, Eddie Rose Sr., Eddie Rose Jr., and Frank Phoenix Sr.; (second row) Kirk Johnson, Condell Sullen, Demond Rose, and Frank Phoenix Jr.; (third row) Steven Whittington Sr., Gregory Wilson, and Claude Johnson; and (fourth row) Reuben Johnson. These men each were either born into or married into the Sullen family. (Courtesy of Tiffany Smith.)

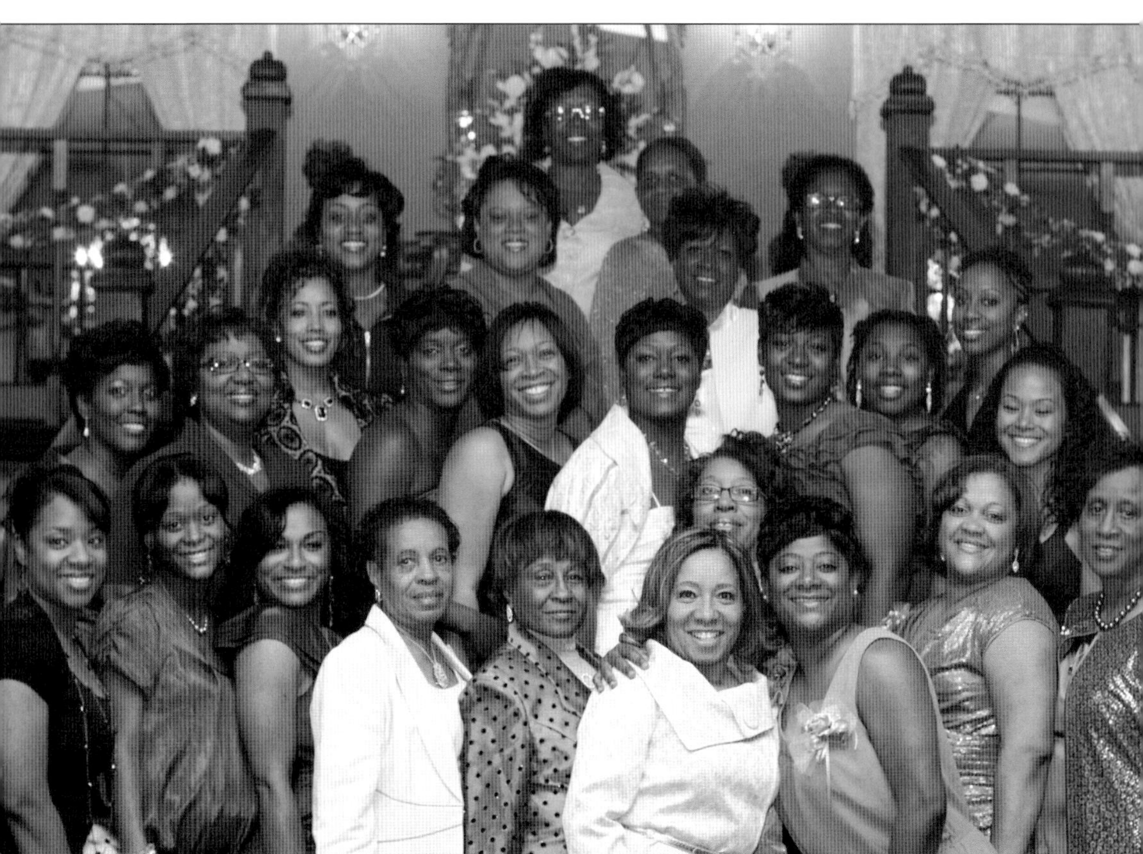

Pictured are, from left to right, (first row) April Johnson, Quran Whittington, Arieal Lasalle, Marylee McDonald, Evelyn Waters, Dena Watkins, Schabandol Johnson, Tiffany Wilson, and Enola Rose; (second row) Tammy Robertson, Mercelyn Sullen, Yashica Joseph, Krishaun Thomas, Bashama Mixon, Schelander Phoenix, Raianna Clark, Tawanya Rivers, and Grace Rose; (third row) Tracy Crear, DDS, and Shante Williams, DDS; (fourth row) Majoria Bowie, Shannon McDonald, and Bernadette Johnson; (fifth row) Eloise Coleman, Bevelyn Manuel, and Gail Langford. These women each were either born into or married into the Sullen family. (Courtesy of Tiffany Smith.)

Robert Lewis Sr., also known as "Pa-Po" to generations that followed, was born in 1895. Robert was beloved by all his grandchildren for his selflessness, as he would offer them food and snacks that others may have denied them. Robert was always full of life, and many in the community speak about how they knew he was nearby by his whistling. (Courtesy of Marylee McDonald.)

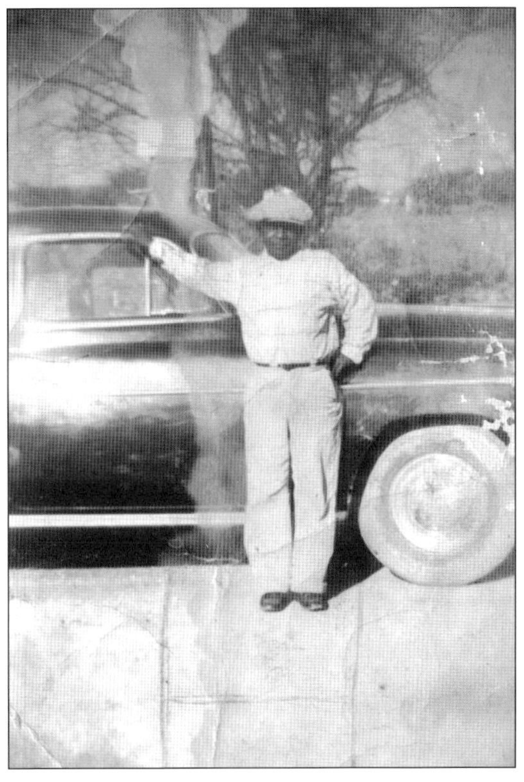

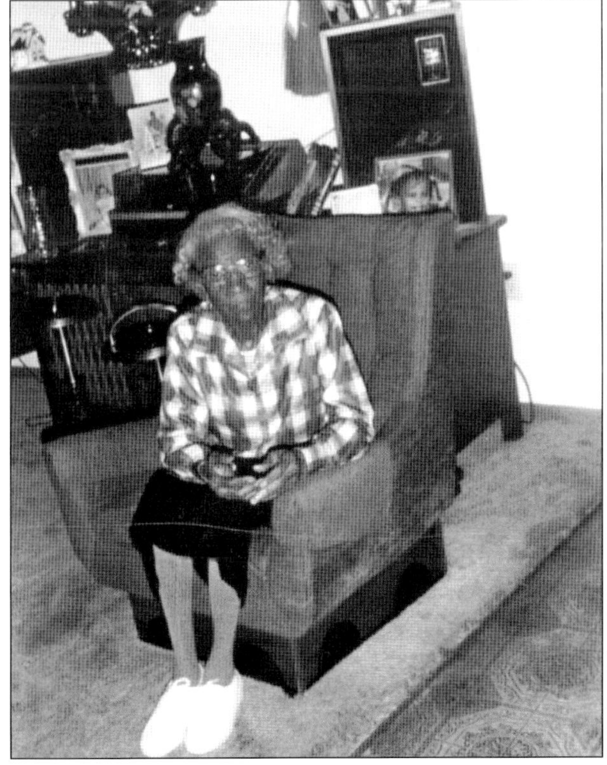

Minerva Lewis was born on January 15, 1900. Minerva worked as a domestic worker for many years before eventually retiring to care for multiple generations of grandchildren. Minerva, wife of Robert Lewis Sr., cared for children until her late 80s, at which point the children felt she was too old in age to continue. After this hobby was taken away, her life began to decline. She passed away at the age of 97 on November 24, 1997. (Courtesy of Gail Langford.)

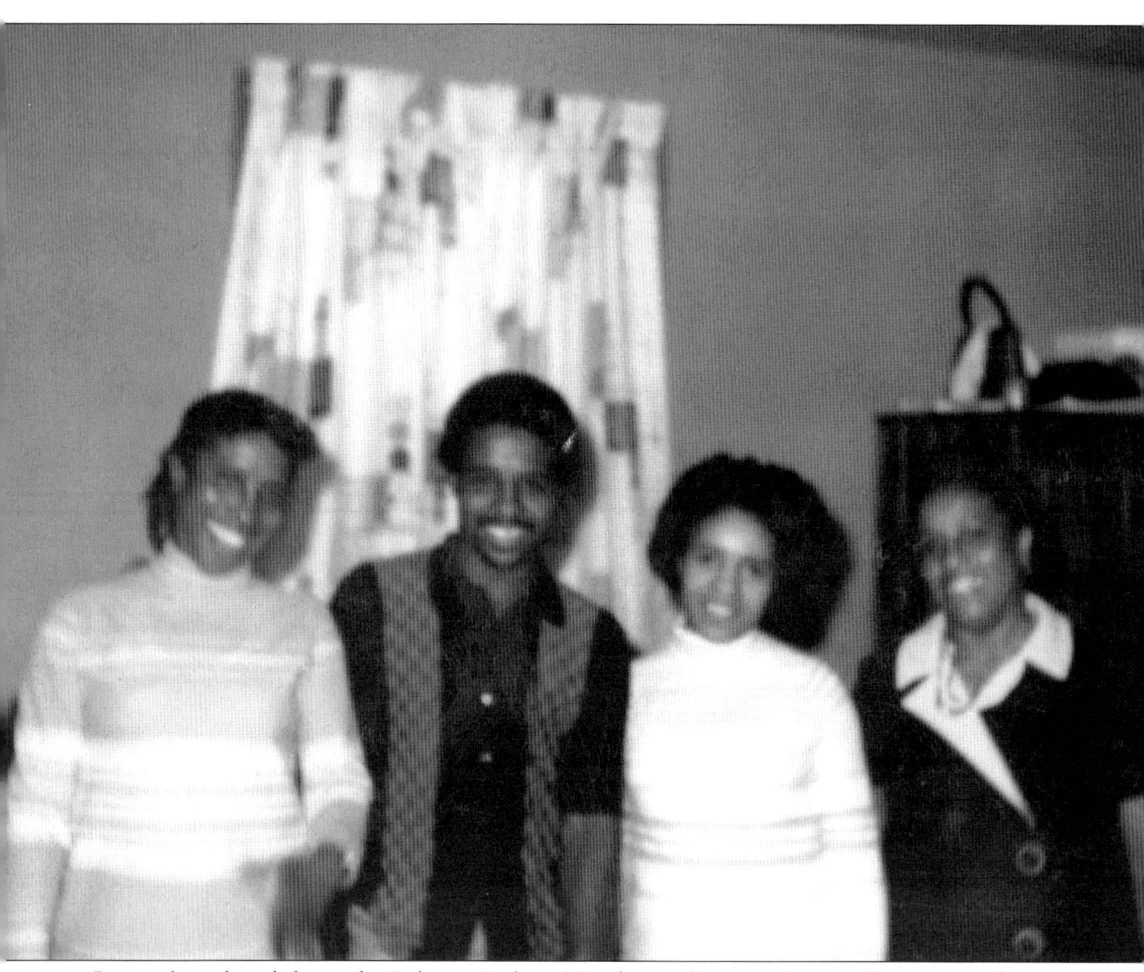

Pictured are, from left to right, Rebecca, Robert, Marylee, and Victoria Lewis. These men and women are the offspring of Minerva Lewis and Robert Lewis Sr. (Courtesy of Marylee McDonald.)

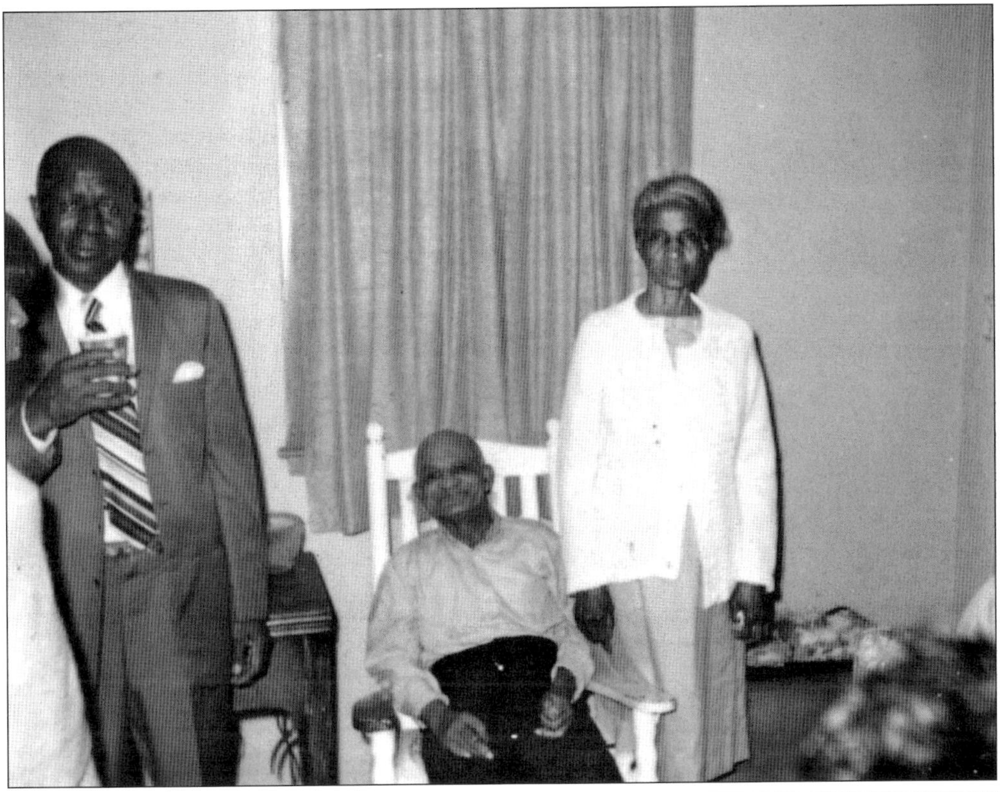

Seen here are, from left to right, William Ross, Robert Lewis, and Minerva Ross. William and Minerva are siblings, while Robert and Minerva are husband and wife. They are pictured here in the 1970s. (Courtesy of Marylee McDonald.)

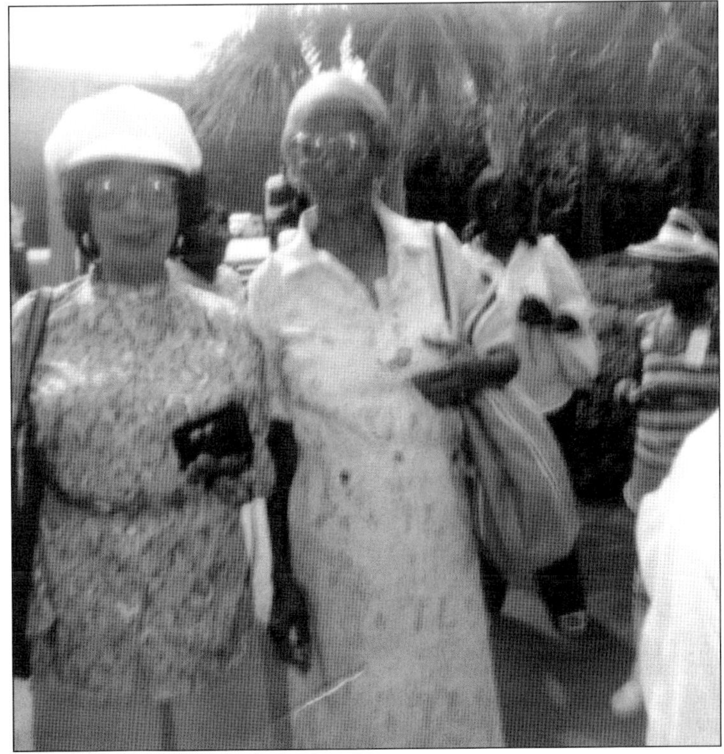

Julia Ross (left) and Minerva Ross are pictured in this 1970s image. Julia was born on July 5, 1918, and married Wesley Rose; they had seven children. Julia was dedicated to her family and her church. She passed way in May 1992. (Courtesy of Bevelyn Manuel.)

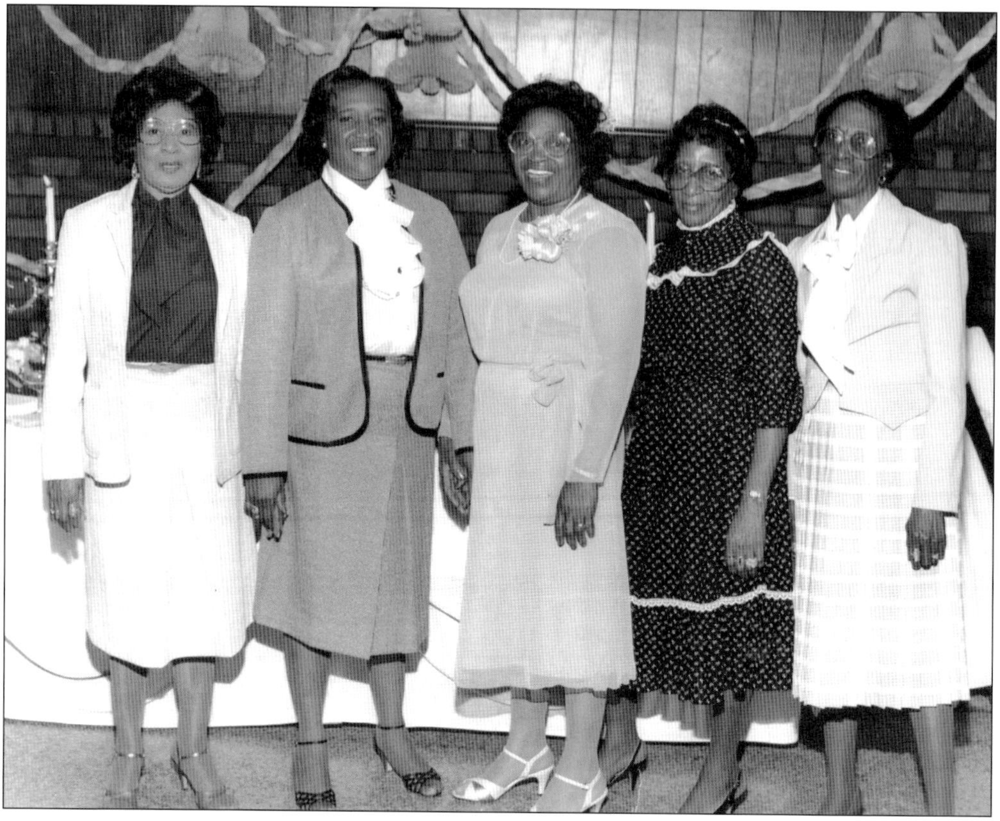

Pictured from left to right are sisters Julia Rose, Selena Ross-Coleman, Annie Mae Ruffin, Gloria Ross, and Virginia Rose. Gloria is the only surviving member of the group. She is in great health and good spirits—at 89 years of age at the time of publication. (Courtesy of Kim Darby.)

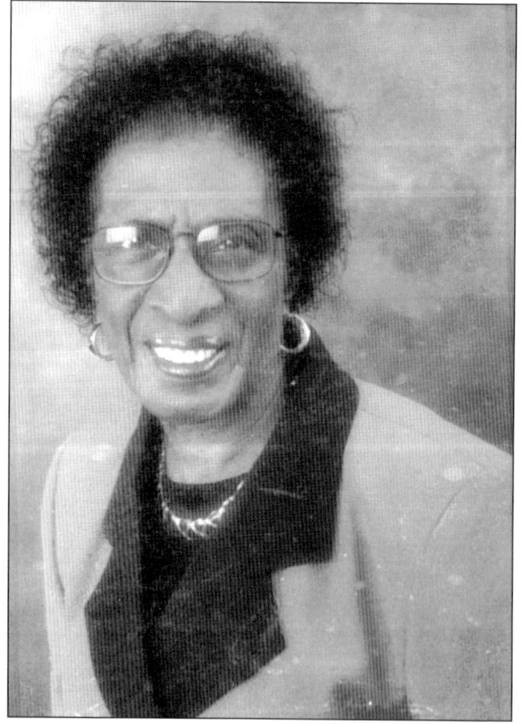

Virginia "Ginny" Ross-Rose was born on February 5, 1923. At an early age in her life, Virginia was baptized in the Mississippi River. She was a devout Christian and a member of the Benevolent Association. Virginia spent 93 years in the community before passing on February 8, 2016. (Courtesy of Anthony Rose.)

Lionel McDonald Jr. (left), Marylee McDonald, and Eugene Ross are pictured in this 1970s photograph. They are captured in semiformal attire of the time. (Courtesy of Marylee McDonald.)

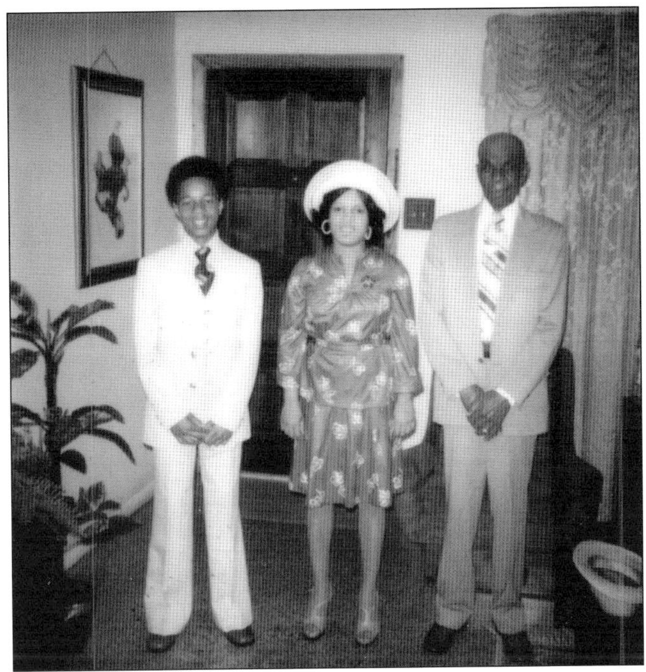

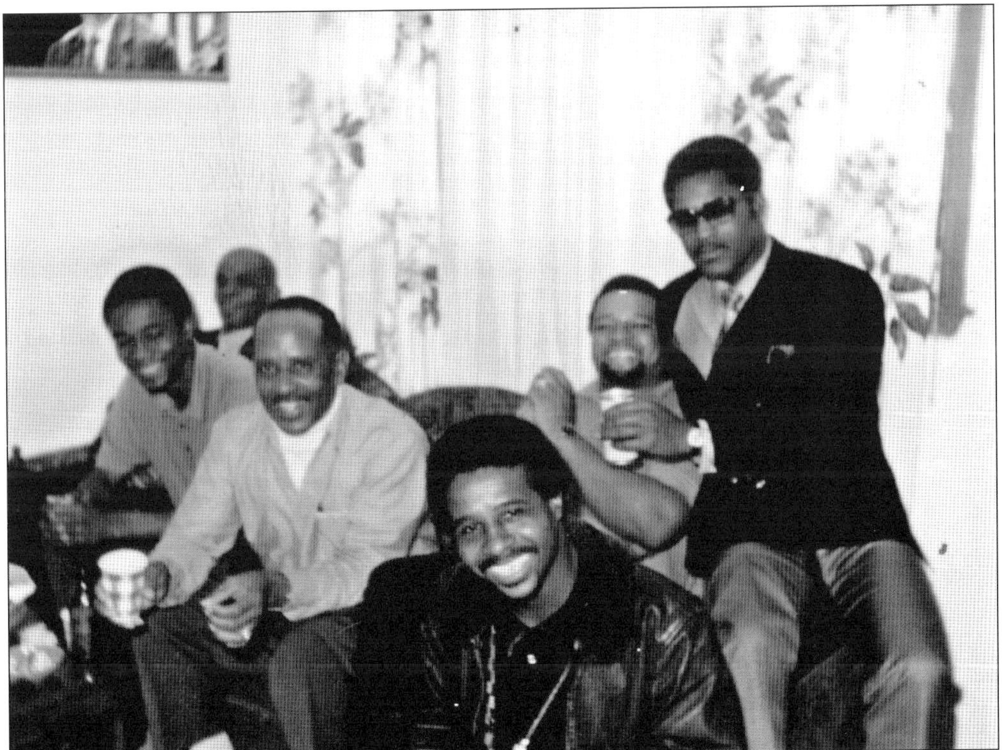

Pictured are, from left to right, Eugene Ross, Frank Wilson Jr., Eli Ross, Robert Lewis, Lionel McDonald, and Eddie Rose Sr. As is custom in the community, they are likely seen in this 1970s image during a conversation about current events while gathered for a meal at someone's home. (Courtesy of Marylee McDonald.)

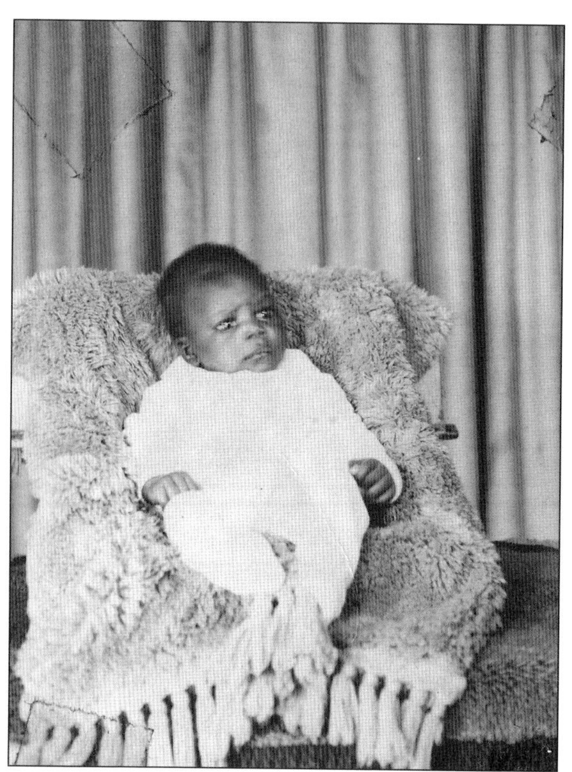

Lionel McDonald Jr. is pictured in this professional photograph taken in the early 1960s. He was the only son of Marylee and Lionel McDonald Sr. (Courtesy of Marylee McDonald.)

Seen here from left to right are Terry Price, Charlene Price, Tammy Manuel, Tracy Manuel, and Dena Manuel. This picture, taken in the 1960s, shows the typical style of dress of children in the neighborhood during this time. (Courtesy of Marylee McDonald.)

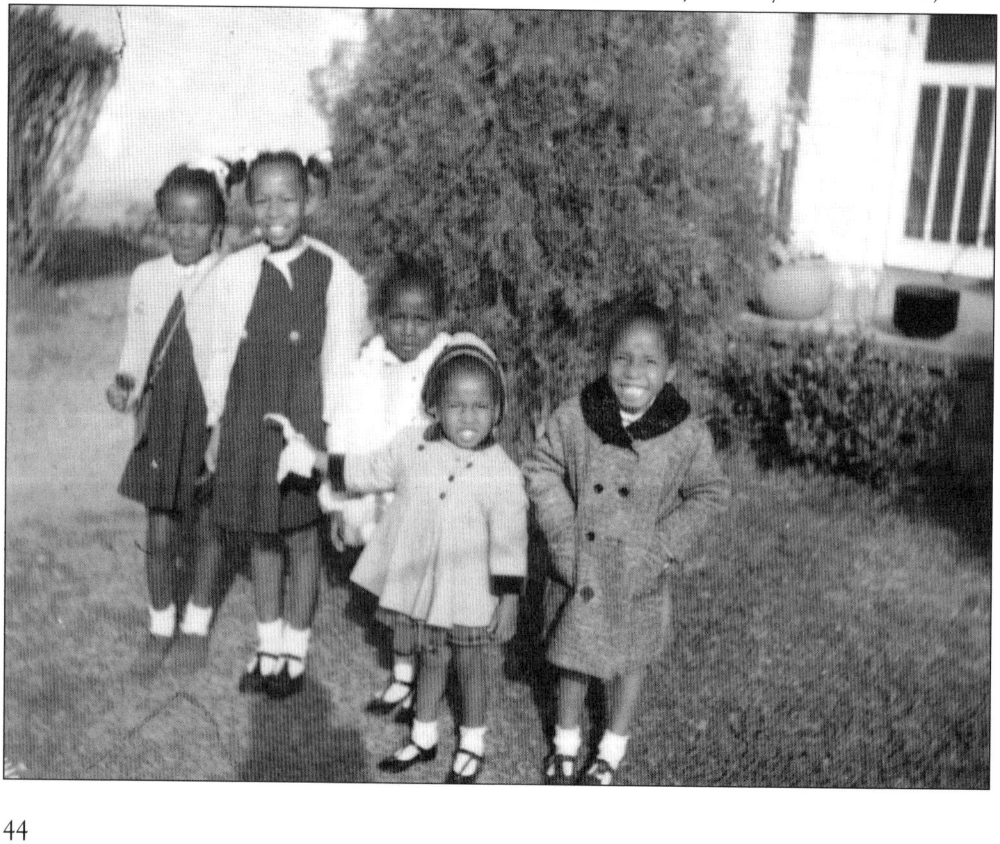

Amelia Washington-Price was born on September 11, 1912, to the union of John "Jack" Phillip Washington and Josephine Brown-Washington. Amelia married Henry Price Sr. in February 1952, and together they had 12 children. Thoroughly devoted in her walk with the Lord, she was called home to be with him on September 20, 1981. (Courtesy of Henry Price Jr.)

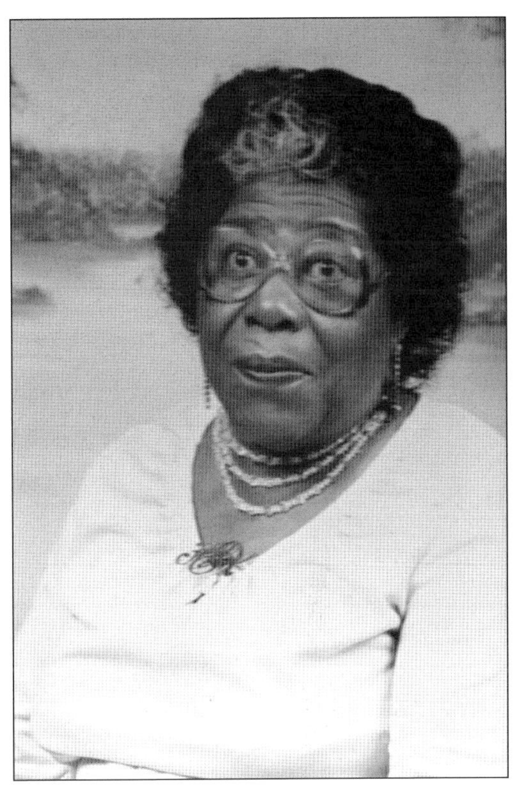

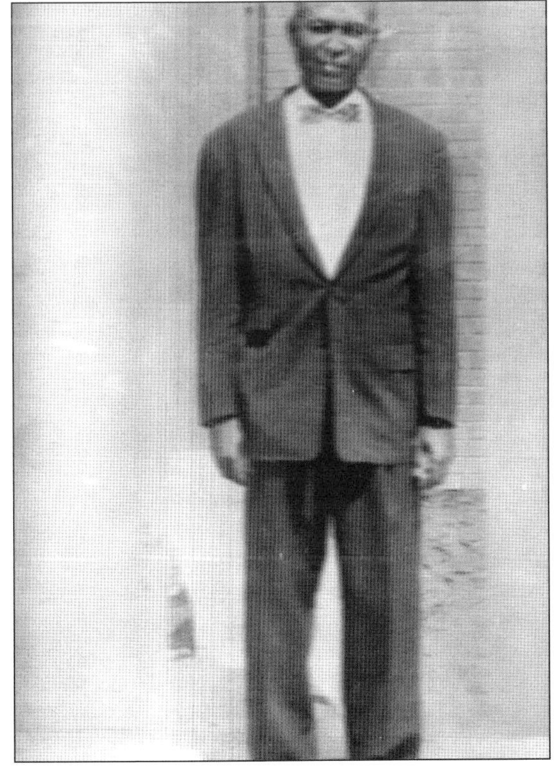

Henry Price Sr. was born on September 5, 1906, to Oliver Price and Amelia Williams. Henry served as secretary and deacon of Second Baptist Church in the 1940s and 1950s. He played a great role in the dedication of the new sanctuary of Second Baptist Church. Henry passed from this life on August 20, 1953. (Courtesy of Henry Price Jr.)

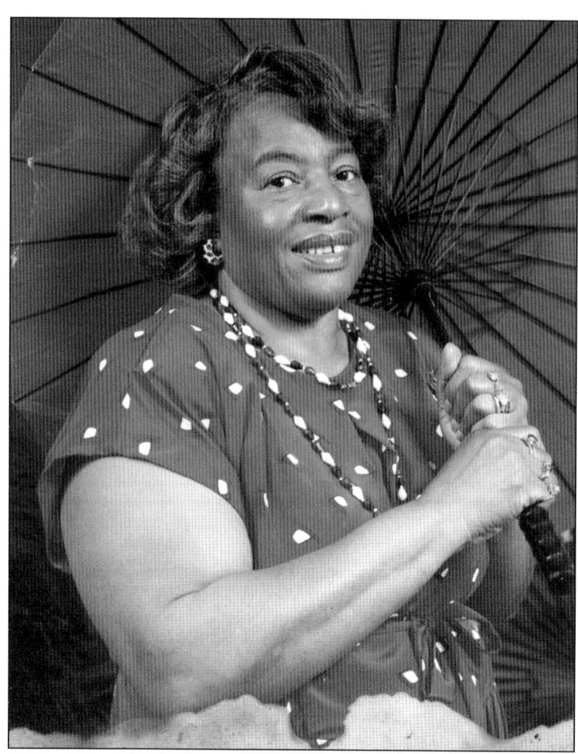

Dorothy Price-Anderson was born on September 23, 1945. Daughter of Amelia Washington-Price and Henry Price Sr., Dorothy was the 10th child of 12. (Courtesy of Henry Price Jr.)

Mabel and Isaiah Williams Sr. were both natives of the Lower Coast of Algiers. Isaiah was born on March 27, 1914, and Mabel was born the same year. They were the parents of five children. Isaiah passed away on January 28, 1989, and Mabel passed on March 27, 2001. (Courtesy of Mabel W. Jones.)

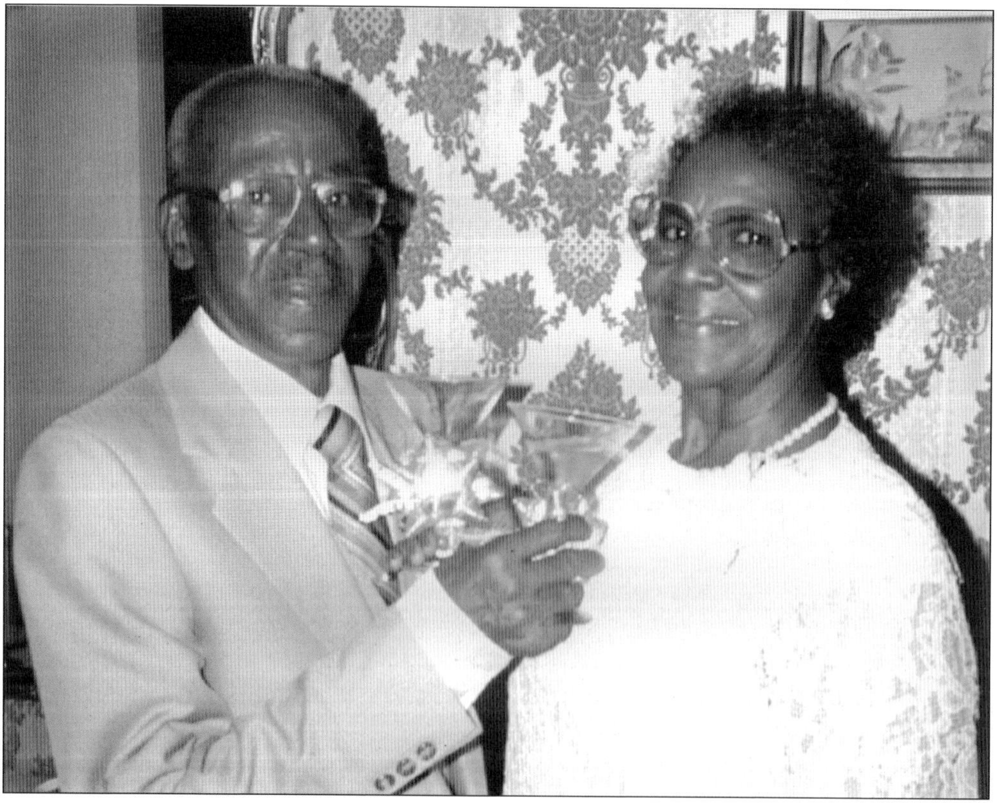

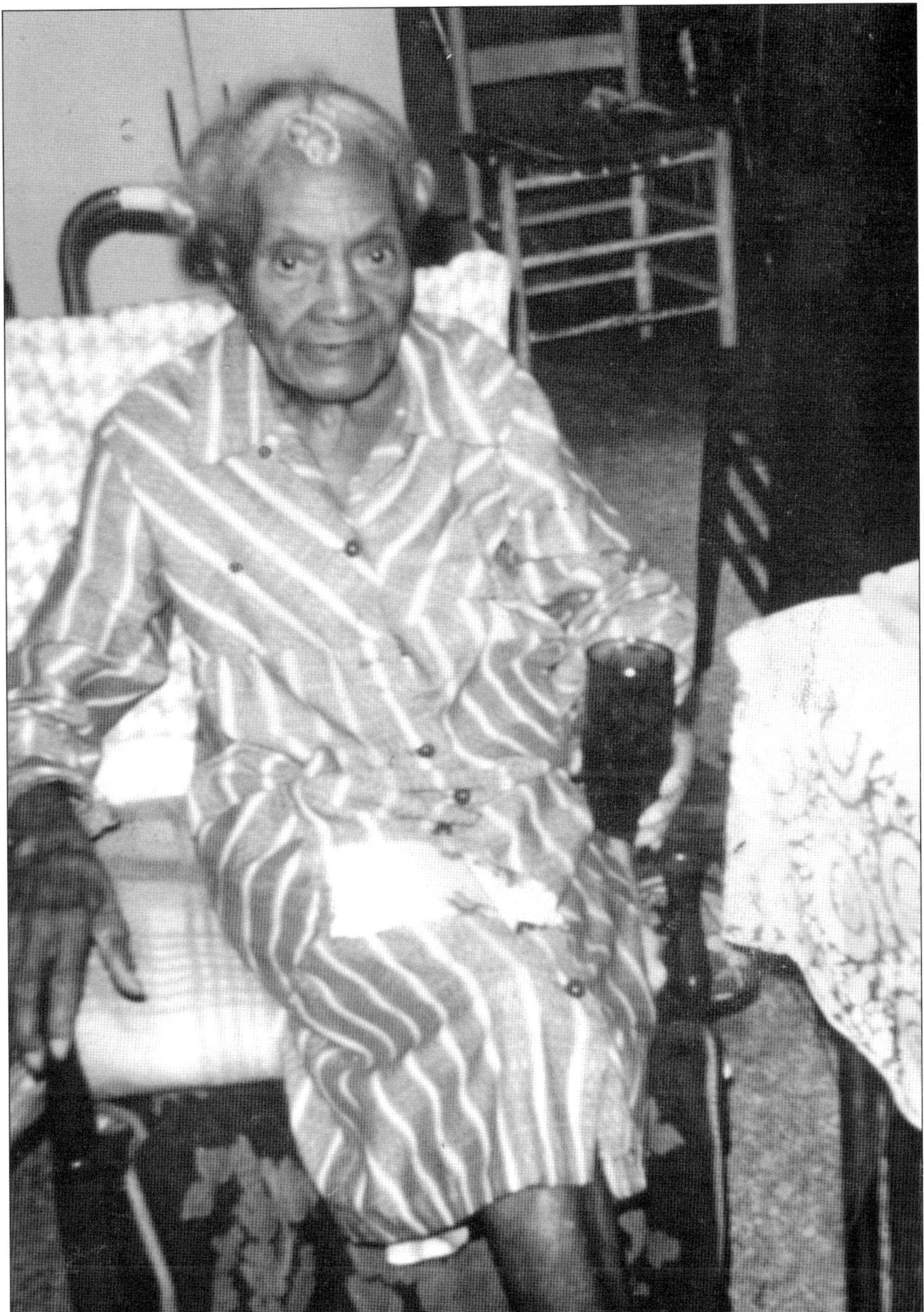

Antoinette Lewis-Jacobs was born April 15, 1879. Born and raised in the Lower Coast of Algiers, Antoinette spent the majority of her life as a homemaker. After the passing of her eldest daughter, Antoinette stepped in to raise her eight grandchildren. She succeeded in this task and passed away years later, on June 26, 1976. (Courtesy of Brenda Marie Gant.)

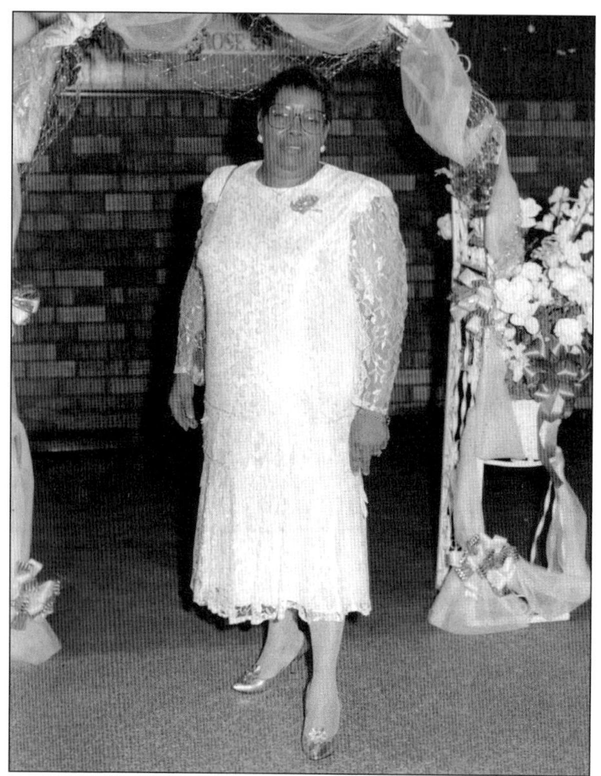

Malinda Benn-Ross was the seventh child to Stella McDonald-Benn and Isaac Benn Sr. She was born on March 25, 1929. Malinda was wed to Eugene Ross, and together they had nine children. Malinda was employed at Mary Joseph Nursing Home, now known as St. Luke Nursing Facilities. She passed away on April 19, 2010. (Courtesy of Lorraine Ross-Price.)

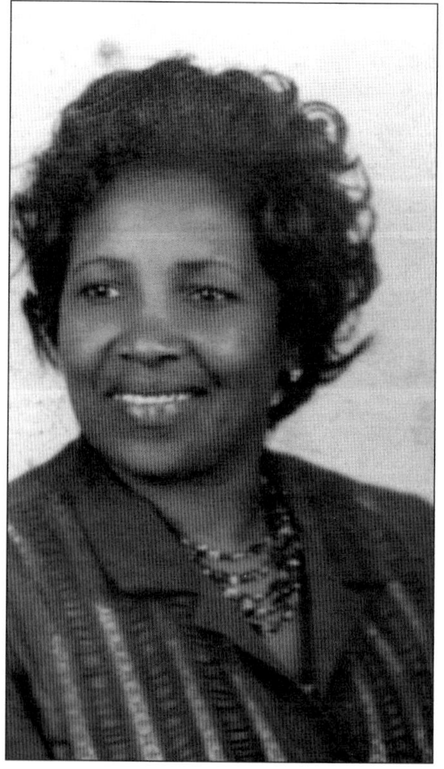

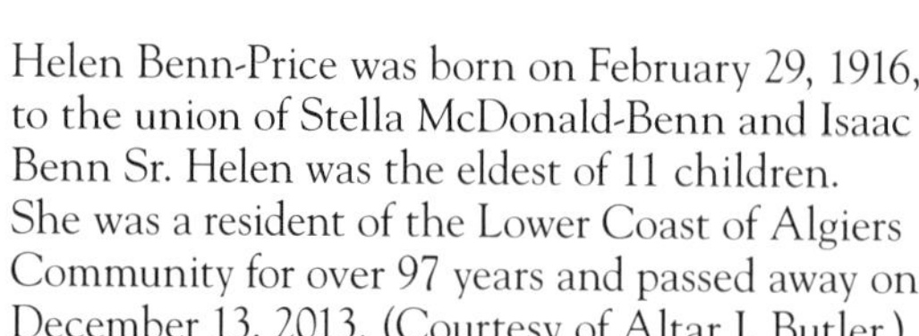

Helen Benn-Price was born on February 29, 1916, to the union of Stella McDonald-Benn and Isaac Benn Sr. Helen was the eldest of 11 children. She was a resident of the Lower Coast of Algiers Community for over 97 years and passed away on December 13, 2013. (Courtesy of Altar J. Butler.)

Bernadine Price was the daughter of Helen and Lawrence Price Sr. Bernadine is pictured in a professional photograph taken in the 1950s. Bernadine was the mother of three daughters and is known in the community for her great talent as a beautician. (Courtesy of Veronica St. Cyr.)

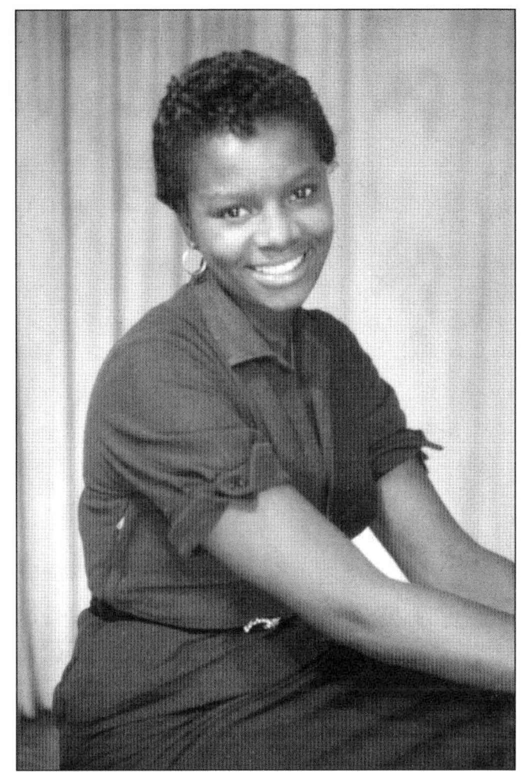

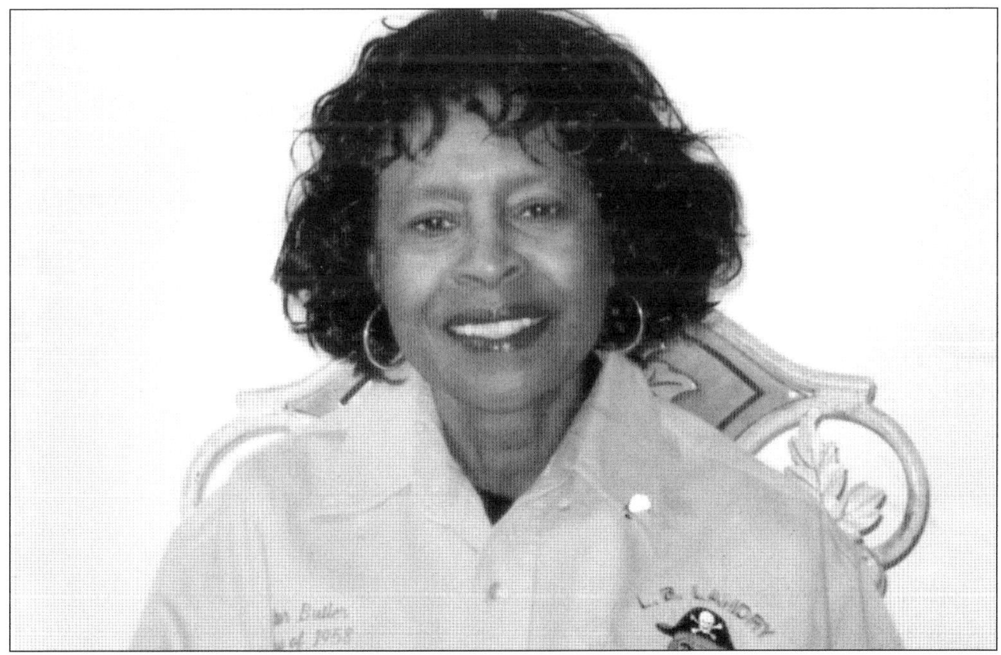

Altar Jacobs-Butler is the daughter of Helen Benn-Price and David "Boyd" Jacobs. Altar was born and raised in the Lower Coast of Algiers, where she attended the old Rosenwald school. Altar is a 1958 graduate of L.B. Landry High School. From L.B. Landry, she went on attend Dillard University. (Courtesy of Altar Jacobs-Butler.)

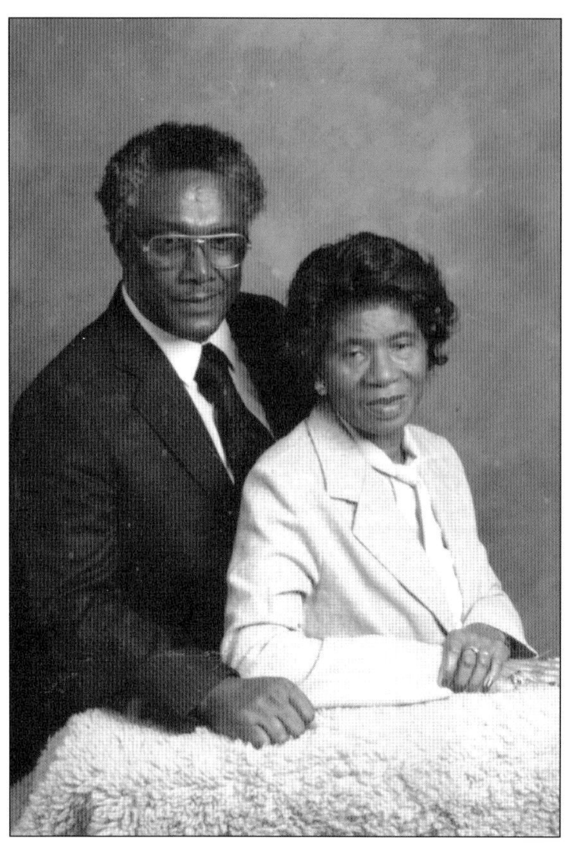

Pictured are Alberta "Bertdu" Riley-Gant and Samuel Gant Sr. Alberta was born March 21, 1923, to the union of Moses and Clara "Classy" Jacob-Riley. She met and married Samuel Gant of Chalmette, Louisiana, and they had 11 children. Alberta served as one of the founding members of the Lower Coast of Algiers Senior Citizen Center that was organized on April 13, 1973, in the home of Irma Taylor. Alberta passed from this life on July 1, 1999. (Courtesy of Brenda Marie Gant.)

Pictured are, from left to right, (first row) Helen Price, Cora Rose, and Bernadine Ross; (second row) Catherine Phoenix, Anna Lou "Shirley" Cosey, Shantell Webb, and Jeneen Graves. Each of these women was born and raised in Algiers's Lower Coast. They are pictured during a 1970s festival. (Courtesy of Veronica St. Cyr.)

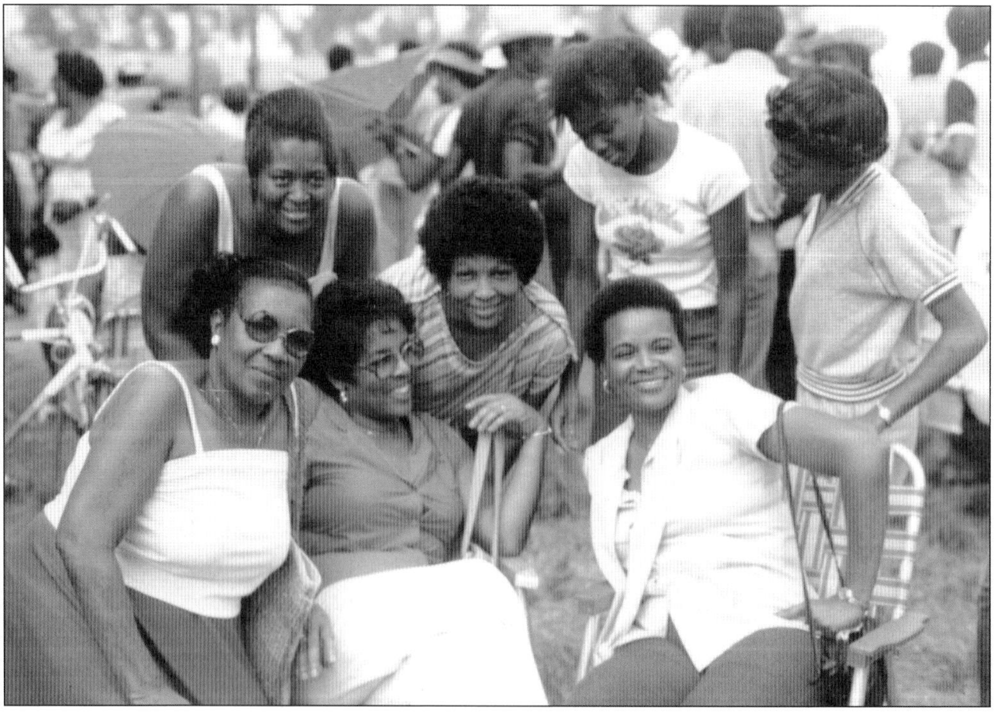

Carolyn Knight-Charles is pictured with her son Dave Charles Jr. This image was taken in the 1970s. (Courtesy of Veronica St. Cyr.)

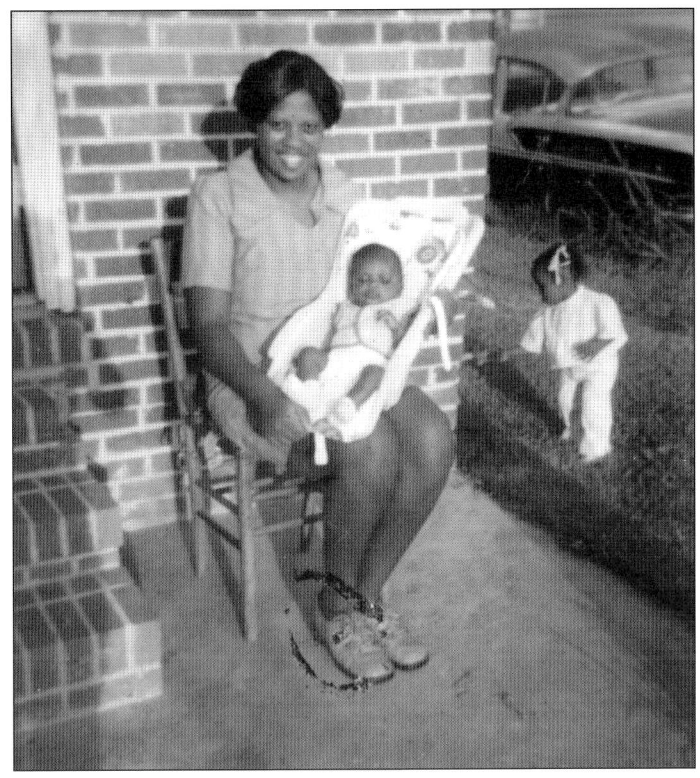

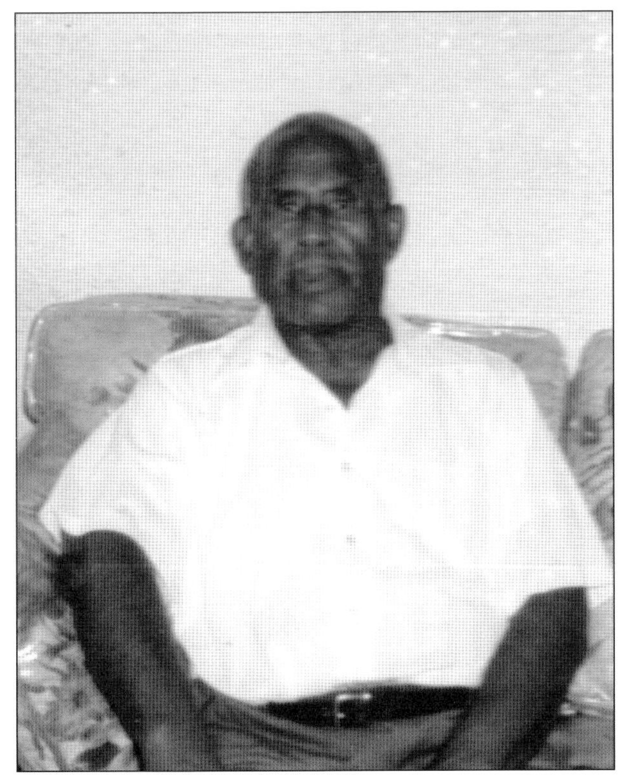

Octave "Chubby" Franklin Sr. was born March 8, 1919, to the union of Della Gray-Franklin and Isaiah Franklin Sr. Chubby attended Rosenwald Elementary School in the late 1920s and served in the Army during World War II. After his tour of duty, he started a civilian career with the National Air Station. He was one of the first candidates for baptism in the newly constructed Second Baptist Church under Rev. Dr. Earl Green. He also held membership and served for a short time as secretary for the Nazarene Benevolent Association. Chubby passed away on October 7, 2015. (Courtesy of Robin Crawford.)

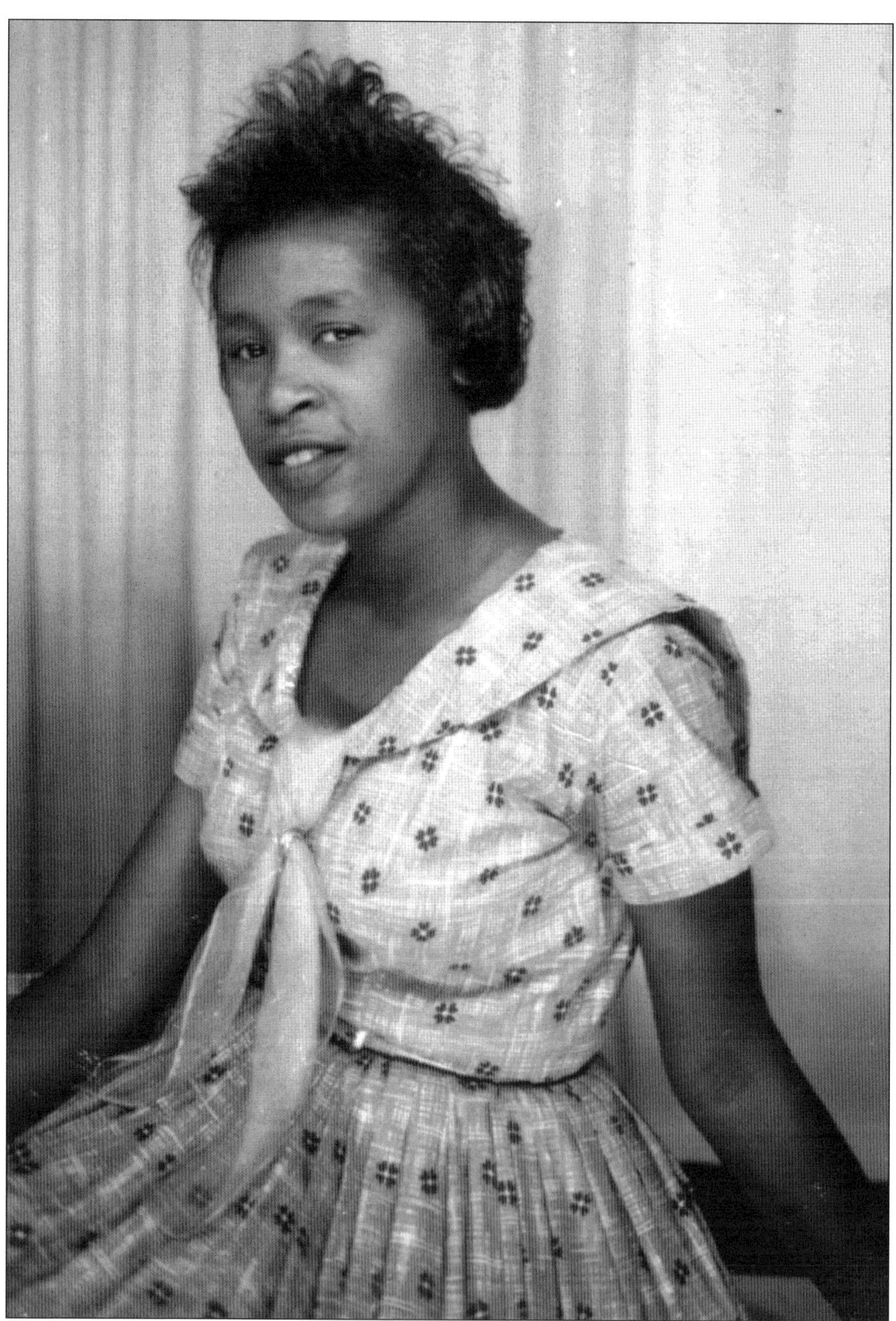

Doris Sullen is pictured in a professional photograph taken in the 1950s. Doris and her husband, Kermit Sullen, were the parents of three daughters: Saundra, Donna, and Kimberly Sullen. (Courtesy of Marylee McDonald.)

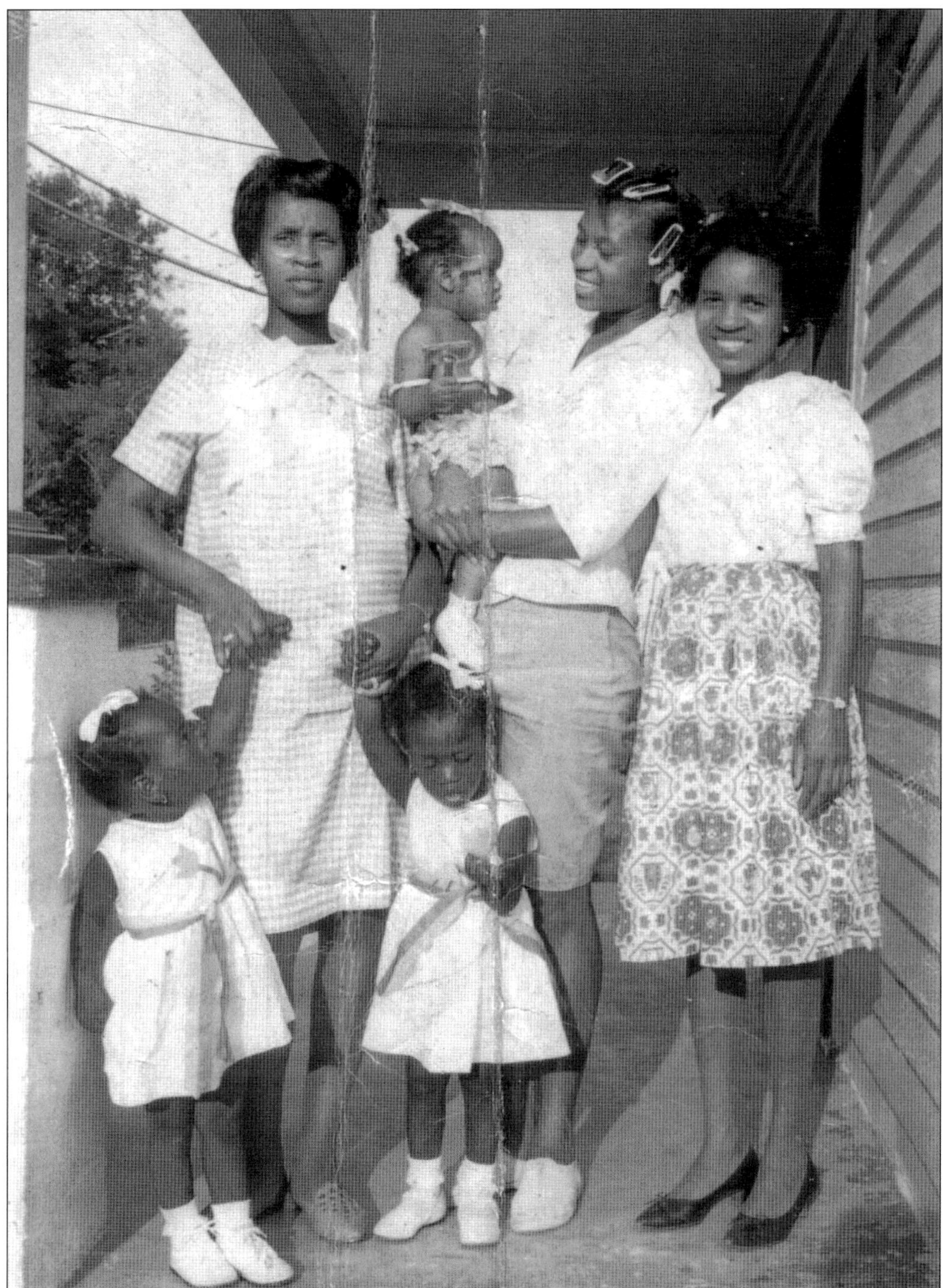

Doris Sullen (left), Nelly Nevil (center), and Mary Lee McDonald are pictured with their young but growing children—from left to right, Donna Sullen, Kim Sullen, and Nyrie Aberdie—on a casual day in 1960s. These women, like many in the area, show great appreciation of one another's company as their children, all similar in age, continue to grow. (Courtesy of Marylee McDonald.)

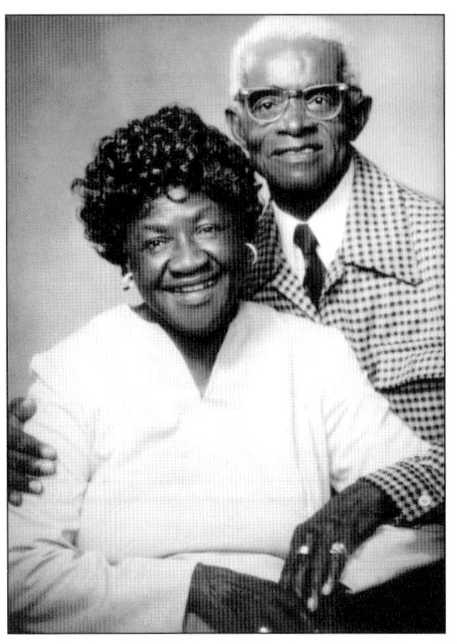

William "Ga-Bee" and Rebecca Phoenix-Ross were born on October 4, 1900, and December 28, 1910, respectively. William was the only man in the community who owned horses. He married Rebecca, and they had nine children. William was a farmer and used his horses to plow his garden, where he planted mustard greens, beans, and okra. He would then harvest them and sell them in the French Market. (Courtesy of Eloise R. Berry and Demetrius Berry.)

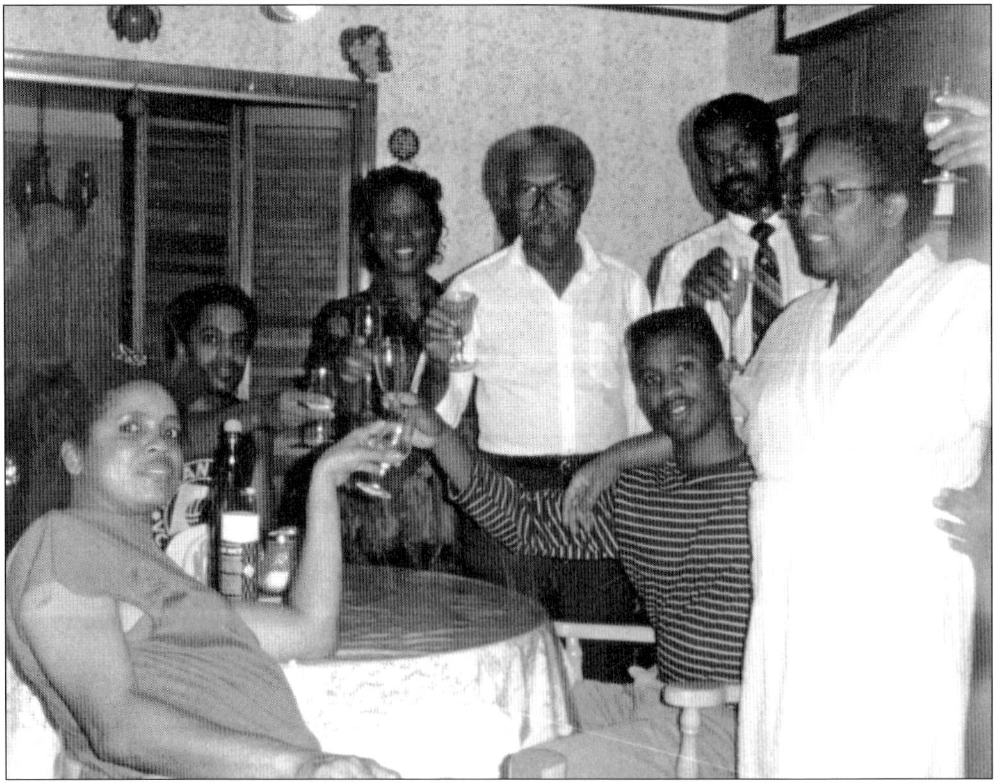

The Rose family is pictured toasting during a Christmas holiday in the 1980s. The patriarch of the family, Percy Rose, is in the center of the photograph with his children and grandchildren surrounding him. Percy is known for his musical talent, with many likening his voice to that of Sam Cook. On this day, as during many other holidays, they celebrate with song and cheer. (Courtesy of Enola Rose.)

Scott and Lillian Charles-Perrymon are shown wearing their lodge uniforms. This photograph was taken in the late 1950s, when many members of the community, particularly men, are known to have joined secret societies. (Courtesy of Robin Crawford.)

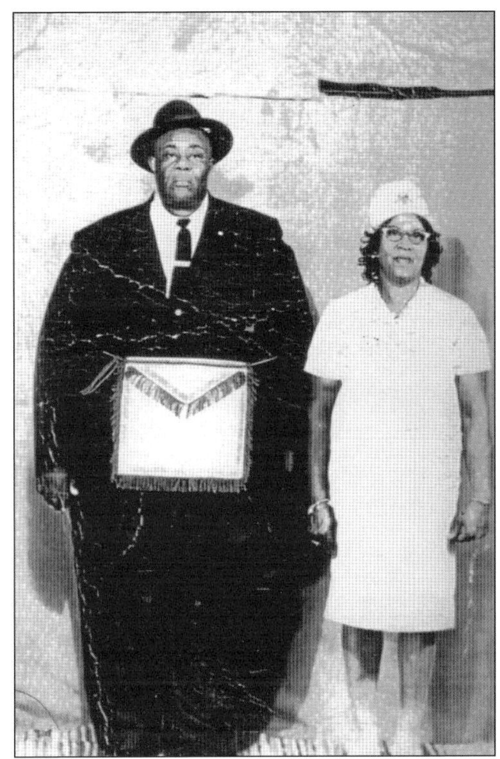

Pictured in this 1950s image are, from left to right, (first row, seated) Eli Jackson and Clarence Walker; (second row) MaryAnn Jackson, Leona Lee, Lillian Perrymon, Scott Perryman, Jean Price, and Grace Lee. (Courtesy of Veronica St. Cyr.)

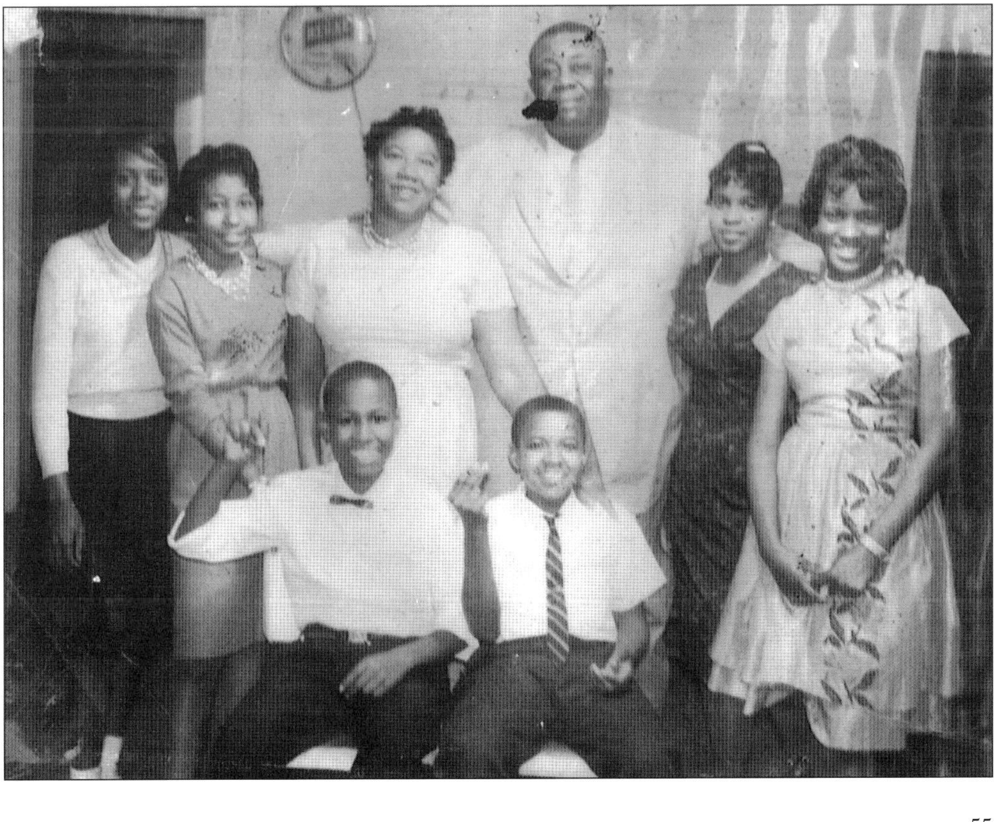

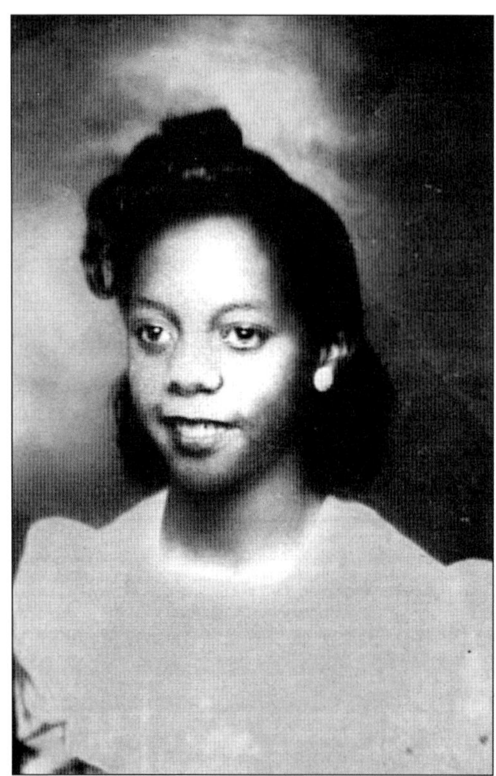

Florence Duplessis-Charles is pictured in this 1940s photograph. Florence was born and raised in the Lower Coast of Algiers. She met and married Leo Charles, and they moved to Columbus, Ohio. They later relocated to Cincinnati, Ohio, where they went on to raise their family. (Courtesy of Valeri Charles.)

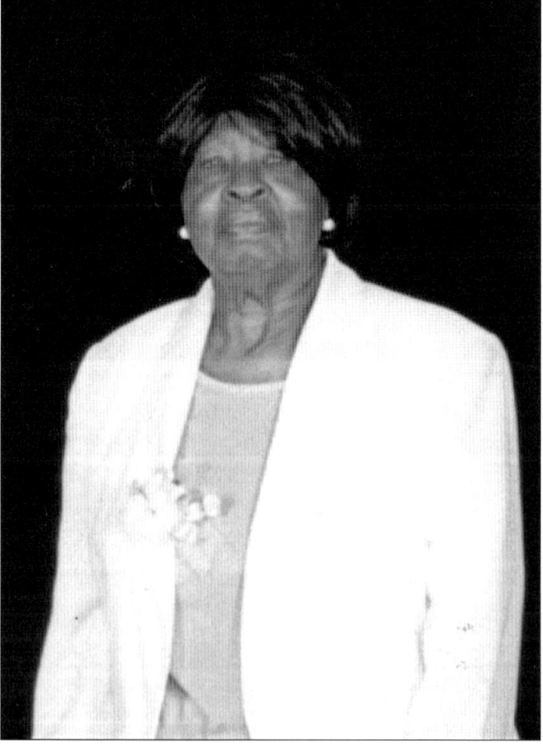

Mary J. Johnson was born May 7, 1920, to the union of Lawrence and Orelia "Mama Felo" Johnson. Mary was very well known in the community as "Peanut-eye." She was most well known in the community for her pecan candy and dress in commemoration of major holidays. Mary was employed by the Orleans Parish public schools for many years. She passed away on November 10, 2005. (Courtesy of Robin Crawford.)

Edward Lee and Louis Davis Sr. are two of the oldest surviving residents in the Lower Coast of Algiers. At the time of publication, both are age 96. Lee is a war veteran and worked as a carpenter for many years. Davis served as the community barber for an extended period of time. (Courtesy of Veronica St. Cyr.)

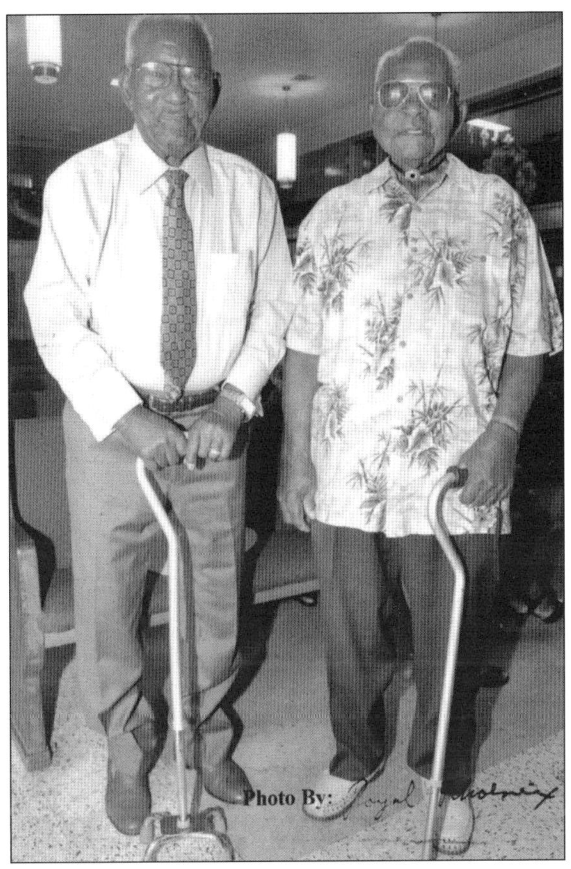

Edward Lee Sr. is pictured with his daughter Veronica and great-grandson Kayvon. Lee, 96 years old in this photograph, served in the Navy during World War II as a chef on a destroyer that was active in the Pacific. After returning home from war, he trained as a carpenter and built his home and many other homes in the area. At the time of the photograph, Veronica was a seamstress servicing many residents in the area and Kayvon was a student at Louisiana State University. (Courtesy of Frederick Weil.)

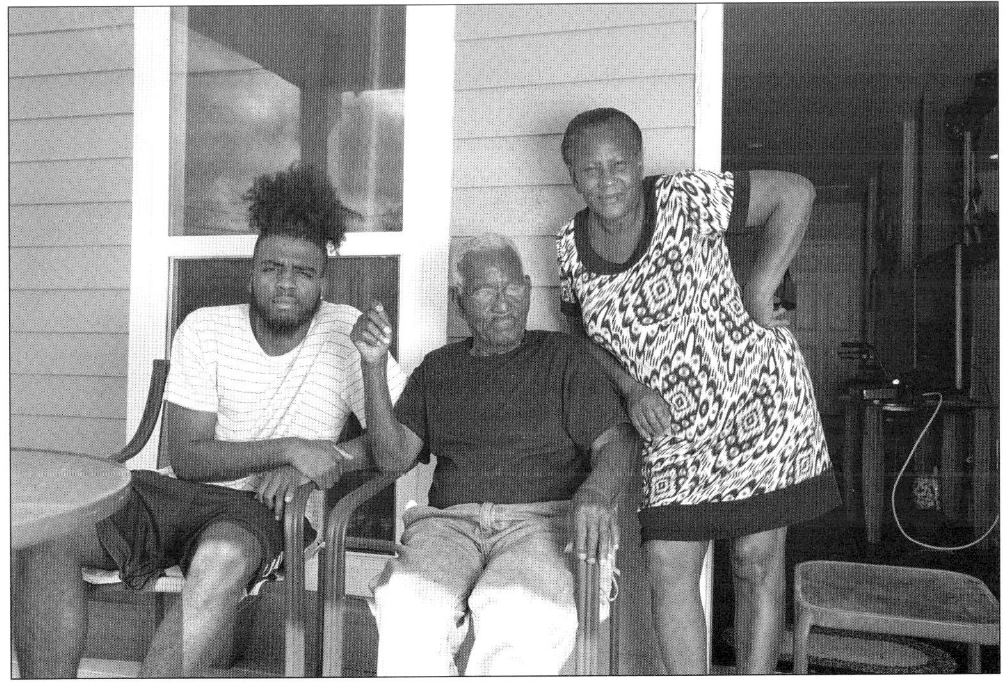

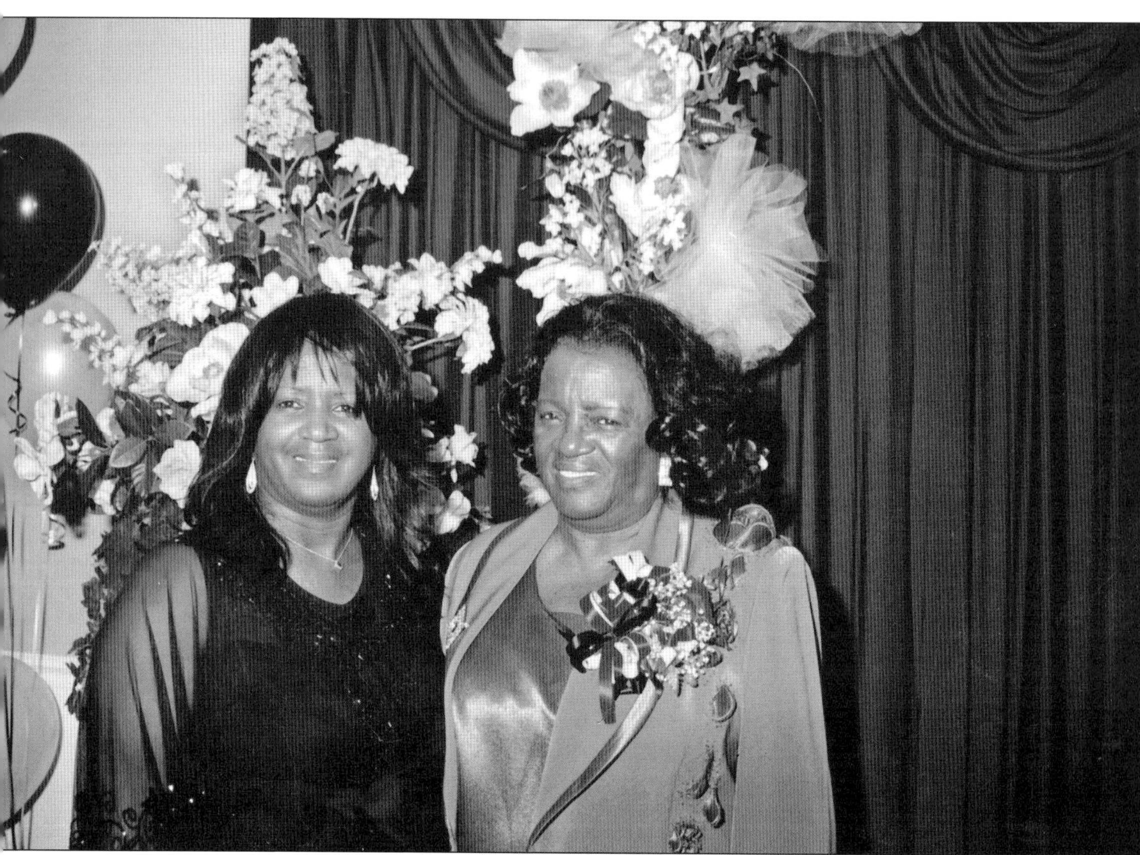

Evelyn McCoy-Gastinell, seen here (at right) with her daughter Melene Williams, was a trailblazer for the Cut-Off community. Born January 10, 1935, to Edward "Eddie" and Angelina Robinson-McCoy, Evelyn worked tirelessly to see justice brought to African American communities. She believed in equality, justice, hard work, integrity, goodwill, and services to others. She stood by these beliefs no matter the repercussions. She founded and was the director of the Lower Coast of Algiers Senior Citizen Center for over 45 years. Evelyn passed from this life on July 24, 2015. (Courtesy of Veronica St. Cyr.)

Two

Faith-Based Institutions

At the Heart of the Community with the Community at Heart

In many African American communities, churches and other faith-based institutions were among the first buildings to be erected in many neighborhoods as a result of collective efforts, be they time, talents, or treasure. In the Lower Coast of Algiers, Second Baptist Church was no exception. Second Baptist was the first of three churches to be come to be constructed in the area. Each of the three churches that currently stand in the community, however, acts as a beacon of hope to the surrounding area and continues the age-old tradition of "loving thy neighbor."

The founders of Second Baptist Church were former slaves from surrounding plantations. Several of the men who had been emancipated from the yoke of slavery gathered together to discuss their deep desire to aid in the spiritual development of mankind. On August 25, 1868, the founders met in a house on Ganascheau plantation (the Orleans subdivision) and elected their first pastor, who went by the name of Brother Jones. Brother Jones was installed as a pastor by the First District Baptist Association, and Second Baptist Church was born.

The church has had only five pastors since its beginning in 1868. Brother Jones pastored for 36 years, before his passing on March 17, 1904. The second pastor, Rev. Reason Boyd, who had been hand-selected by Reverend Jones prior to his passing, was ordained and installed as pastor of the congregation on October 2, 1904. During Reverend Boyd's 51 years of service to the congregation, the country engaged in two world wars, the Great Depression, and several wars against communist aggressors. When Reverend Boyd passed from this life on April 23, 1955, he was succeeded by his adopted son Rev. Dr. Earl Green. A new sanctuary was erected under the leadership of Reverend Green in 1967, and the Reason Boyd Memorial Annex was dedicated in memory of his predecessor.

Just prior to the passing of Rev. Earl Green in May 1994, Rev. Taza Green was installed as the fourth pastor of Second Baptist Church. Under Rev. Taza Green's leadership, Second Baptist grew both numerically and spiritually. His teaching ministry brought spiritual enlightenment to both the church and the community. Taza Green passed away on September 16, 2015, after a hard-fought battle with cancer and was succeeded by the current pastor, Rev. Andre Sigler.

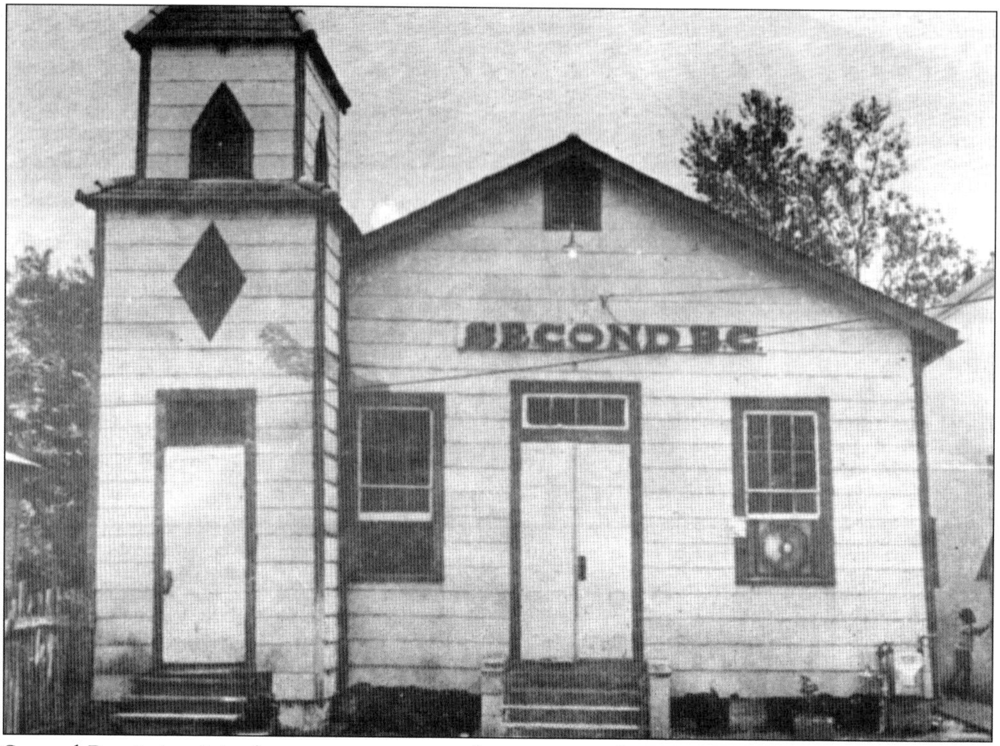

Second Baptist's original structure was a single-room, wood structure positioned on a small lot on Simpson Place. Despite its modesty, members from the community would gather to receive expository preaching as well as to participate in other social, cultural, and educational events. (Courtesy of Mercelyn Sullen.)

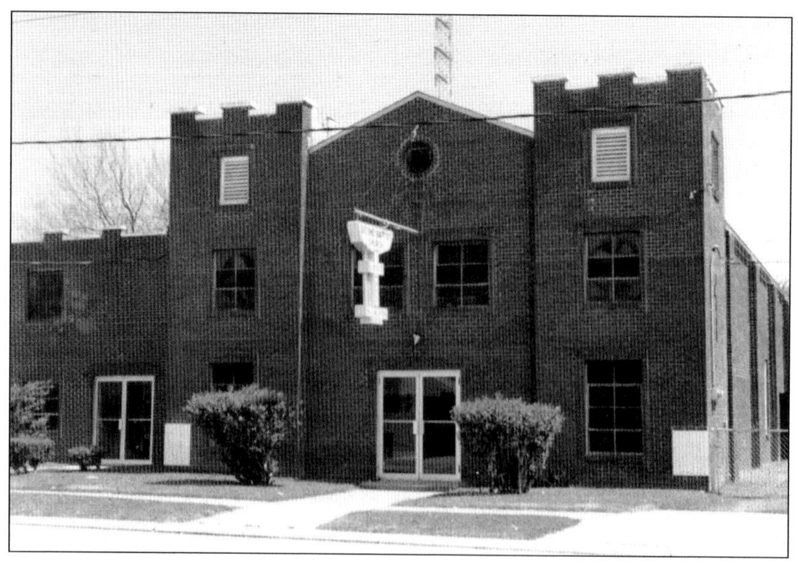

Second Baptist's new brick building was erected in 1957. The Reason Boyd Memorial Annex was constructed and dedicated in 1967, in memory of the late pastor. (Courtesy of Charlie Benn Jr.)

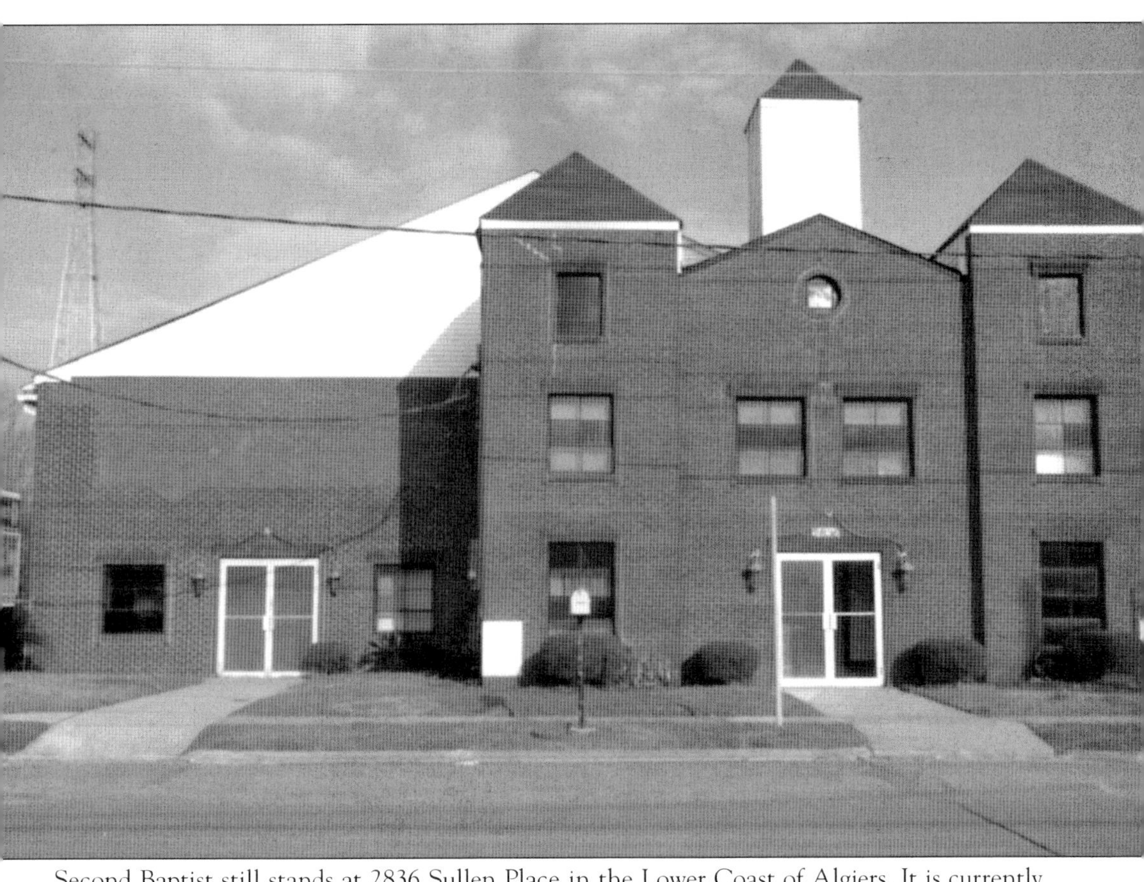

Second Baptist still stands at 2836 Sullen Place in the Lower Coast of Algiers. It is currently under the leadership of Rev. Andre Sigler. (Courtesy of Robin Crawford.)

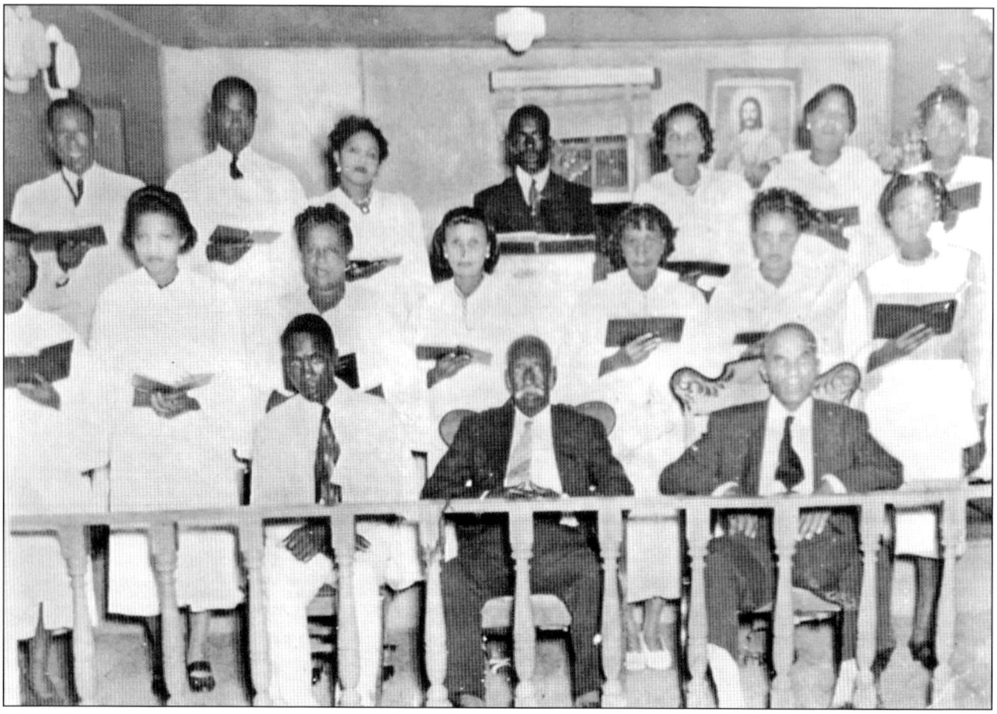

This photograph was taken in the early 1950s in the original Second Baptist Church structure. This image shows the choir, which includes, from left to right, (first row) Wesley Ruffin, Rev. Reason Boyd, and Rev. Morris Gastinell; (second row) Eartha Ross, Myrtle Williams, Anita Cook, Julia Rose, Glory Mae Ross, and Odetta Wilson (organist); (third row) Herbert Sullen (director), Dood Johnson Sr., Helen Price, Rev. Earl Green, Lillian Green, Hennie Phoenix, and Hannah Green. During this time, the Reverend Boyd served as senior pastor, with Morris Gastinell serving as assistant pastor. (Courtesy of Leroy "Royal" Phoenix.)

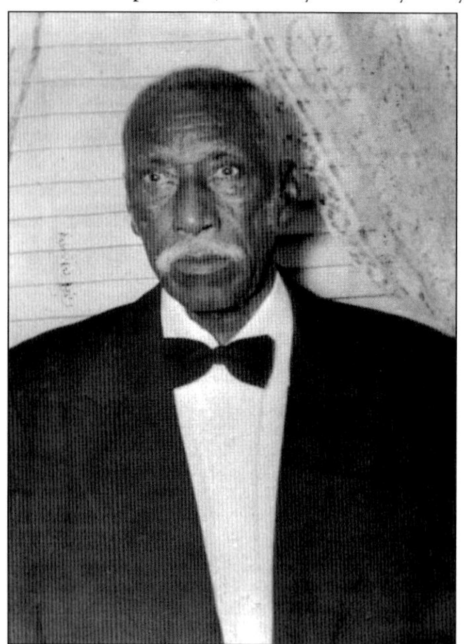

Rev. Dr. Reason Boyd was born on February 19, 1870, to the union of Sally and John Boyd. Reverend Boyd served for over 50 years as the second pastor of Second Baptist Church. Reverend Boyd was known as "Doc" in the community. Boyd Street, which sits just behind Second Baptist Church, was named in his honor. Though he passed away many years ago, on April 23, 1955, his legacy still lives on. (Courtesy of Leroy "Royal" Phoenix.)

Rev. Dr. Earl Green was the husband of Lillian Green. He was also the father of Thomas Green Sr., Charles Green, and Geraldine Green. (Courtesy of Robin Crawford.)

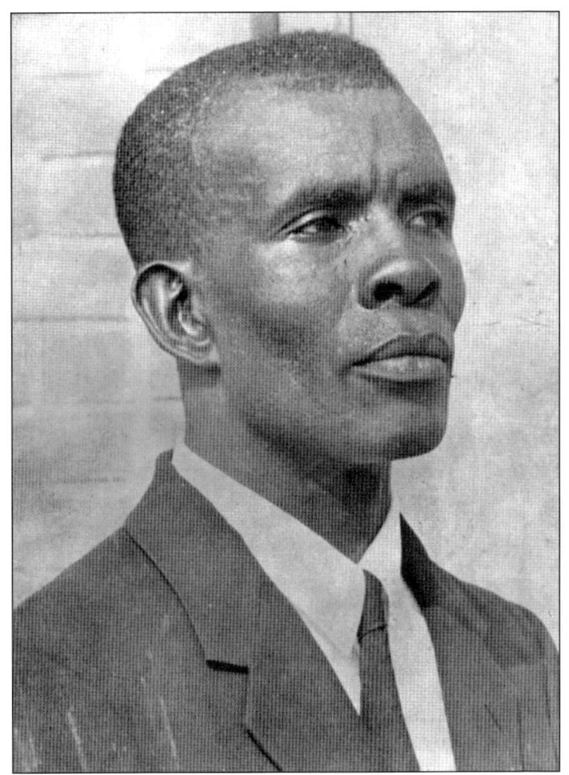

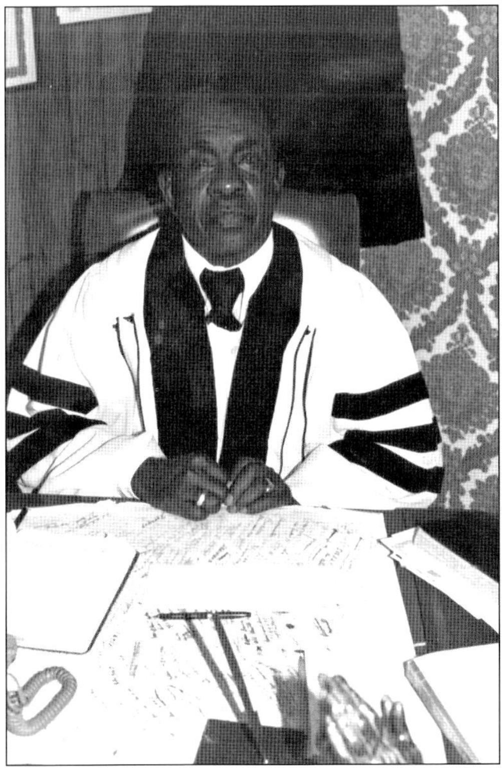

Rev. Earl Green was ordained as a pastor of Second Baptist Church in 1955. He was not only a spiritual leader in the local area but also served as a civic leader. Reverend Green often met with local politicians to ensure that the community had paved streets and running water. Reverend Green is remembered in the community as a civic leader with deep love for the Algiers and the Cut-Off community. (Courtesy of Charlie Benn Jr.)

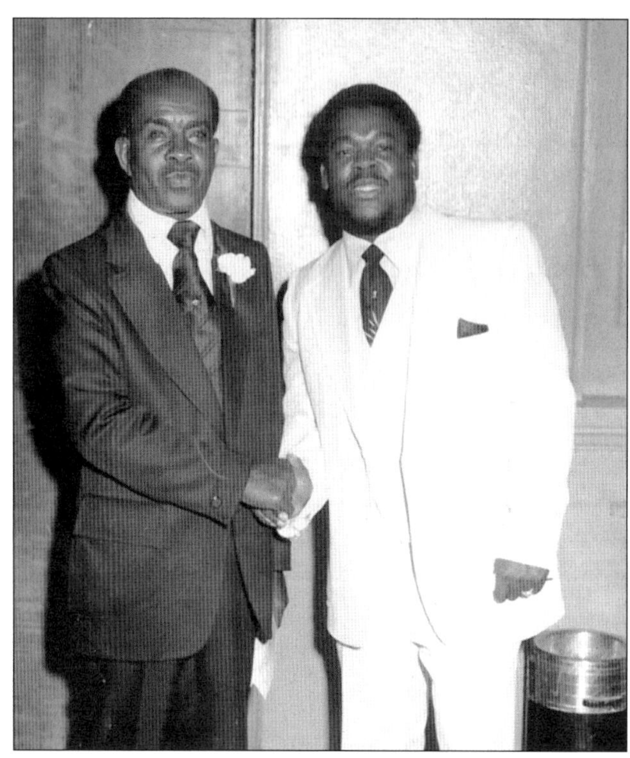

Rev. Earl Green (left) is pictured with Clarence "Frogman" Henry in this 1980s photograph. The two used their platform to bring awareness regarding situations in the community. (Courtesy of Clarence Henry Jr.)

Pictured is Rev. Dr. Earl Green performing the wedding ceremony of Olivia Landry-Ruffin and Wesley Ruffin Sr. at Second Baptist Church. Eugene Gastinell Sr. and Lola Mae Ross stand as witnesses. (Courtesy of Wesley Ruffin Jr.)

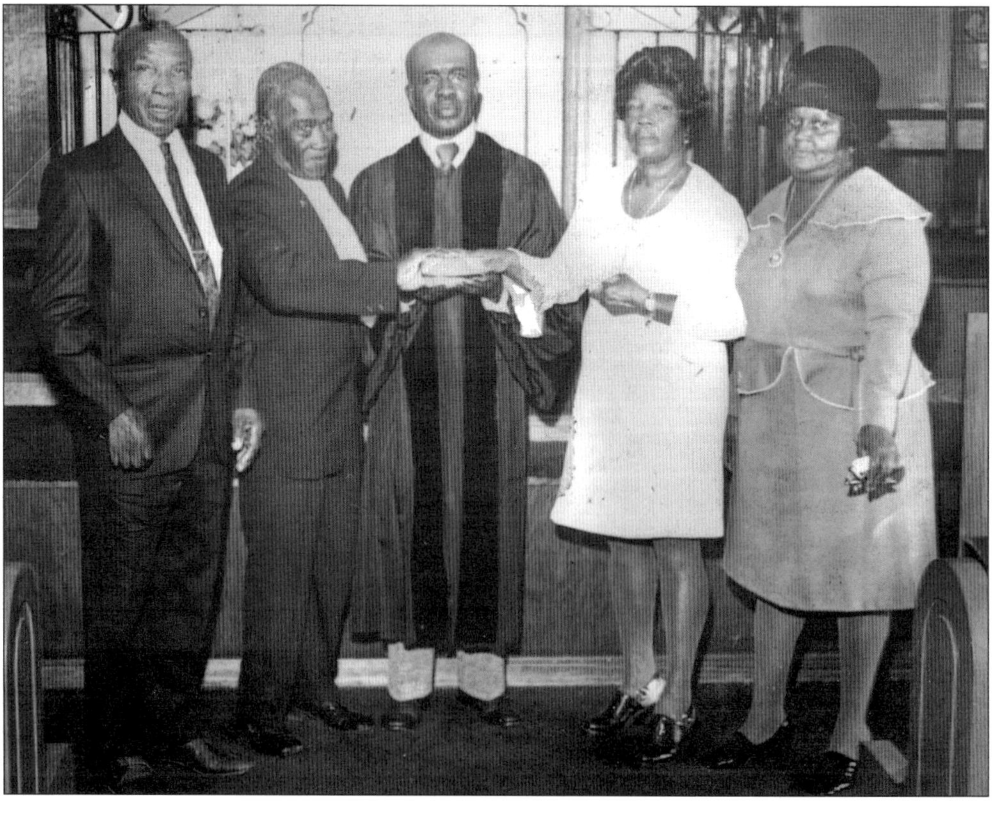

Pastor Taza Green Sr. was born on January 6, 1959, to Claudette Landry-Green and Thomas Green Sr. He was employed as an educator with the Jefferson Parish public schools until his retirement in 1994. Having realized several years earlier there was a higher calling in his life, he announced his intention, on July 4, 1988, to become a pastor and was ordained in April 1989. On April 26, 1994, he was installed as pastor of Second Baptist Church, where he served faithfully until his passing on September 16, 2016. Aside from being a great pastor and community leader, Reverend Green was a devoted husband to Ira C. Smith Green and a loving father to his children Taza Jr. and Tira E. Green. (Right, courtesy of Robin Crawford; below, courtesy of Ira Green.)

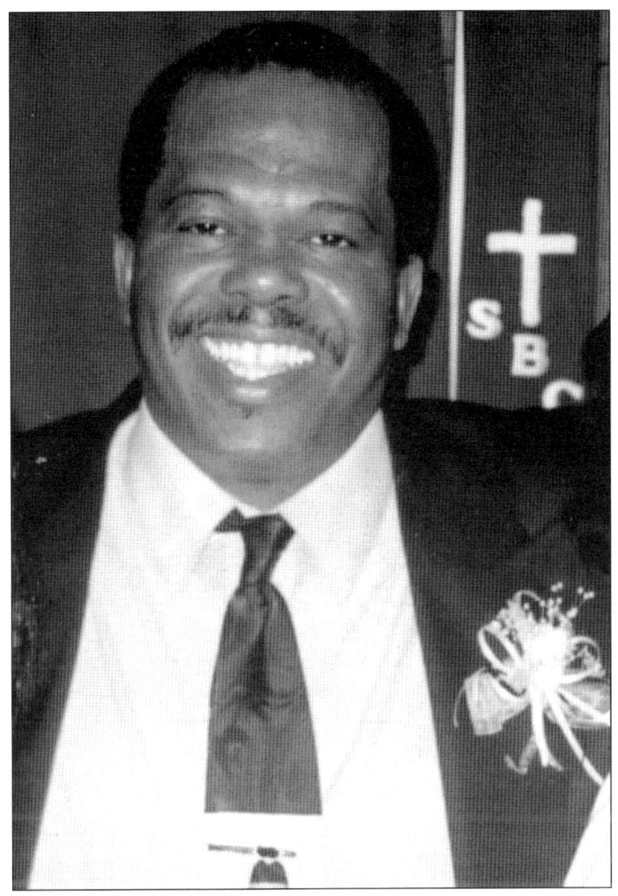

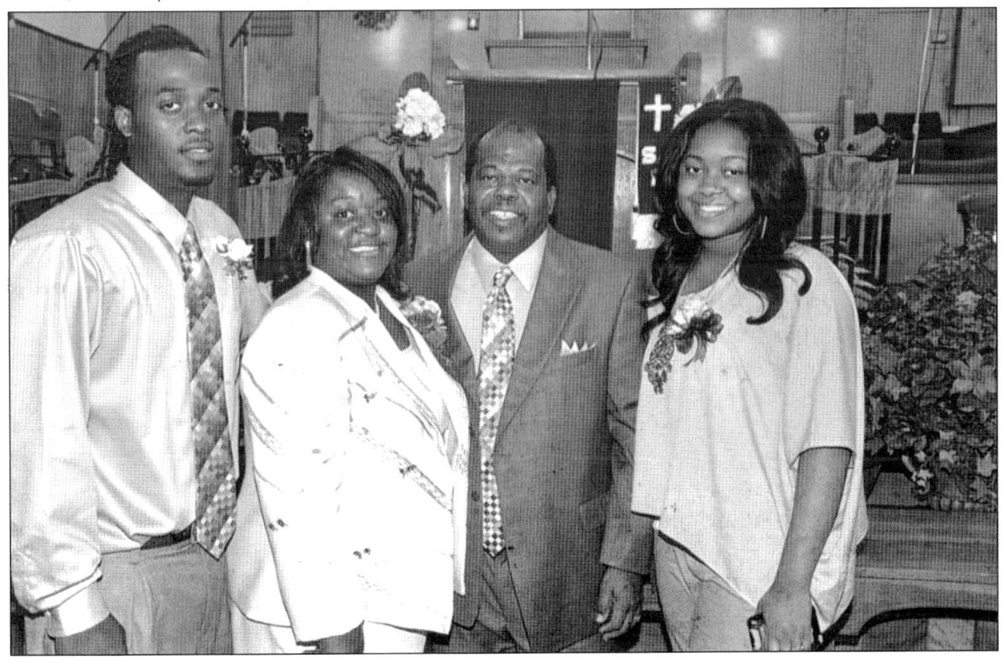

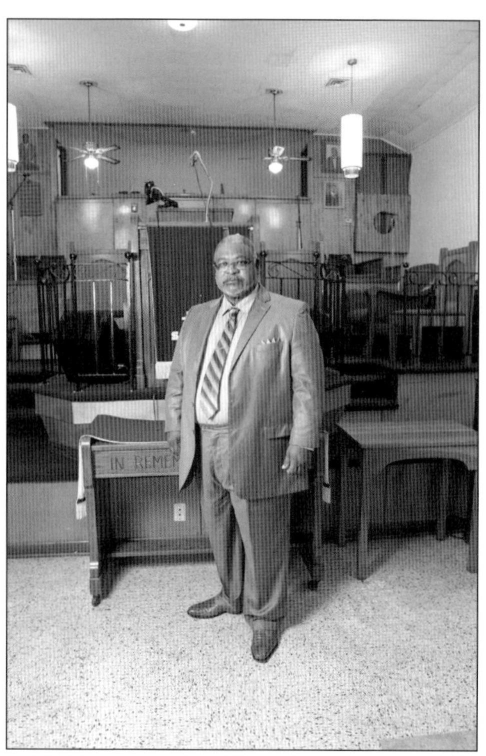

Pastor Andre Sigler is the current pastor of Second Baptist Church. He is also the leader of Pure Light Baptist Church, located in Greater New Orleans. (Courtesy of Frederick Weil.)

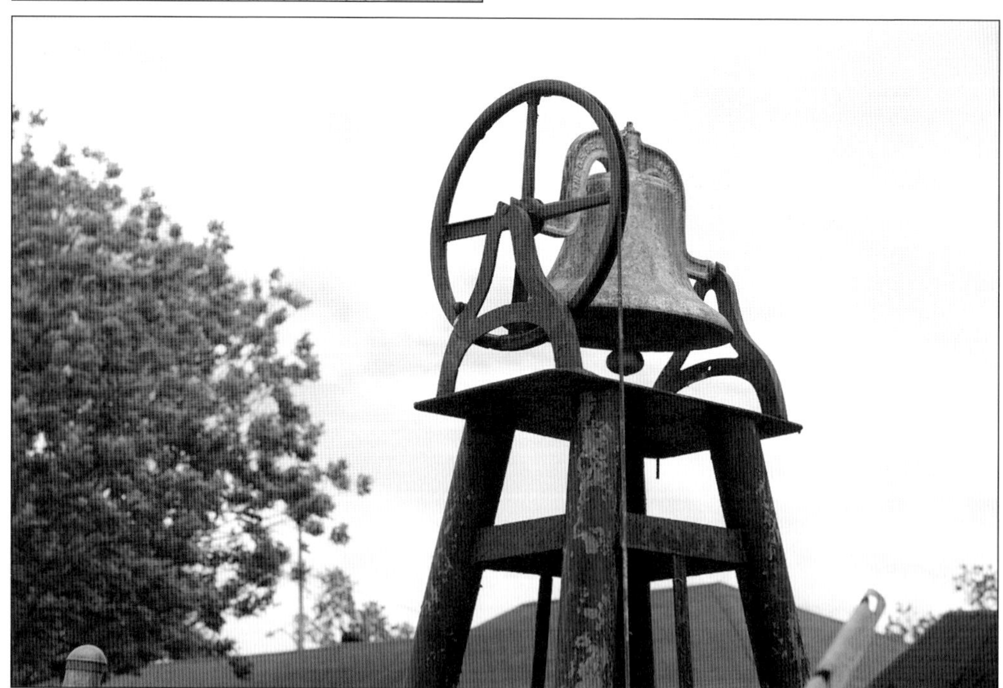

This church bell has been a vital part of the community since 1868. The bell was used to signify the time for worshippers to gather. Different tones were used to distinguish between the type of celebration that was to take place. This bell still rings out from the church today. (Courtesy of Frederick Weil.)

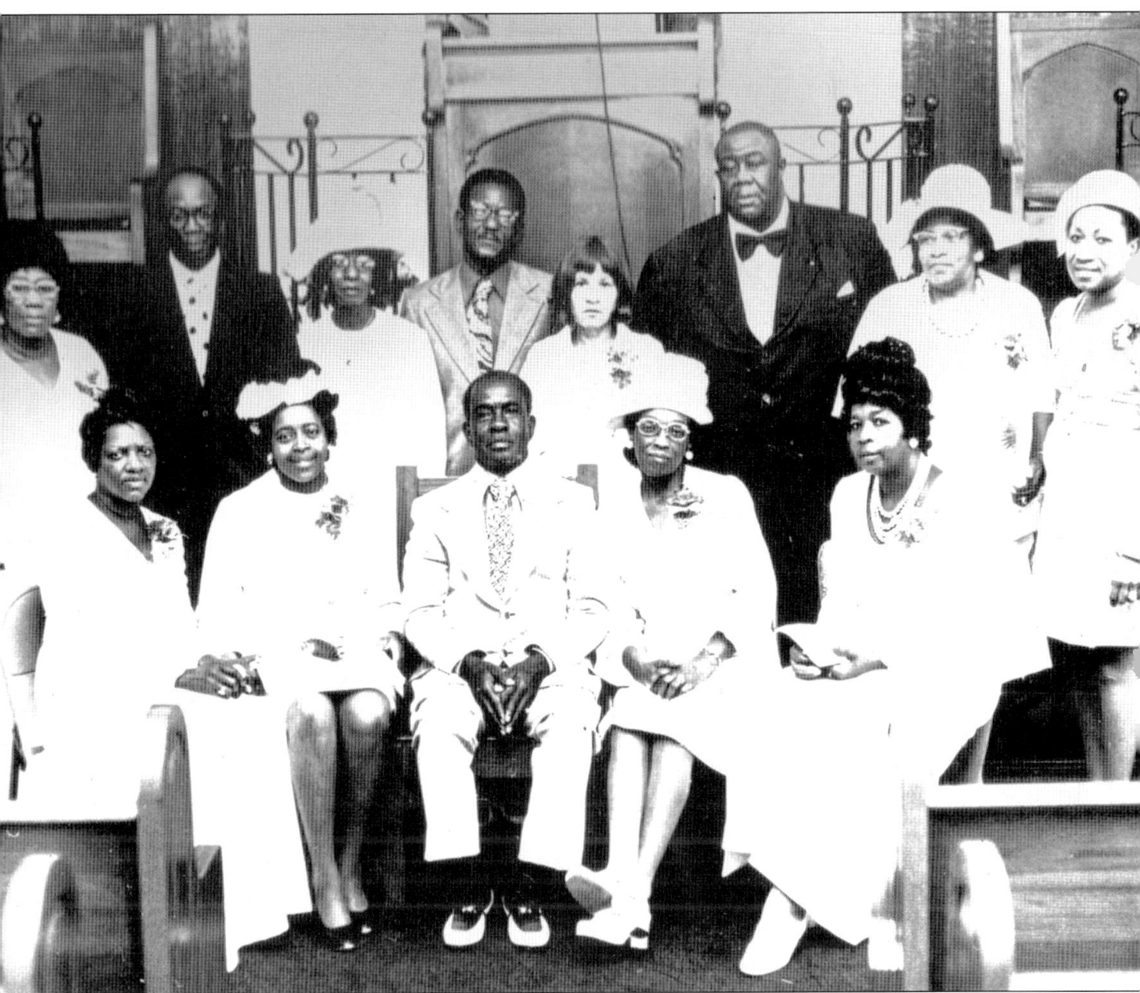

Pictured in this image are, from left to right, (sitting) Clementine G. Benn, Eartha Rose, Rev. Dr. Earl Green, Lillian G. Green, and Louise Cazano; (standing) Isabel Berry, John Phoenix, Rebecca Ellison, Edward Lee, Scott Perrymon, Amelia Price, and Elinese Simmons. This photograph was taken during Woman's Day at Second Baptist Church. (Courtesy of Robin Crawford.)

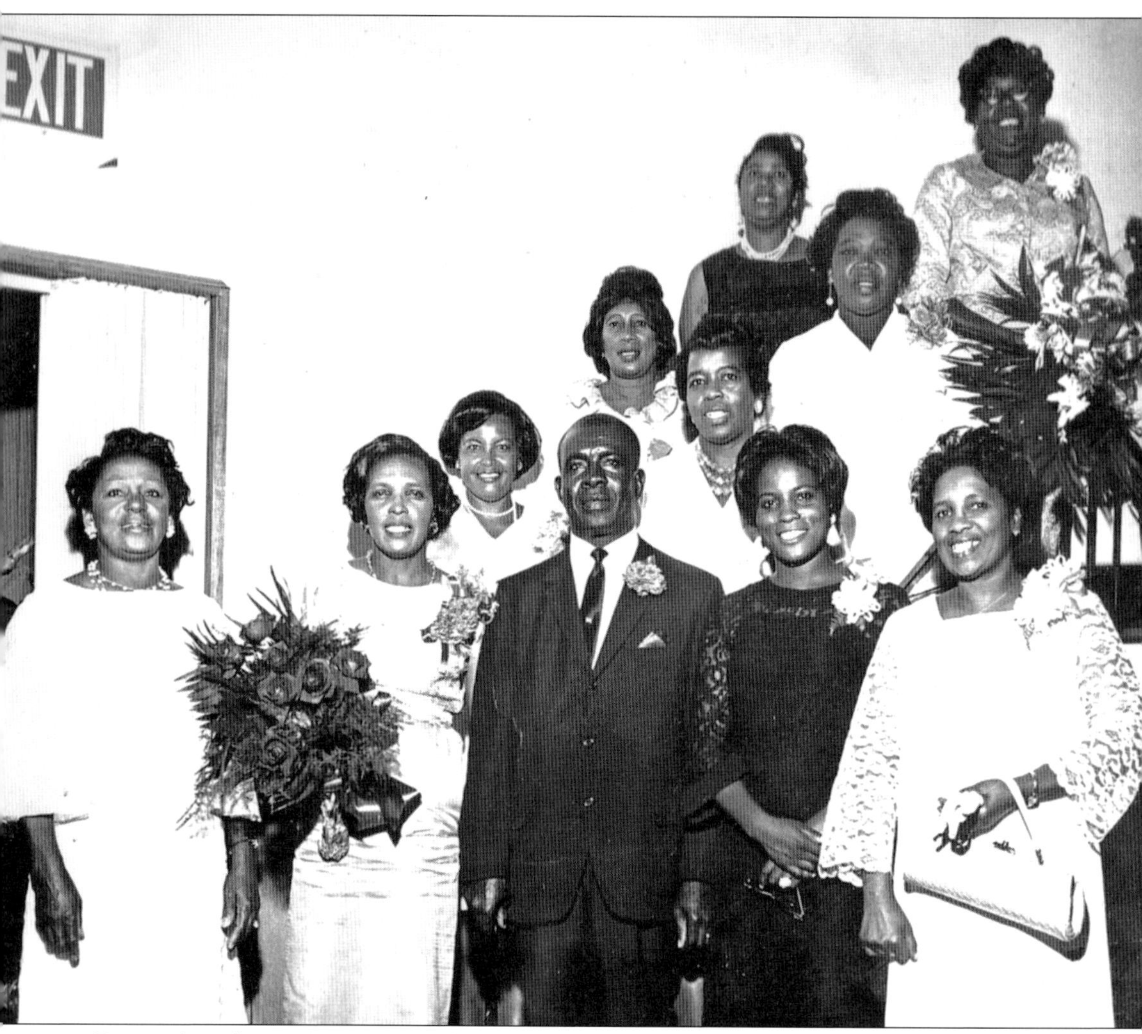

Pictured in this 1960s image is the Pastor's Aide Committee commemorating the pastoral anniversary of Rev. Dr. Earl Green. Shown are, from left to right, (first row) Kitty Robinson, Lillian Green, Reverend Green, Grace Lee, and Cora Rose; (second row) Mildred Phoenix and Louise Cazano; (third row) Isabell Berry and Alberta Franklin; (fourth row) Rebecca Sullen and Hennie Phoenix. (Courtesy of Doris Phoenix.)

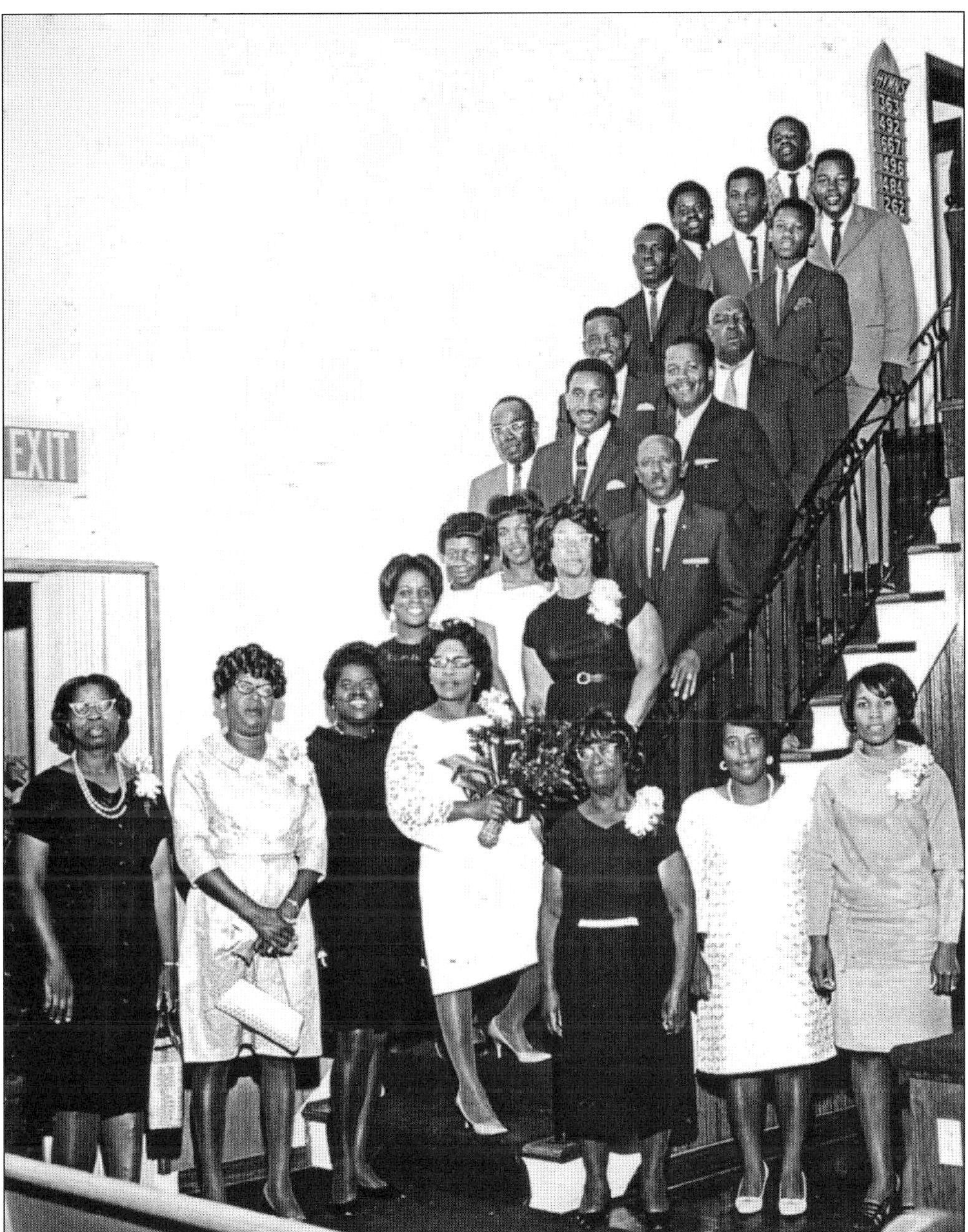

Pictured in this 1960s image taken at Second Baptist Church are, from left to right, (first row) Ethel Knight, Hennie Phoenix, Yvonne Berry, Cora Rose, Anita Cook, Eartha Rose, and Audrey Green; (second row) Grace Lee, Selina Banks, Elvira Martin, and Hazel Smith; (third row) Eli Ross, Lawrence Price, and John Phoenix; (fourth row) Royal "Leroy' Phoenix and Edward Lee; (fifth row) Alexander Washington, Charles Green, Roger Lee, and Michael Franklin; (sixth row) Rene Ross, Alfred Ross, and Dale Williams. (Courtesy of Doris Phoenix.)

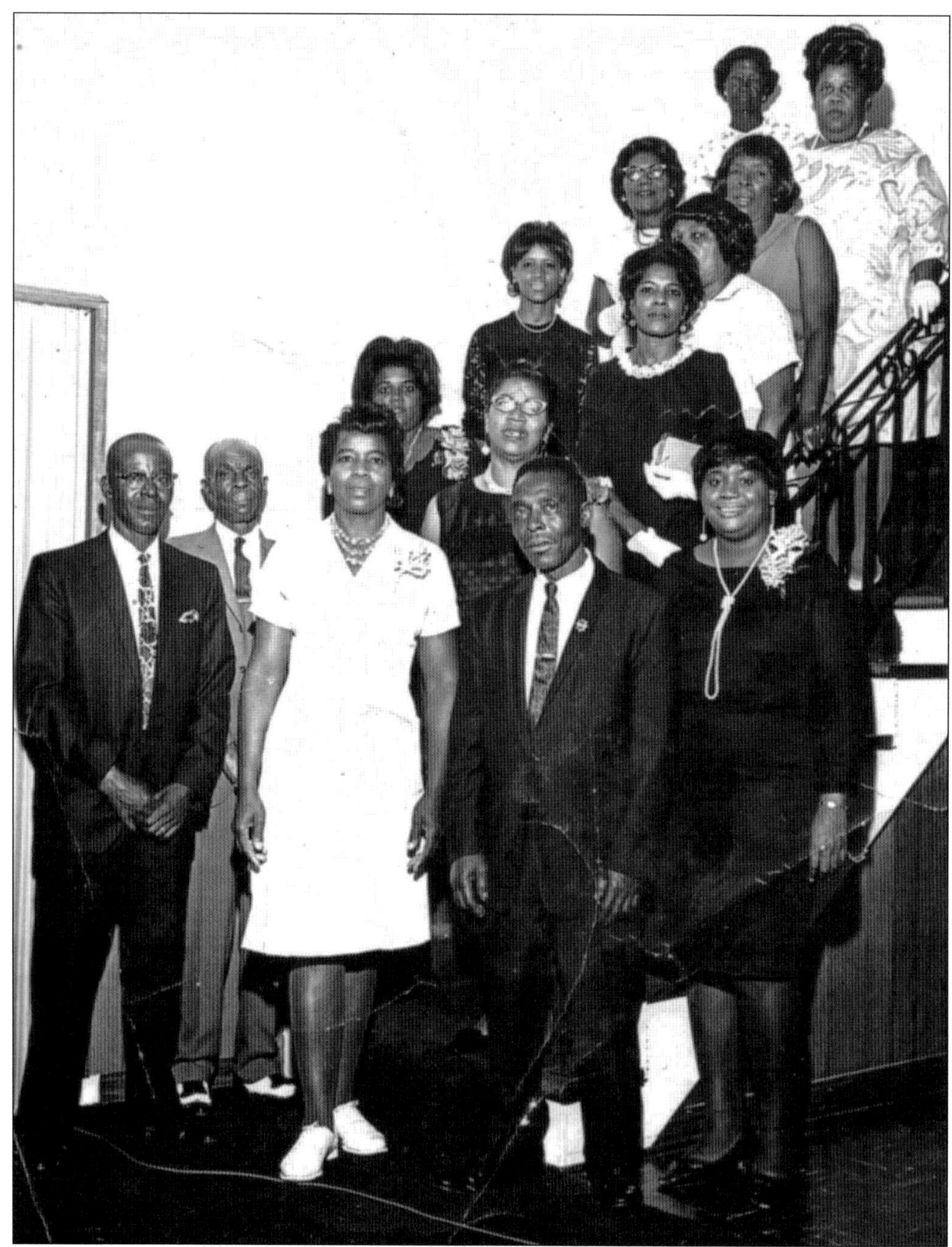

Pictured in this 1960s image is a group of Second Baptist Church ushers. This group includes, from left to right, (first row) Isaiah Williams, Eugene Ross, Louise Cazano, Ernest Cook Sr., and Emogene Smith; (second row) Lola Mae Ross and Lillian Perrymon; (third row) Diane Davis, Grace Lee, Mercedes Noil, Ernestine Carter, Orelia Johnson, and two unidentified persons. (Courtesy of Doris Phoenix.)

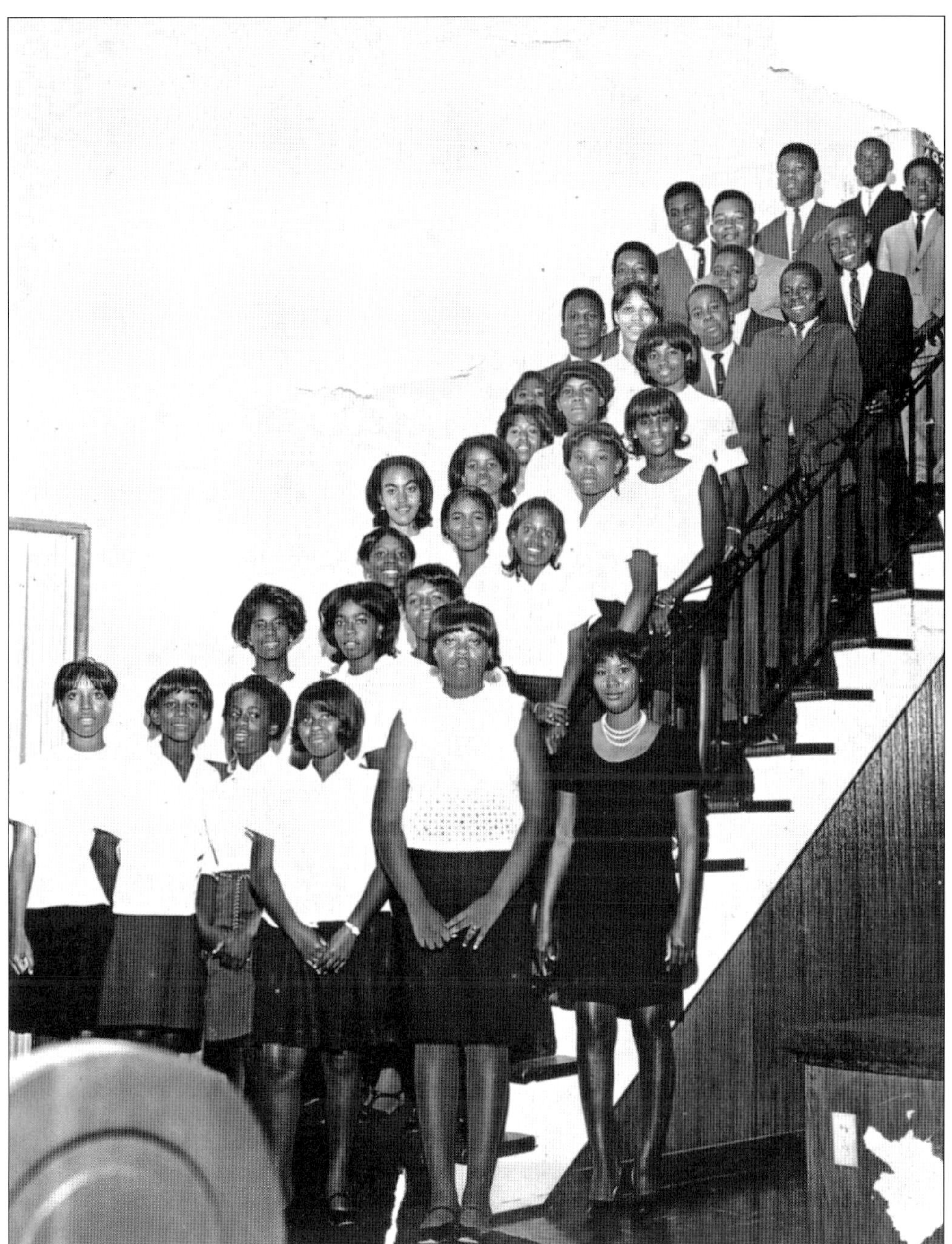

Pictured in this 1960s image are the youth of Second Baptist Church. This group includes Schelander Sullen, Veronica Lee, Cynthia Jackson, Carolyn Knight, Doris Phoenix, Sherlyn Rogers, Cynthia Riley, Gaynelle Green, Gail Sullen, Janice Benn, Bernadette Sullen, Jacquelyn Phoenix, Stella Dale Rose, Joel Franklin, Jean Marie Gary, Marcell Ruffin, Marcella Jackson, Elaine Ross, Sandra Rose, Barbara Knight, Rickey Williams, Charlie Benn Jr., Richard Smith, Dale Williams, Vernon Gastinell, Gregory Franklin, Condell Sullen, Ray Lee, Roger Lee, Michael Franklin, and Donald Sullen. (Courtesy of Doris Phoenix.)

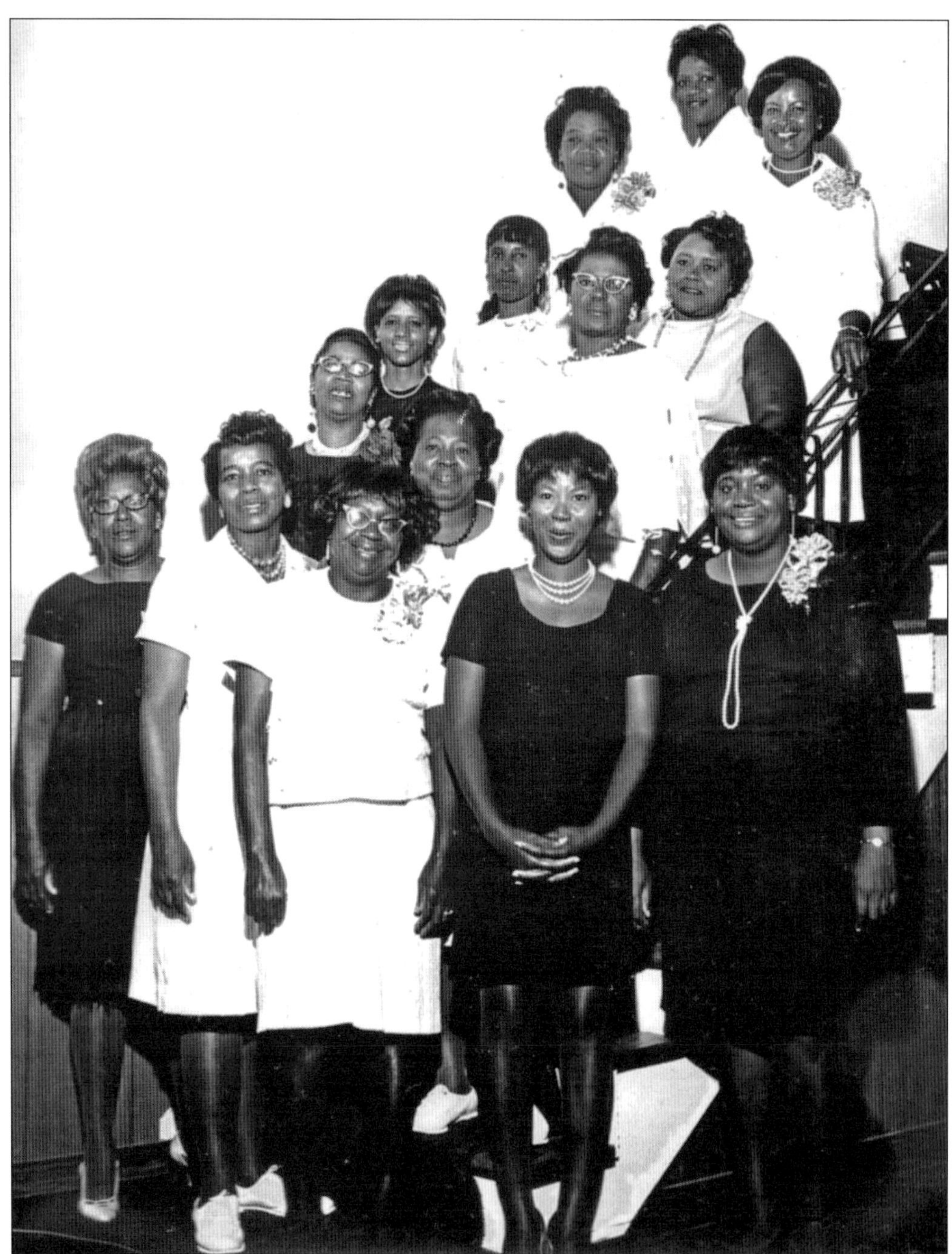

Pictured in this 1960s image is the Second Baptist Church Women's Usher Ministry. Choir members include, from left to right, (first row) Imogene Smith, Doris Phoenix, and Sophie Charles; (second row) Mary Johnson; (third row) Kitty Robinson, Diane Davis, and Lillian Perrymon; (fourth row) Mathilda Cook and Rebecca Sullen; (fifth row) Mildred Phoenix, Clementine Benn, and Alberta Franklin. (Courtesy of Doris Phoenix.)

Amelia King was born December 10, 1879, to the union of Phillip and Delia Elsey-Jones. Amelia is remembered in the community for her tireless fight against Jim Crow and toward social justice and equity in American society. As a young lady at the age of 20, she worked as a servant. She later became a part of the Equal Justice Social and Pleasure Club and Eureka Benevolent Association. She is pictured here with her son Rev. Dr. Dan King Jr. and Ernestine Pierre-Carter during Rev. Dr. Earl Green's pastoral anniversary. Amelia passed away on January 26, 1973. (Courtesy of Doris Phoenix.)

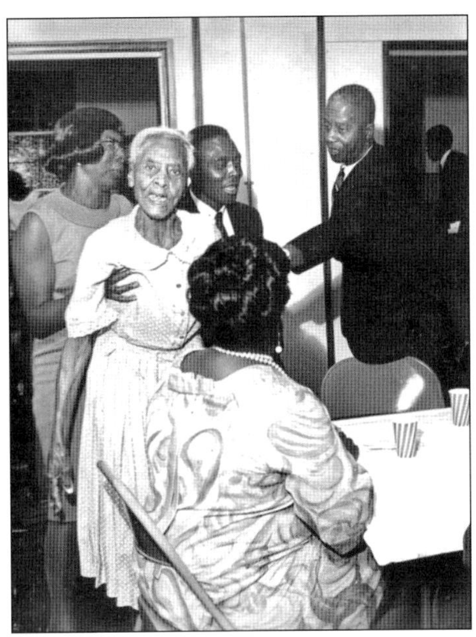

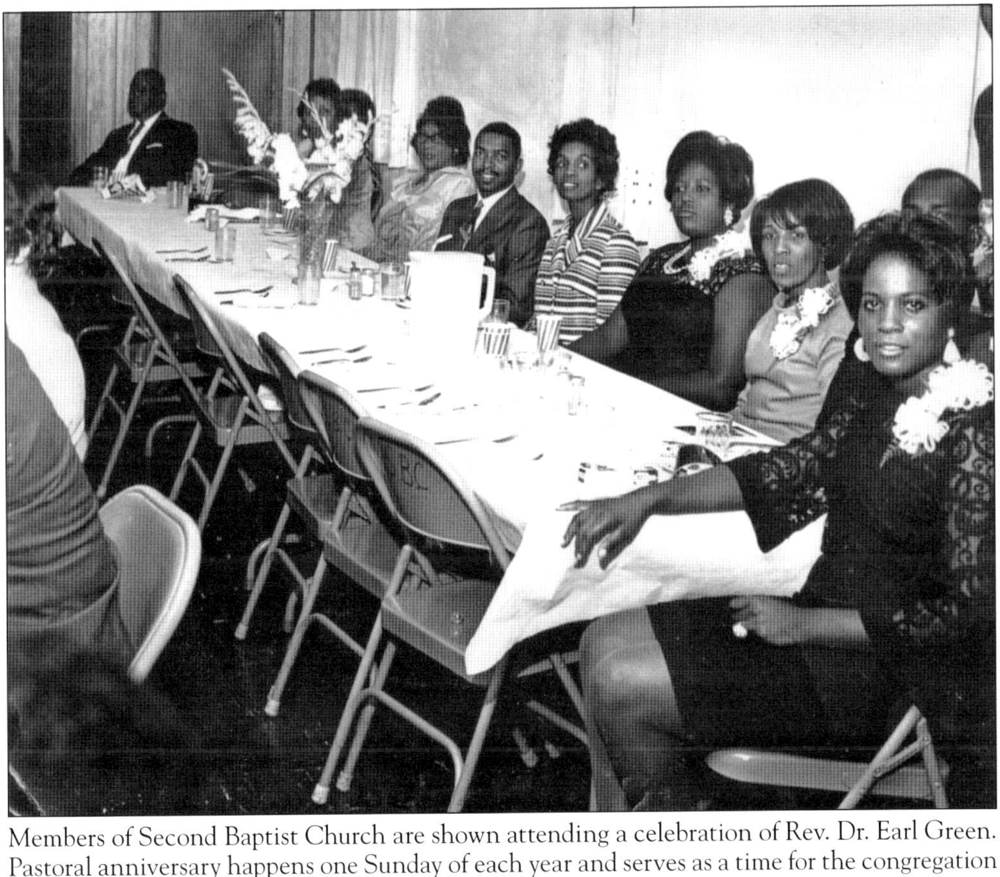

Members of Second Baptist Church are shown attending a celebration of Rev. Dr. Earl Green. Pastoral anniversary happens one Sunday of each year and serves as a time for the congregation to say "thank you" to the pastor and build unity around the church's vision. (Courtesy of Doris Phoenix.)

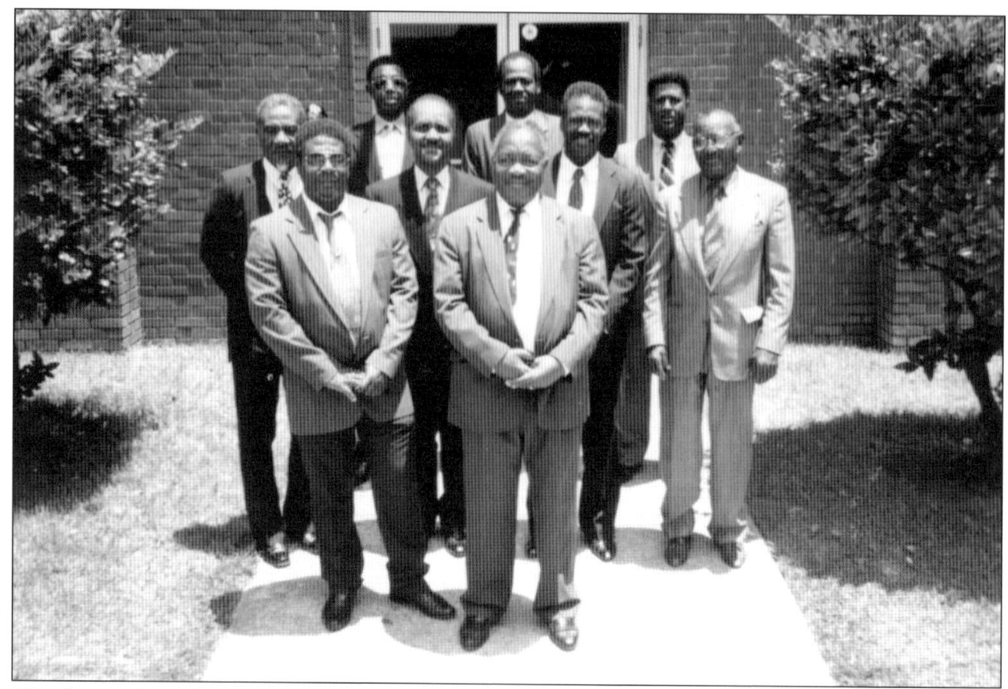

The deacon board of Second Baptist Church is pictured in the early 1990s. This image includes, from left to right, Caesar Ruffin Sr., Alvin Gant, Isaiah Riley, Vernon Lewis, Roy Jackson, Edward Lee, Rodney Price, Leroy "Royal" Phoenix, and Willie Peoples. (Courtesy of Robin Crawford.)

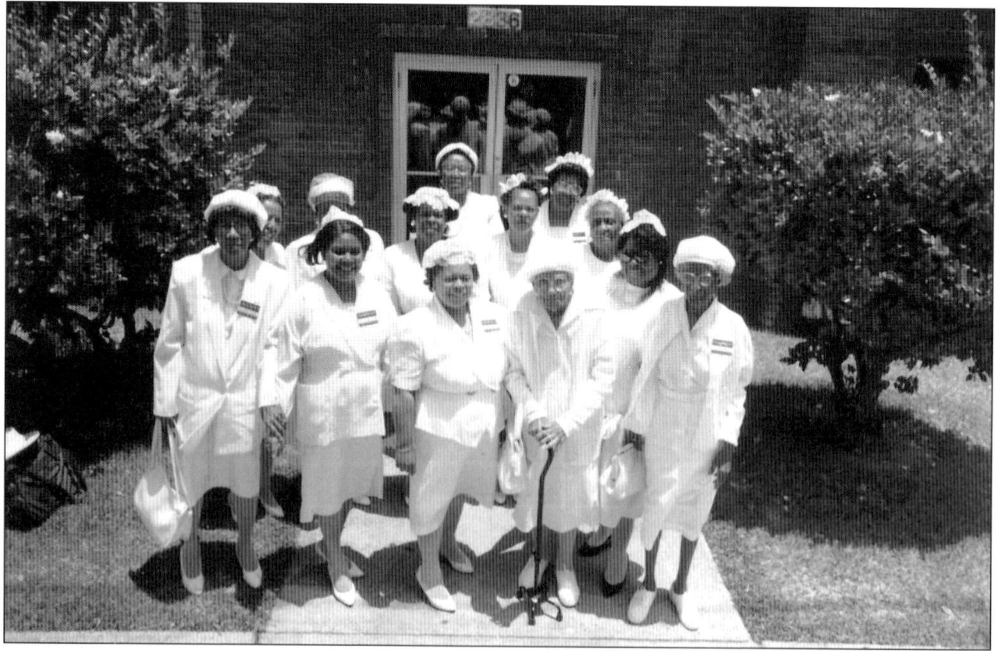

The deaconess board of the early 1990s is pictured here. This image includes (first row) Alberta Gant, Joyce Lewis, Barbara Johnson, Louise Wright, and Minerva Lewis; (second row) two unidentified, Roselle Bridges, Doretha Butler, Mae West, and Orelia Noil; (third row) Edna Lloyd and WillieMae Decluit. (Courtesy of Leroy "Royal" Phoenix.)

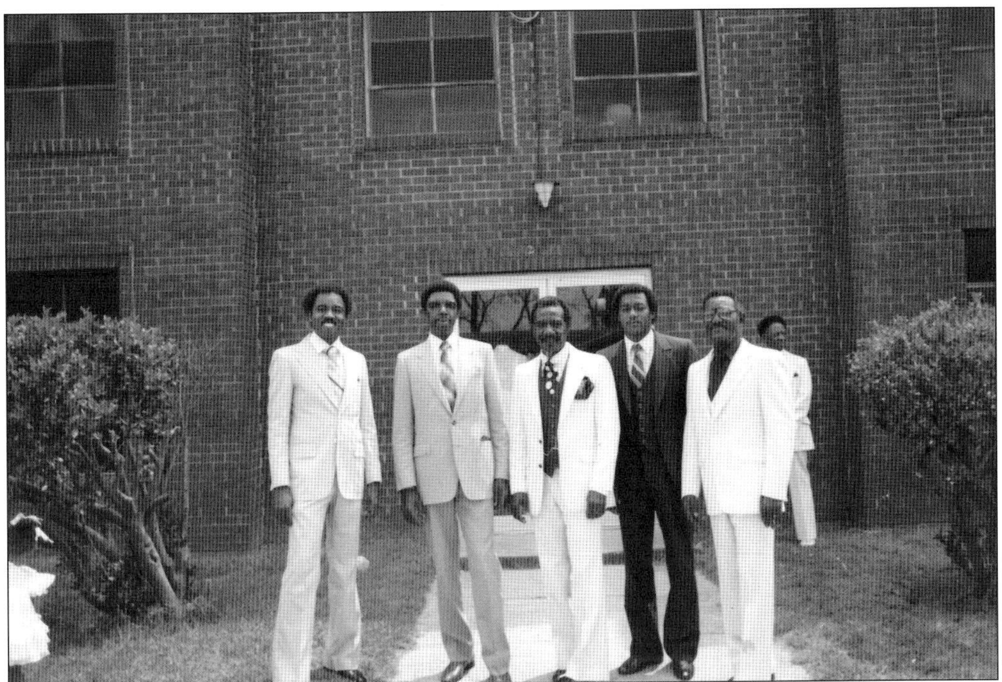

This photograph of deacons that served at Second Baptist Church was taken in the 1980s. This image includes, from left to right, Percy Rose, Frank Peoples, Isaiah Riley, Clarence Lovelace, and Edward Lee. (Courtesy of Veronica St. Cyr.)

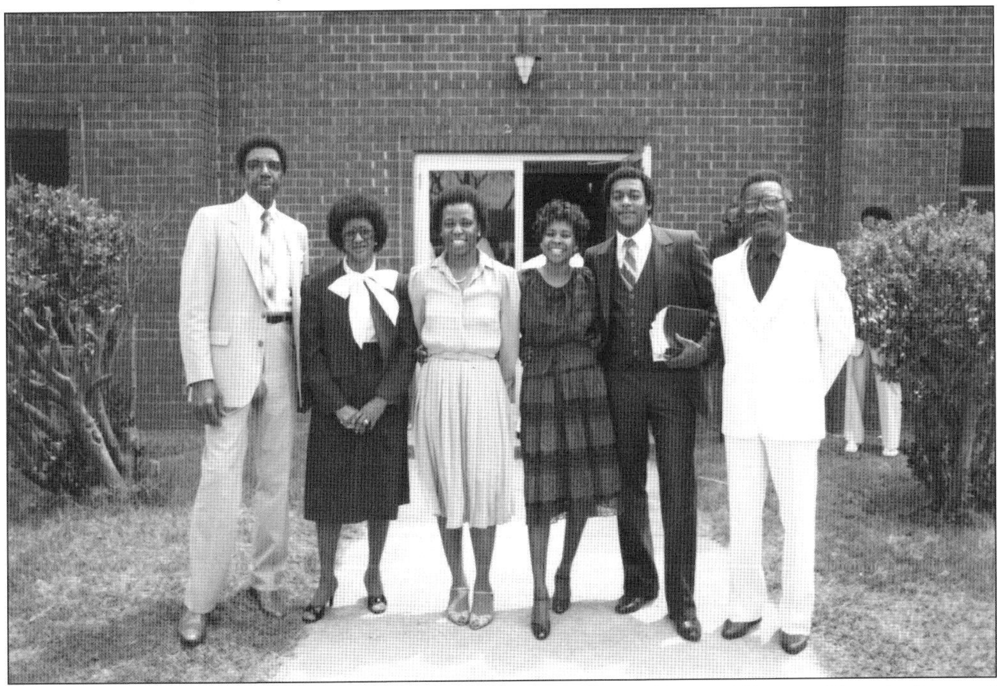

Captured in this 1980s image are the Sunday school teachers of Second Baptist Church. Pictured from left to right are Frank Peoples, Leola Anchor, Elsie Rose, Alta Butler, Clarence Lovelace, and Edward Lee. (Courtesy of Veronica St. Cyr.)

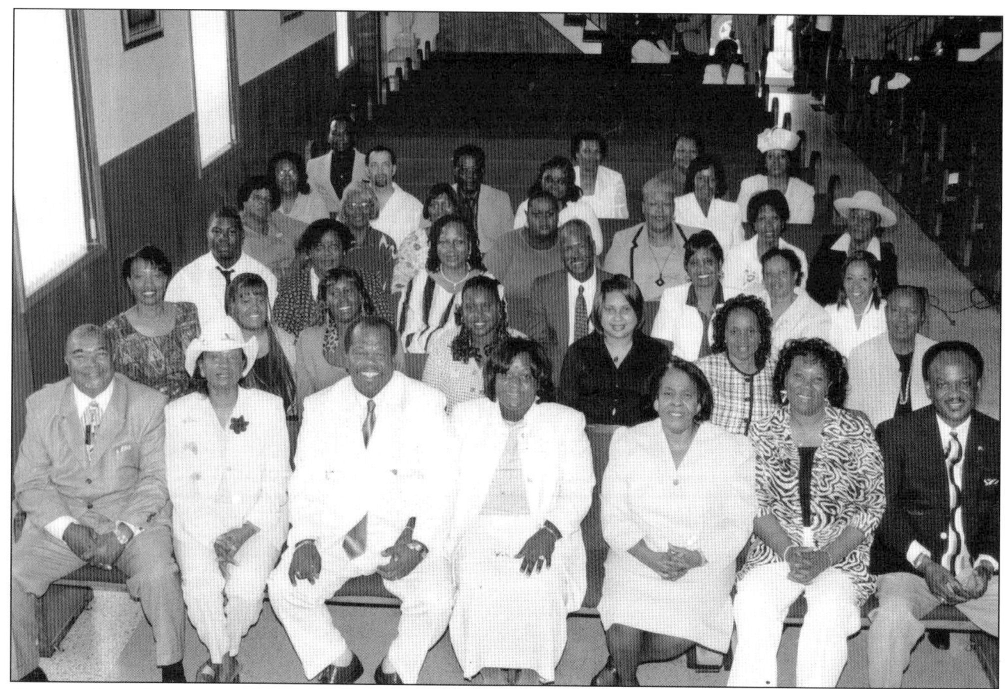

Captured in this 1990s photograph is the deaconess board ministry of Second Baptist Church. These women served not only in the church but also in the community. (Courtesy of Rosey Garrett.)

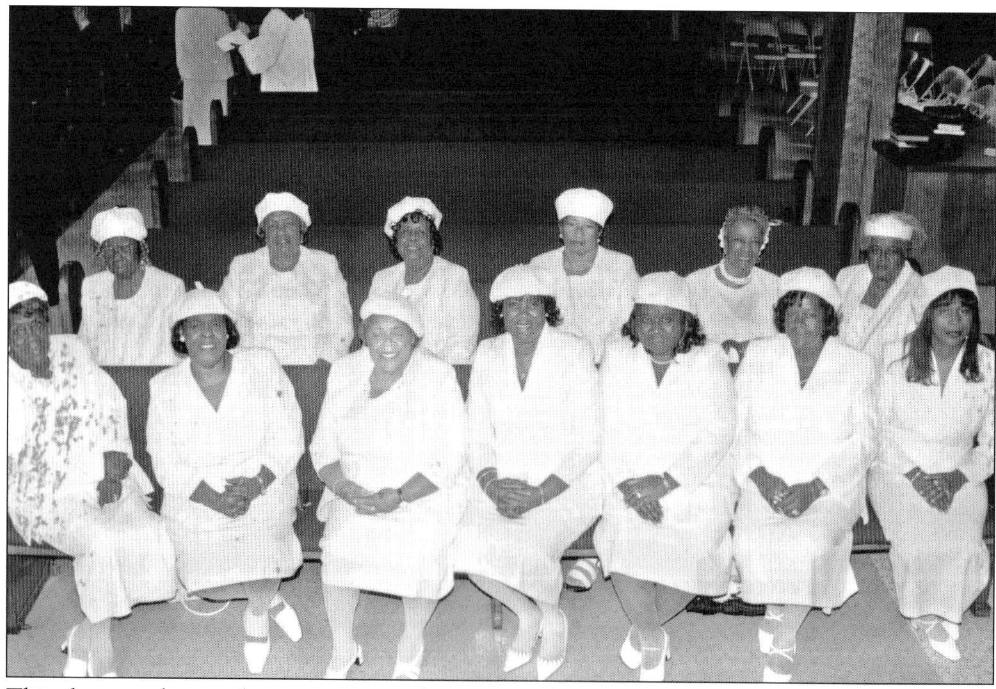

This photograph was taken sometime in the 2000s and shows the Second Baptist deaconess board. The deaconesses of the church help with prayer service, communion, baptism, and membership in Second Baptist Church. (Courtesy of Ira Green.)

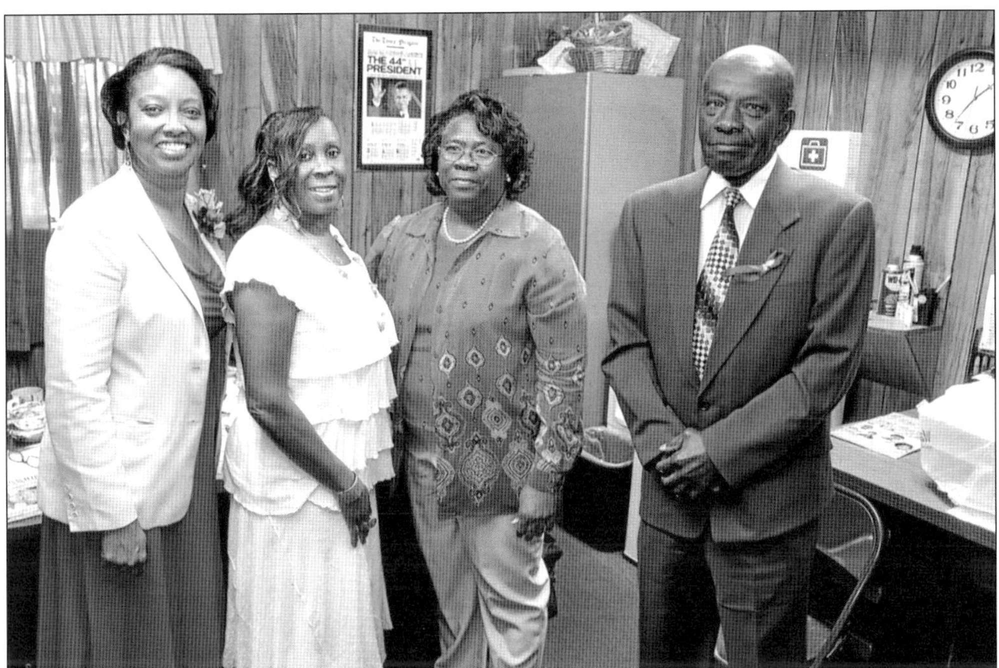

Pictured are, from left to right, Rosie Garrett, Paulette LeBlanc-Green, Brenda Gant, and Charlie Green. These individuals served as support staff of the church, ensuring that things run smoothly behind the scenes. (Courtesy of Rosie Garrett.)

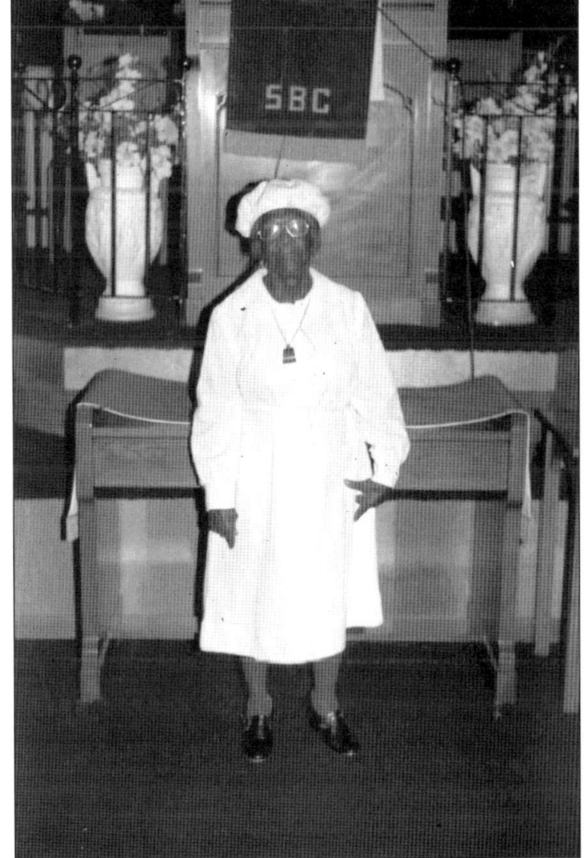

Coretta "Tee-Tee" Green is pictured in this 1980s image in the center aisle of Second Baptist Church. Members pass through this space in the center of the church to participate in communion and offerings. (Courtesy of Veronica St. Cyr.)

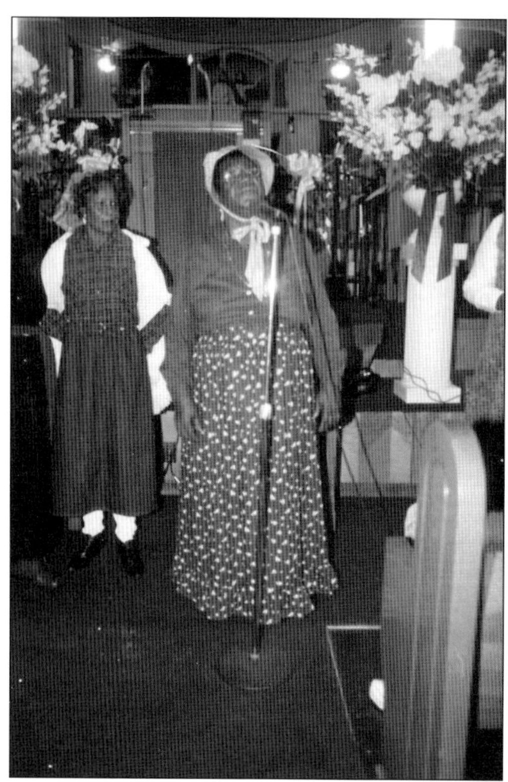

After slaves were emancipated in the Algiers area, many moved from various plantations (such as Stanton, Shamrock, Ganascheau, Norman, and Point Beka plantations) and settled on what came to be known as Cut-Off Village. Second Baptist Church hosts an annual Black History Month program where members of the community remember the lives of their ancestors and Africans throughout the diaspora. In these images, these women commemorate the lives that have gone before them through song and poem. (Both, courtesy of Leroy "Royal" Phoenix.)

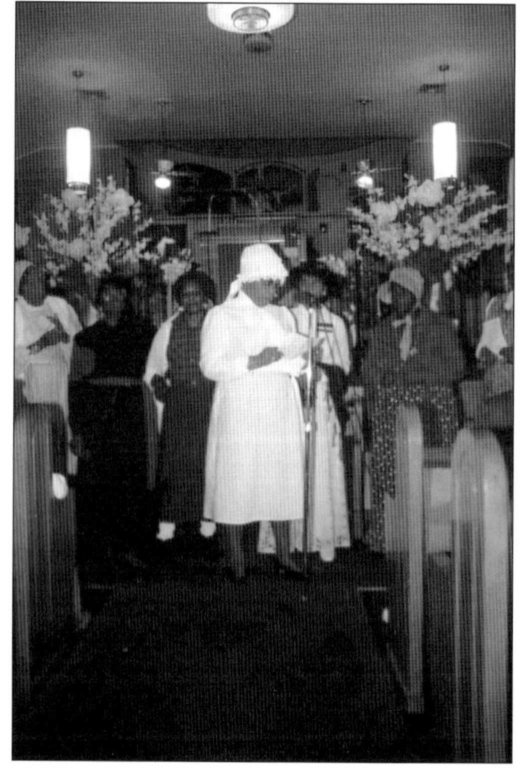

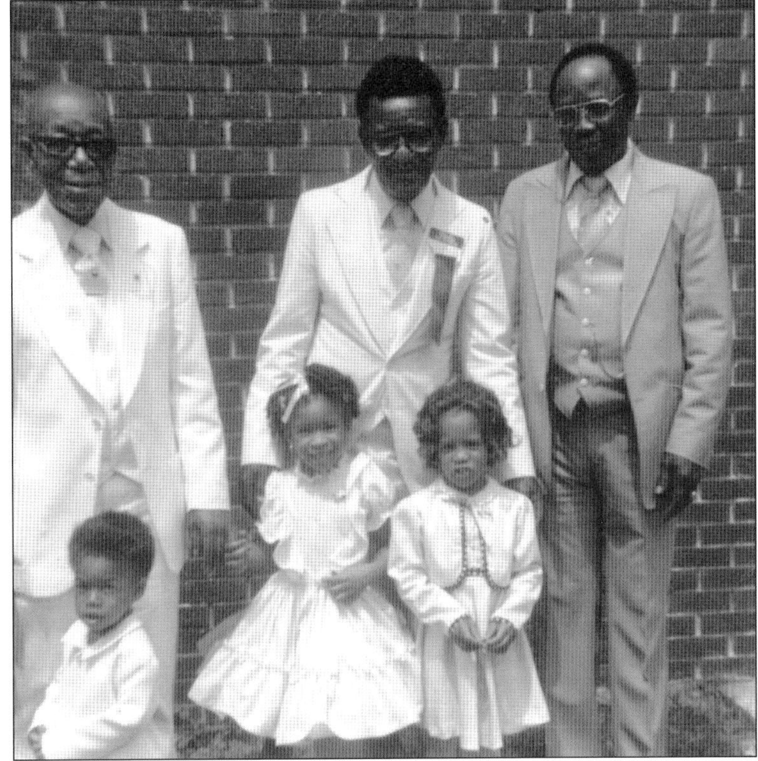

Church leaders are pictured with the next generation of leaders in this 1970s photograph. Pictured are (first row) Frank Phoenix Jr., Krishaun Phoenix, and Shannon McDonald; (second row) Herbert Sullen Sr., Edward Lee, and John Phoenix. (Courtesy of Marylee McDonald.)

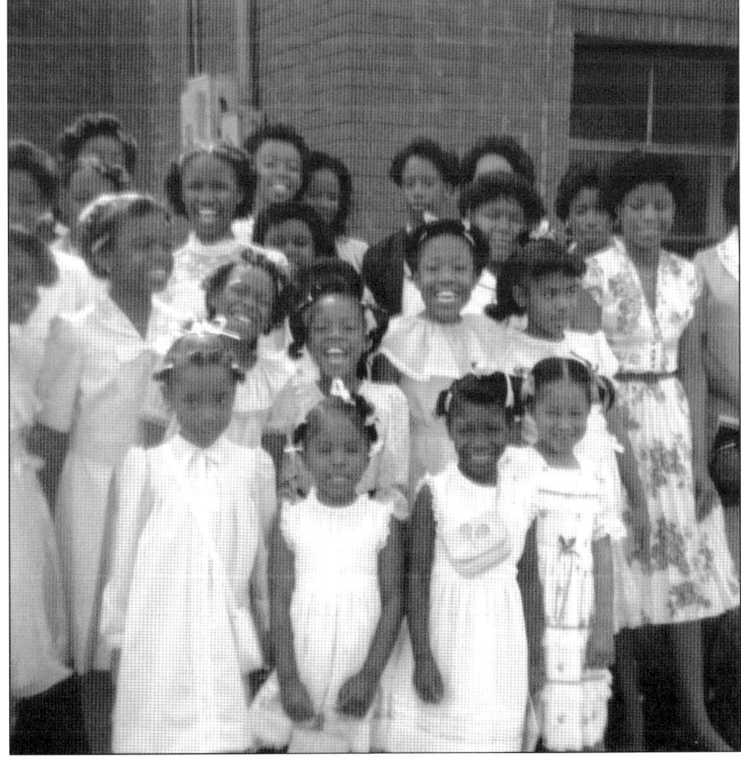

This image of a children's Sunday school class was taken in the 1980s. These classes are centered around religious instruction and play an integral role in reaching the youth of the community. (Courtesy of Leroy "Royal" Phoenix.)

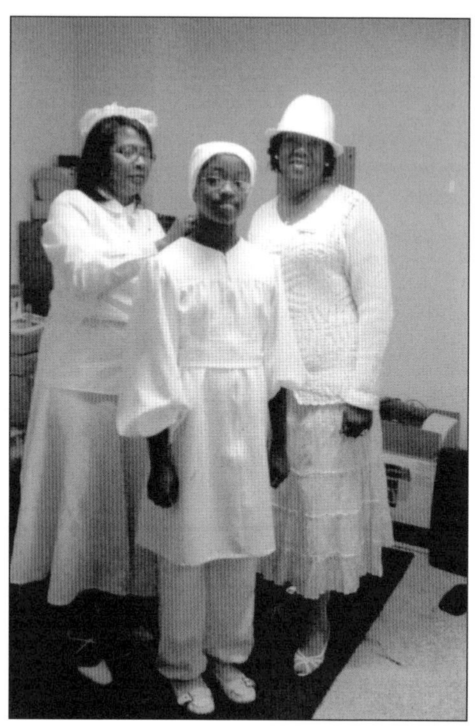

Lydia G. Phoenix (left) and Ruth Phoenix (right) are pictured as they dress Kawanza Livas in preparation for baptism. This baptism was performed by Taza Green Sr. (Courtesy of Robin Crawford.)

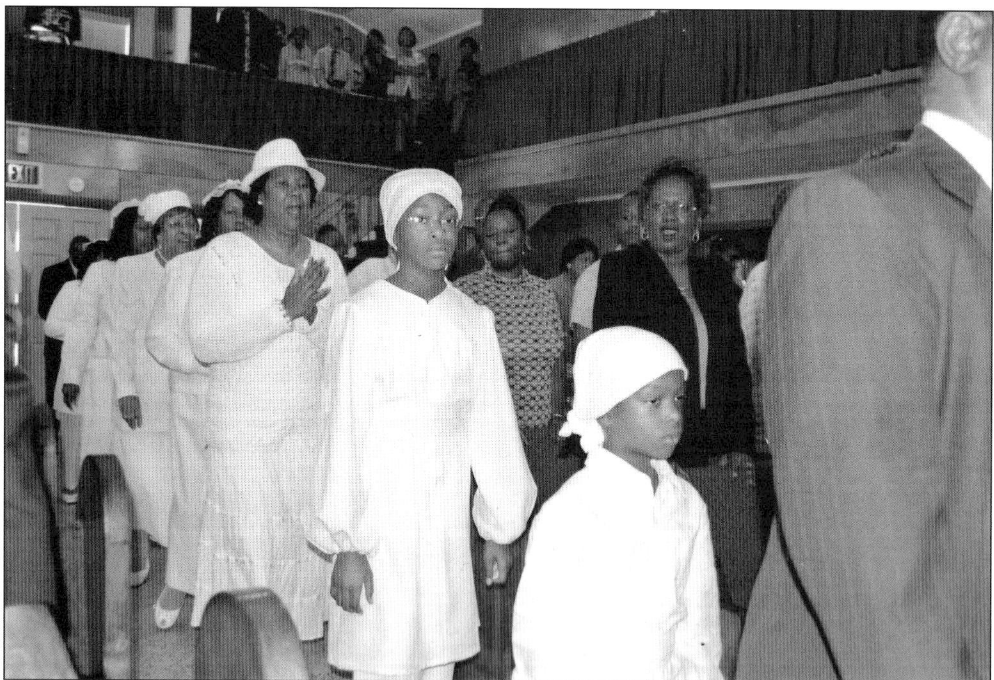

A church tradition from the early 1900s was for baptism candidates to walk around the church building with the deacons and deaconesses as they sang "We Will March Through the Streets of the City." This act was previously done in the actual streets that surrounded the community as a public declaration and celebration of faith. Pictured are baptism candidates Edwin Joseph Jr. (in front) and Kawanza Livas. (Courtesy of Robin Crawford.)

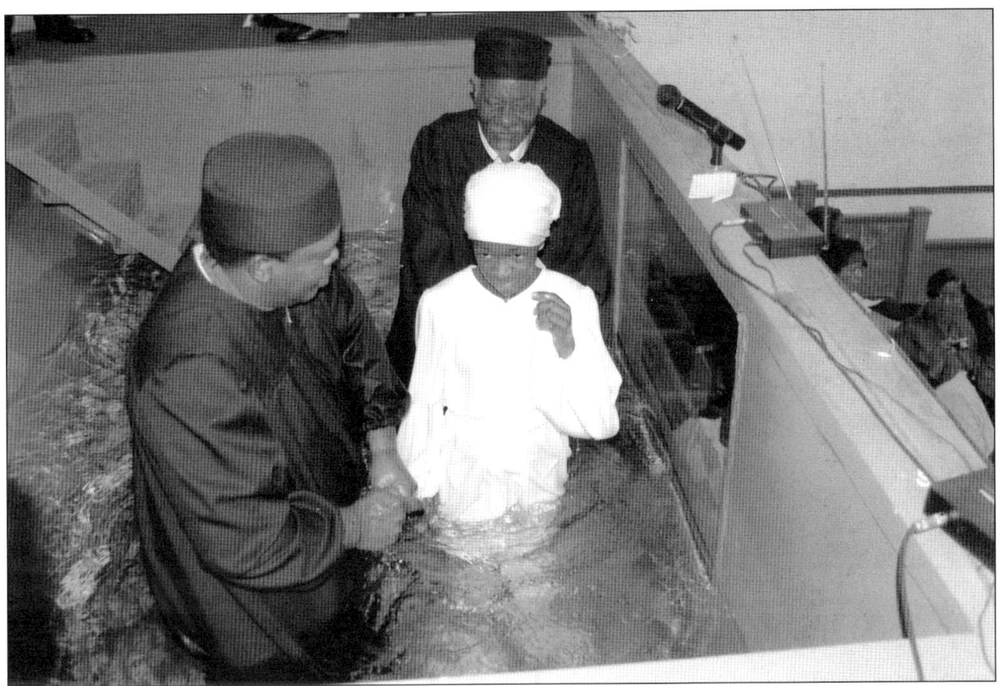

Pastor Taza Green Sr. (left), Brother Isaiah Riley (right), and baptism candidate Kawanza Livas are pictured in this photograph. The men are preparing to baptize this young woman in a small pool of water as a public declaration of her profession of faith. In the early 1900s, this act took place exclusively in the Mississippi River. Since moving indoors, the tradition has now become for young children to move into the choir stands, which are just in front of the pool to watch family and friends be baptized. (Both, courtesy of Robin Crawford.)

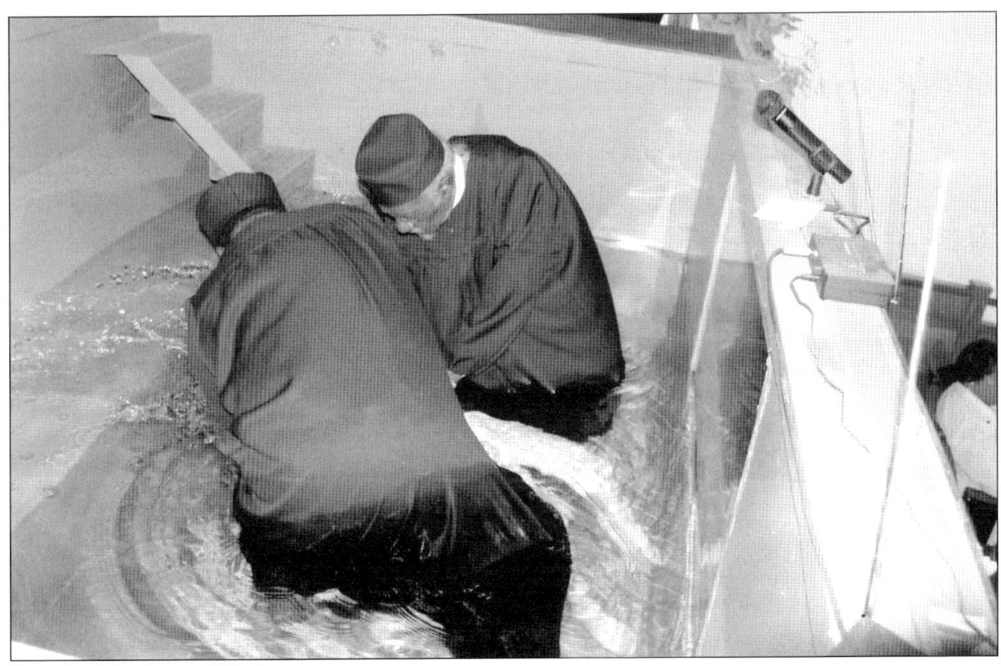

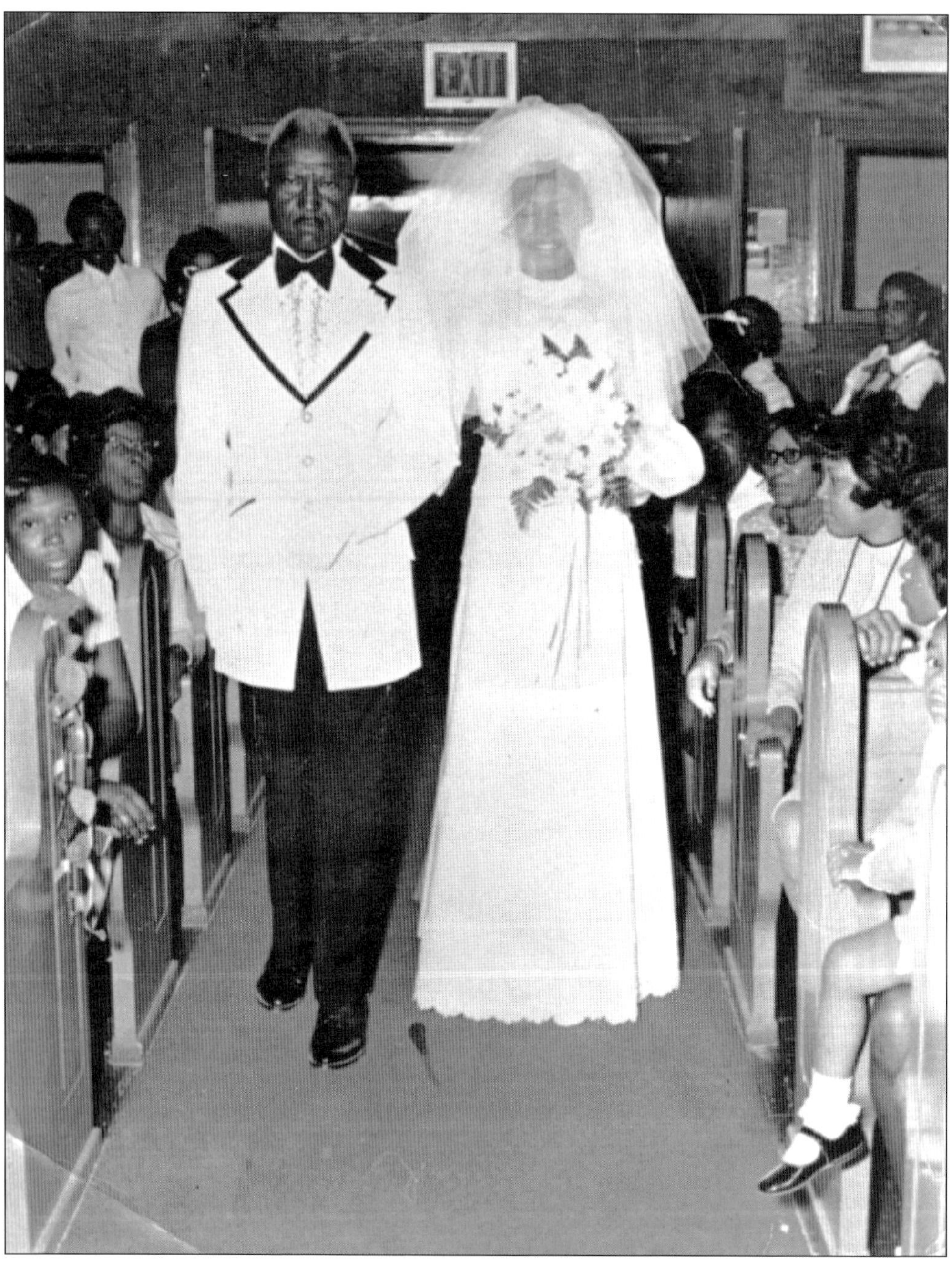

Altus Lee Sr. was the husband of Hennie Lee; together, they produced Altus Lee Jr. and Marcella Lee. The elder Altus is pictured walking his daughter Marcella Lee down the aisle in Second Baptist Church to be wed to Ronald Ross. (Courtesy of Veronica St. Cyr.)

Leroy "Royal" Phoenix has been a member of Second Baptist Church since he was a young boy. Royal serves in many capacities in the church. He is a deacon, a member of the male chorus, and the church photographer and videographer. (Courtesy of Robin Crawford.)

Isaiah Riley is a devout Christian and has served in many capacities in the church. Brother Riley was active in the church from a very young age. He served as the superintendent of the Sunday school department and in the male chorus and now serves as a deacon. (Courtesy of Frederick Weil.)

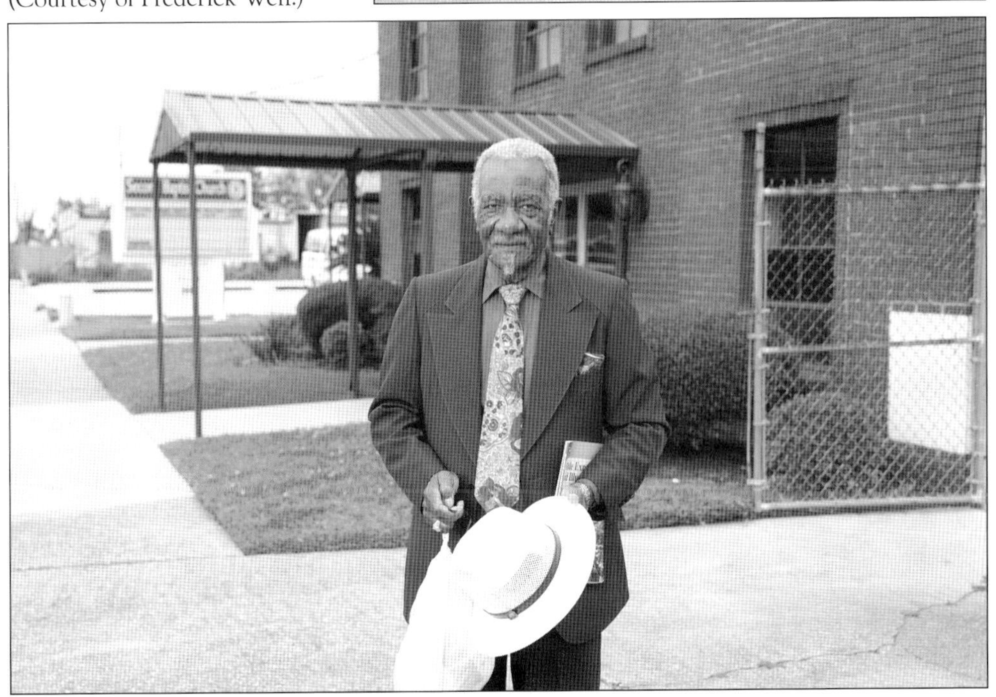

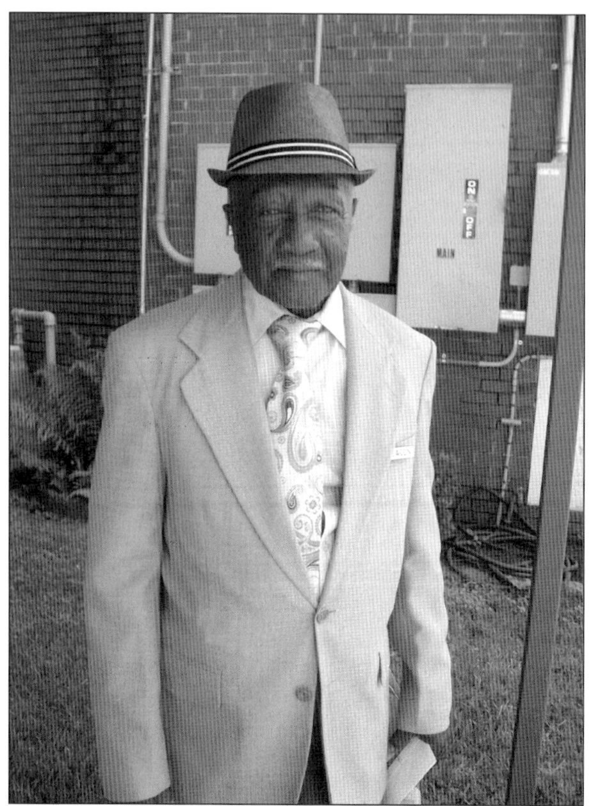

Wesley Ruffin Jr. serves as chairman of the deacon board of Second Baptist Church, as did his father, Wesley Ruffin Sr. (now deceased), and brother Caesar Ruffin Sr. (Courtesy of Robin Crawford.)

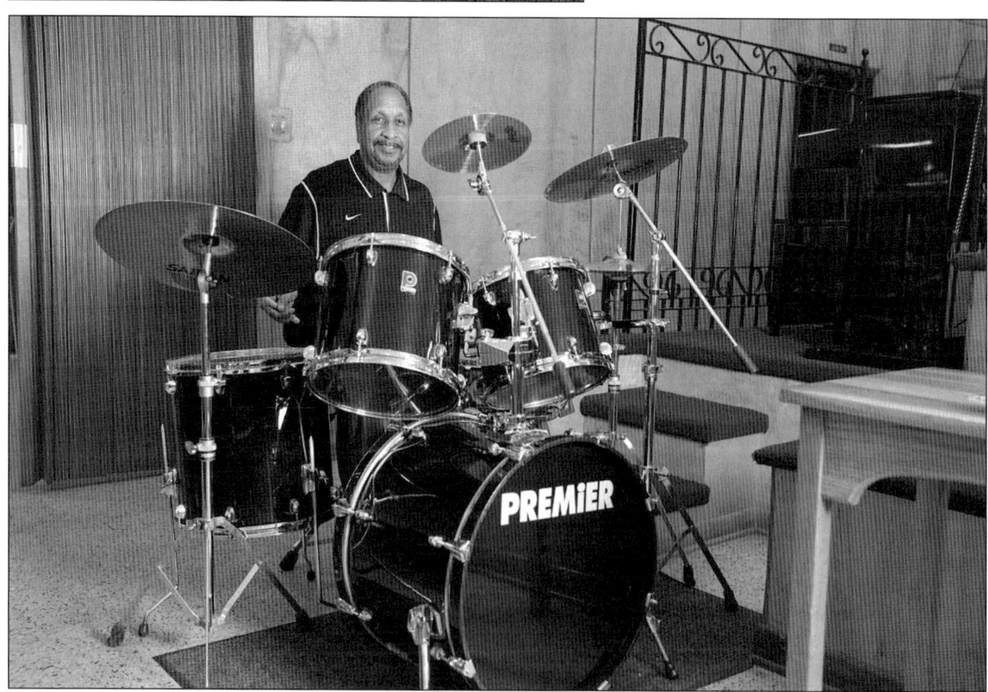

Alvin Rose serves as a deacon of Second Baptist Church and is the head of the music ministry. Alvin has served as the church drummer for many years. (Courtesy of Frederick Weil.)

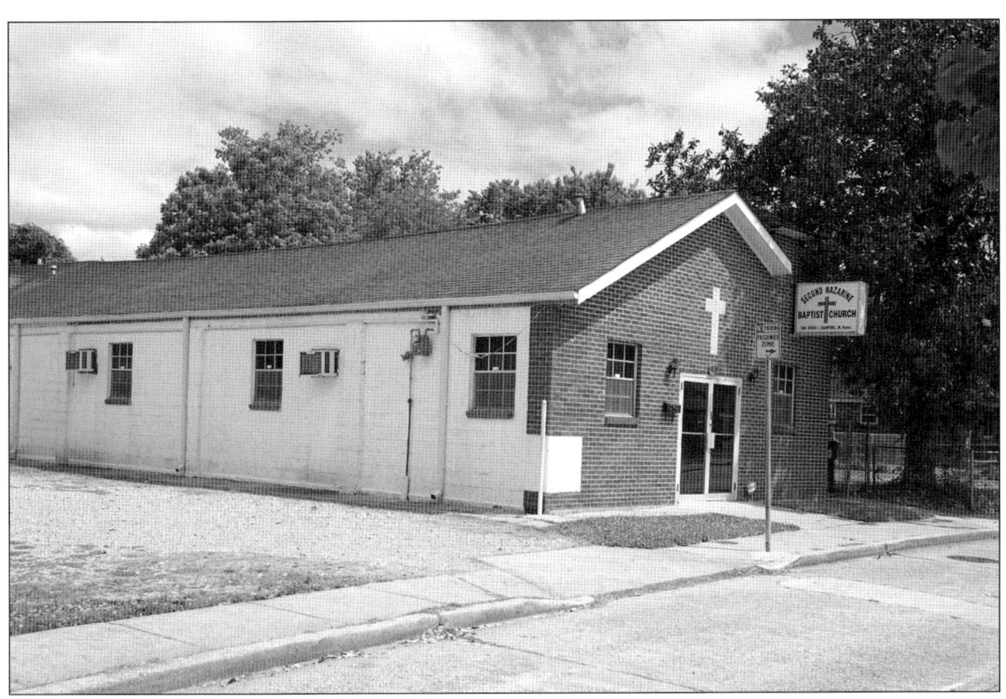

Second Nazarene Baptist Church was organized on April 8, 1883, on the Stanton plantation. After moving from Stanton plantation, the original members who gathered purchased the land to build a new church at 3062 Isadore Street, which has since been renamed Boyd Street. The original wood structure was reconstructed in the late 1960s. (Courtesy of Frederick Weil.)

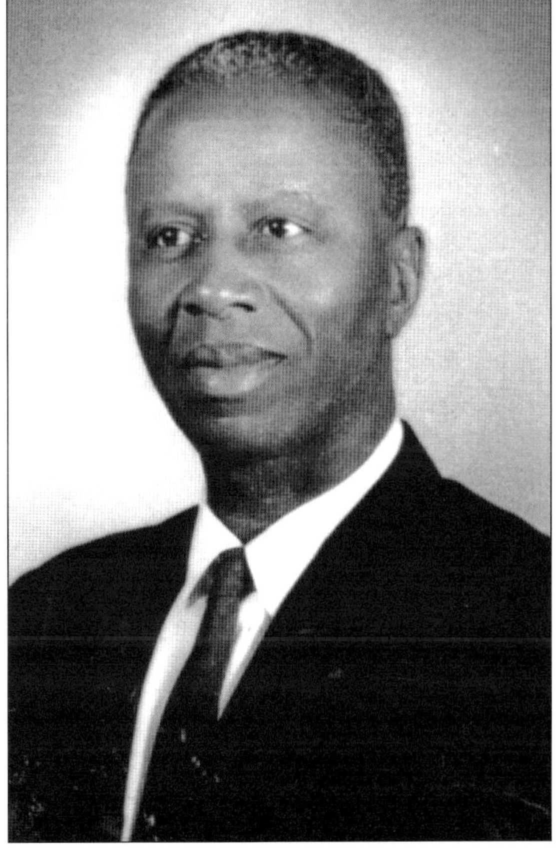

Rev. Daniel King Jr. was the son of Amelia and Dan King Sr. He was born and raised in the Lower Coast of Algiers. As a young man, he served in the US Army and was stationed in El Paso, Texas, in 1944. During this time, he began to sense a call to ministry and returned home to be ordained as a minister after his discharge. (Courtesy of Robin Crawford.)

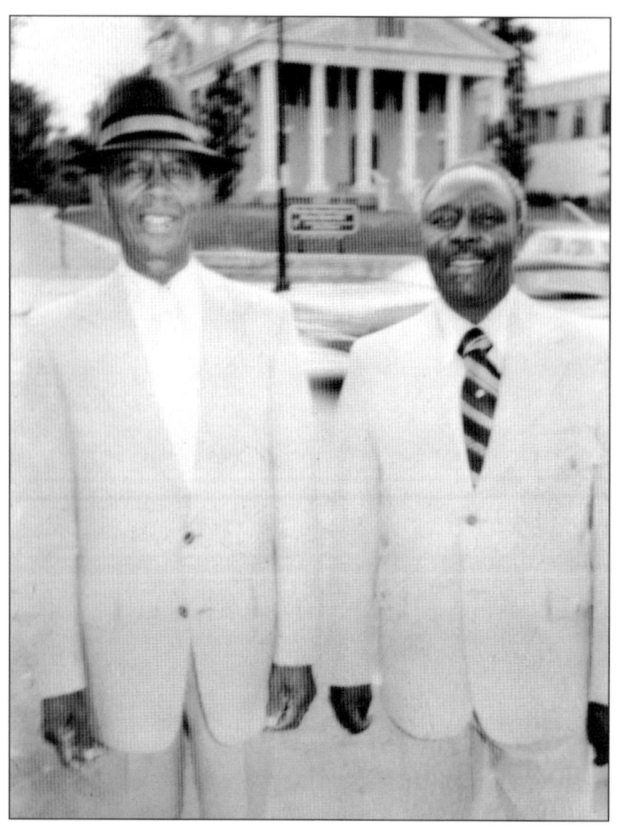

Rev. Dan King Jr. (left) was baptized and given a ministerial license to preach by Rev. Reason Boyd and was first ordained as pastor of Mount Olive Baptist Church in Algiers. In 1967, he was elected by the First District Association and made pastor of Second Nazarene Baptist Church. Reverend King held positions in both churches until he passed away in 1993. The man on the right is unidentified. (Courtesy of Veronica St. Cyr.)

Rev. Daniel "Dan" King is pictured with Frances King, Ernestine Carter, and Ernest Cook. This picture was taken in the 1970s. (Courtesy of Veronica St. Cyr.)

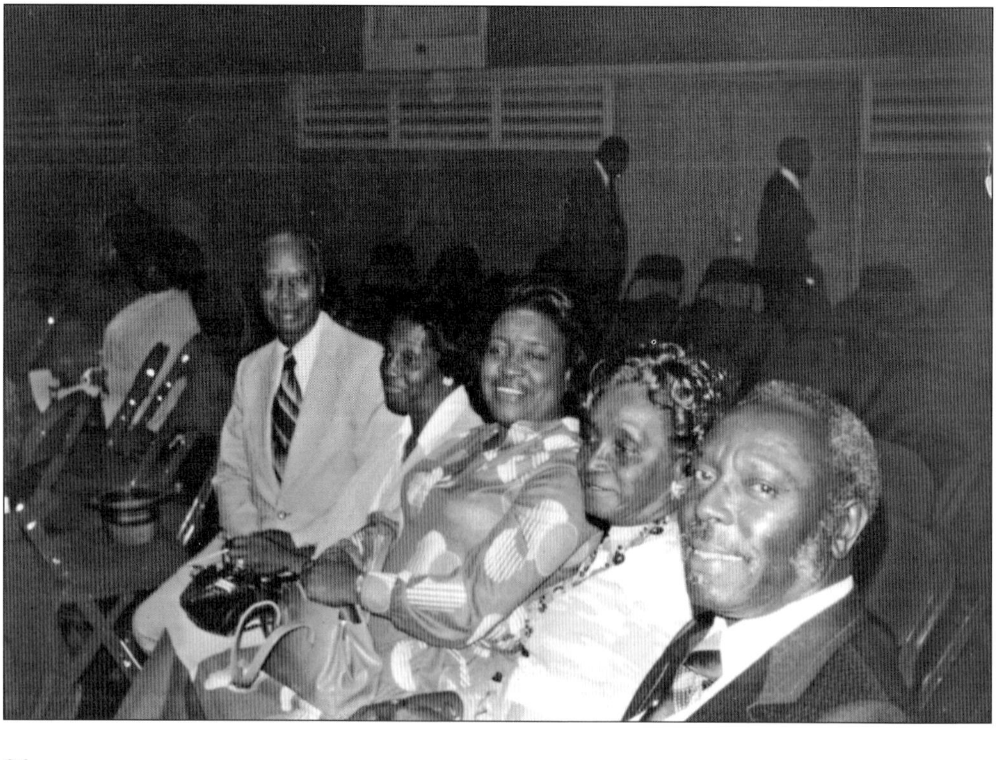

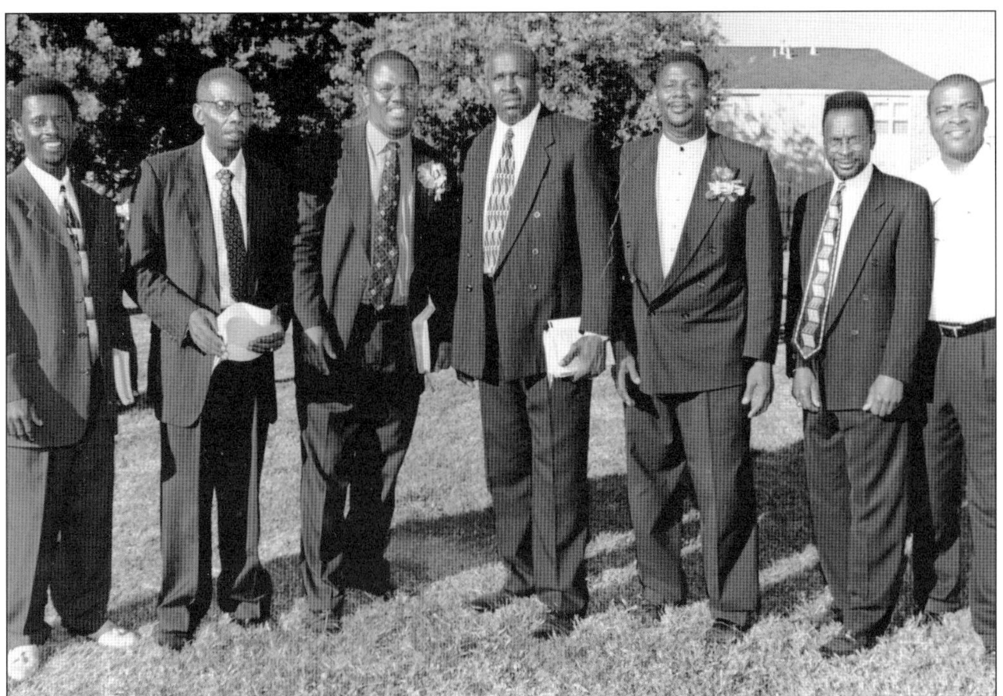

Among those pictured in this image taken in 1999 is pastor Peter L. Crawford Jr. He is shown with the deacon board ministry of the time. The photograph includes, from left to right, Anthony Ruffin Sr., Cardell Nunnery, Pastor Crawford, Clarence Ross, Randolph Crawford, Gary Williams, and Lawrence Lee Jr. These men were attending a note-burning ceremony for the new site of Second Nazarene Baptist Church. (Courtesy of Robin Crawford.)

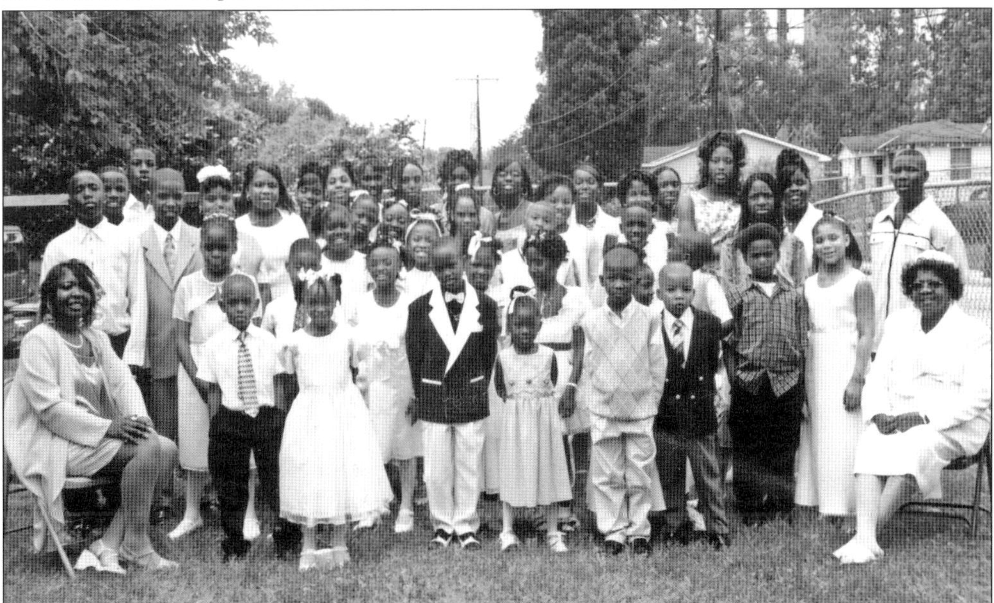

This photograph of the Second Nazarene Baptist Church Youth Choir was taken in the 1990s. Chrissandra Cook served as the choir director, and Stella H. Jimcoily was the director of the youth ministry. (Courtesy of Robin Crawford.)

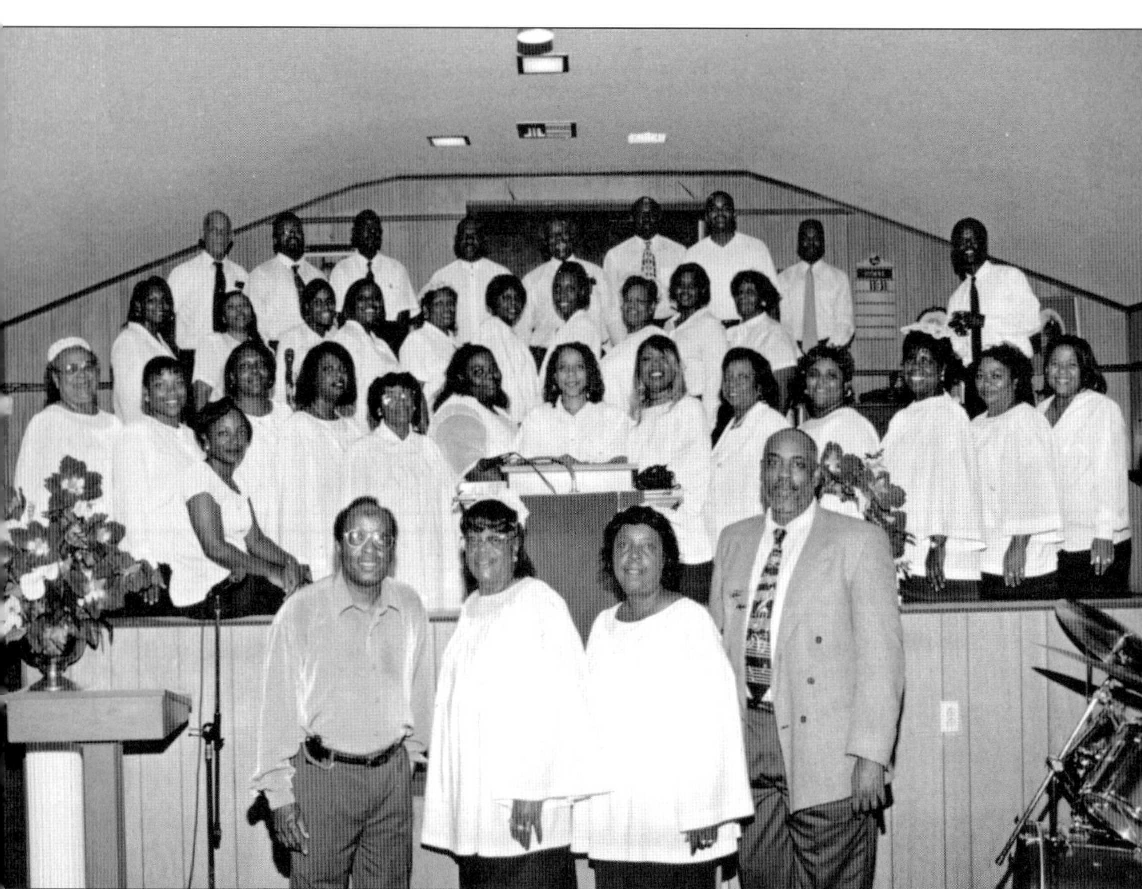

This image is of the Second Nazarene Baptist Church Mass Choir in the 1990s. Seen from left to right in the front row, Alton "T.C." Hawkins (director), Rachel Ross (president), Augustine H. Cook (director), and Will Norflin (organist) served the ministry of music. (Courtesy of Robin Crawford.)

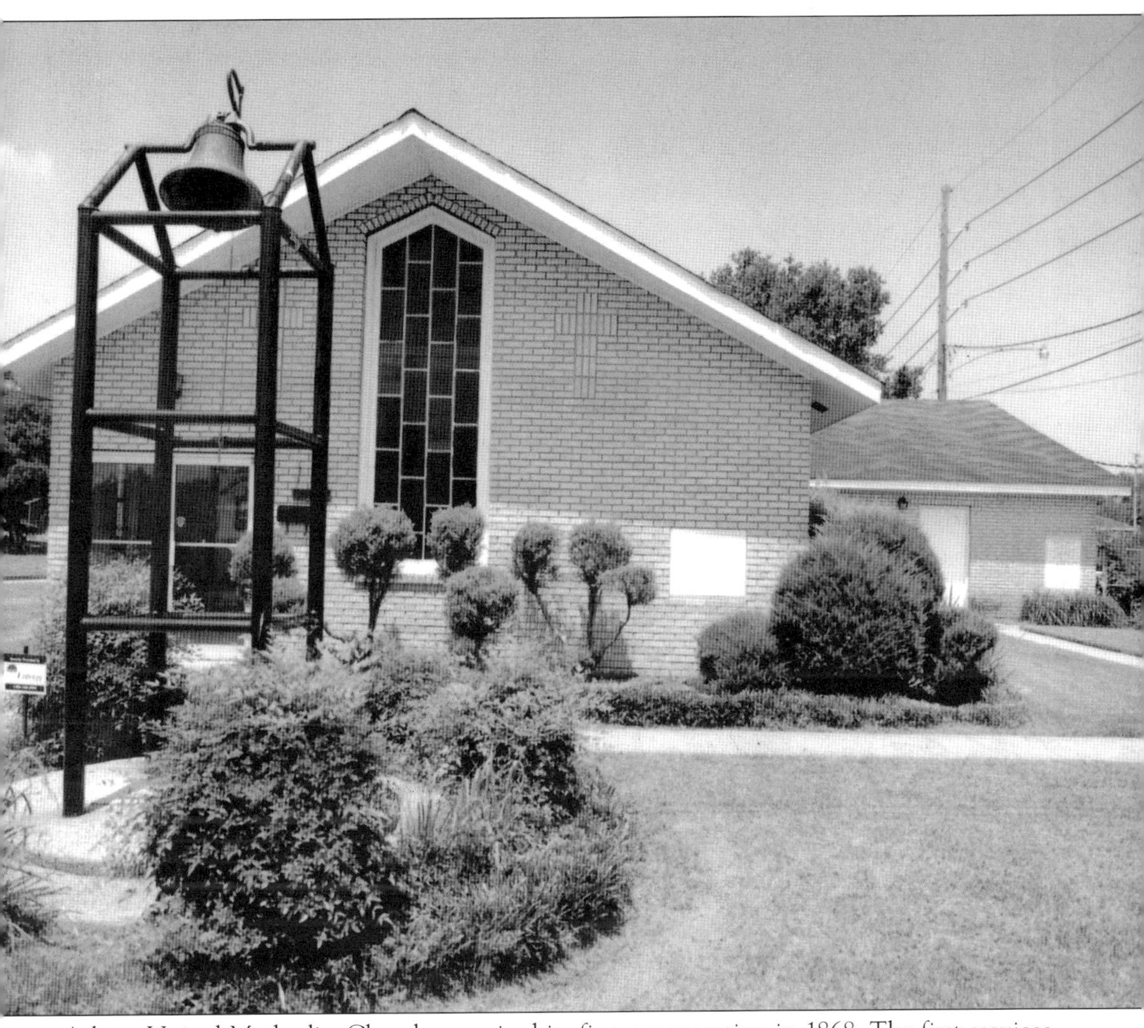

Asbury United Methodist Church organized its first congregation in 1868. The first services were led by Rev. John Brock under a brush arbor until the next pastor, Rev. James M. Bryant, purchased the property on which the church was built in the 1870s. In 1940, the church was destroyed by a storm and rebuilt by Moses Riley, Edward Duplessis, and Ben Charles under the leadership of Rev. A.L. Franklin. Moses and Edward were compensated $35, and Ben received $40. The structure was remodeled again in 1970 under the leadership of Rev. H.J. Rhyan, and an extension was added in 1984 under the leadership of Rev. William Jones. On July 11, 1993, the congregation choose to remodel the building once more. Plans for building began in 1996, and the facilities were finalized in October 2001 under the leadership of Rev. Andrew Douglas. (Courtesy of Charlie Benn Jr.)

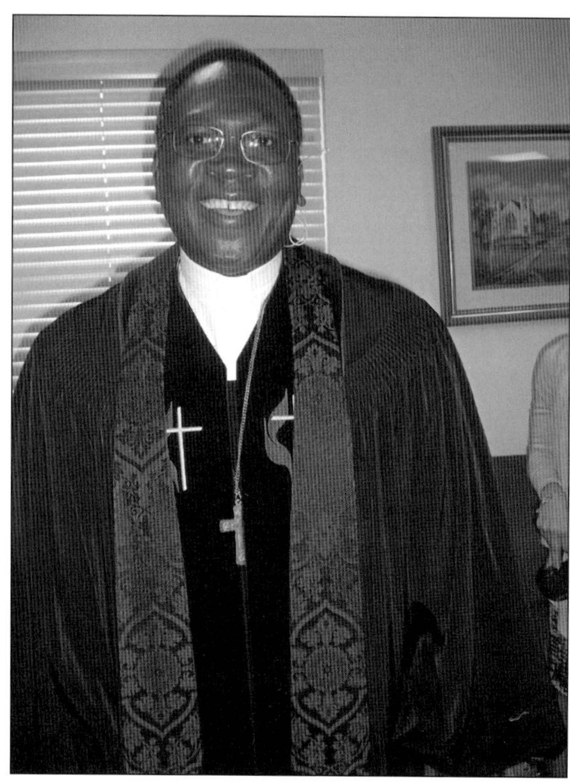

Rev. Simon Chigumira is the current pastor of Asbury United Methodist Church. Reverend Chigumira attended Candler School of Theology at Emory University. He is a man who never tires of preaching the gospel, and the church has seen many lives changed, souls saved, and numerous ministries birthed under his leadership. (Courtesy of Robin Crawford.)

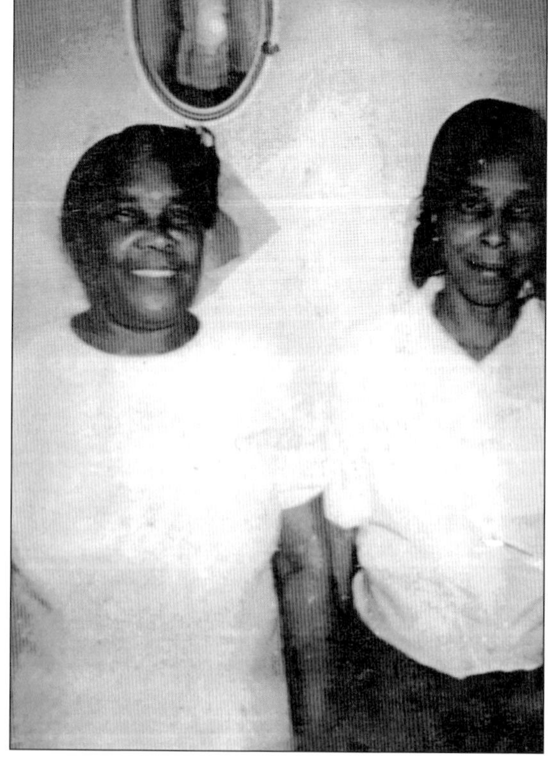

Mary Jane Anderson-Ross (left) was born July 27, 1907. Mary Jane was a member of Asbury United Methodist Church where she served as an usher. She was one of the founding members of the church when it began on Adrian Street. The church later moved to Ernest Street. Her daughter Hannah Ross-Johnson (right) was born February 17, 1926, and also served as an usher. (Courtesy of Kathleen Roberson.)

Three

Businesses, Landmarks, and Educational Institutions

He Who Learns, Teaches

Prior to the building of a Rosenwald school in the Lower Coast of Algiers, many of the residents had never been introduced to formalized education. Parents in the area would train their children at home by way of oral traditions and indigenous knowledge. After the construction of Second Baptist Church, parents would occasionally use that space for more formal corporate learning (children gathered in large groups) as well.

The Julius Rosenwald Fund brought the first formal educational institution to the Cut-Off community in 1920s. Interested in social issues, particularly the education of African Americans in the rural South, this program required African American communities to raise funds or donate property and labor to construct local schools, at which point the (white) school board would agree to match the funds and handle the operating costs. The Cut-Off was one of more than 5,000 schools that participated in matching funds to ensure that the chronically underfunded public education of African American students was enhanced.

The Rosenwald school was built on what was then known as Simpson Place but is now known as Sullen Place, and it served for many years as the community school. The community took great pride in the school, not only for the education that children received but also because residents had played a large role in its construction.

Whether or not formally educated, the members of the community have always boasted of their self-sufficiency and entrepreneurial endeavors. This chapter explores several of the institutions that helped them remain self-sustaining for many years.

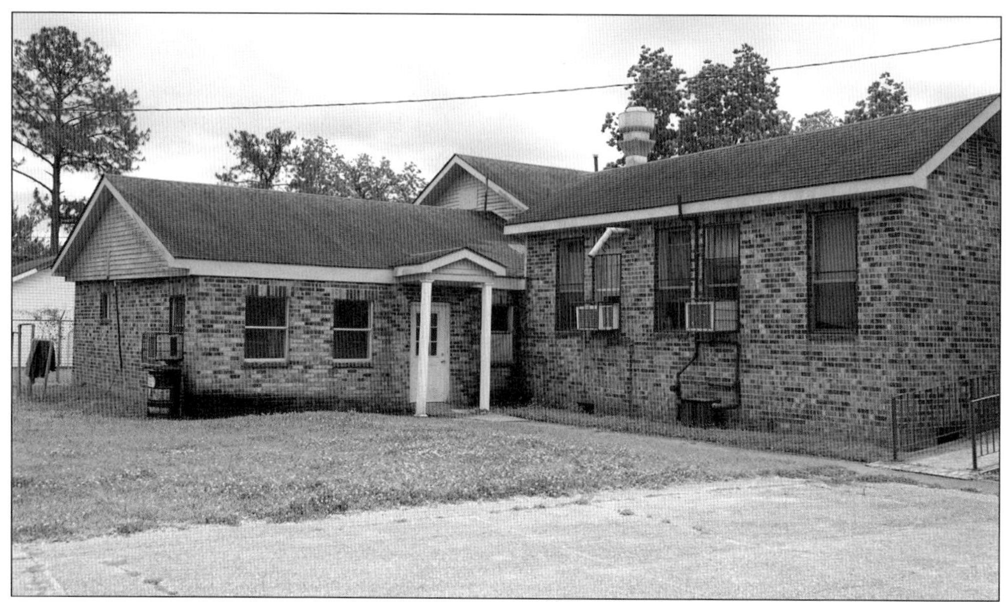

Rosenwald Elementary in the Lower Coast of Algiers was one of many Rosenwald campuses founded by Julius P. Rosenwald. Rosenwald gathered with members of the community and pulled together resources to purchase a property on what was then known as Simpson Place (now known as Sullen Place) to build the original schoolhouse. Many years after its completion, the school burned. In 1975, Second Baptist Church purchased the nonfunctioning schoolhouse and made many structural improvements to both the exterior and interior of the building. (Courtesy of Frederick Weil.)

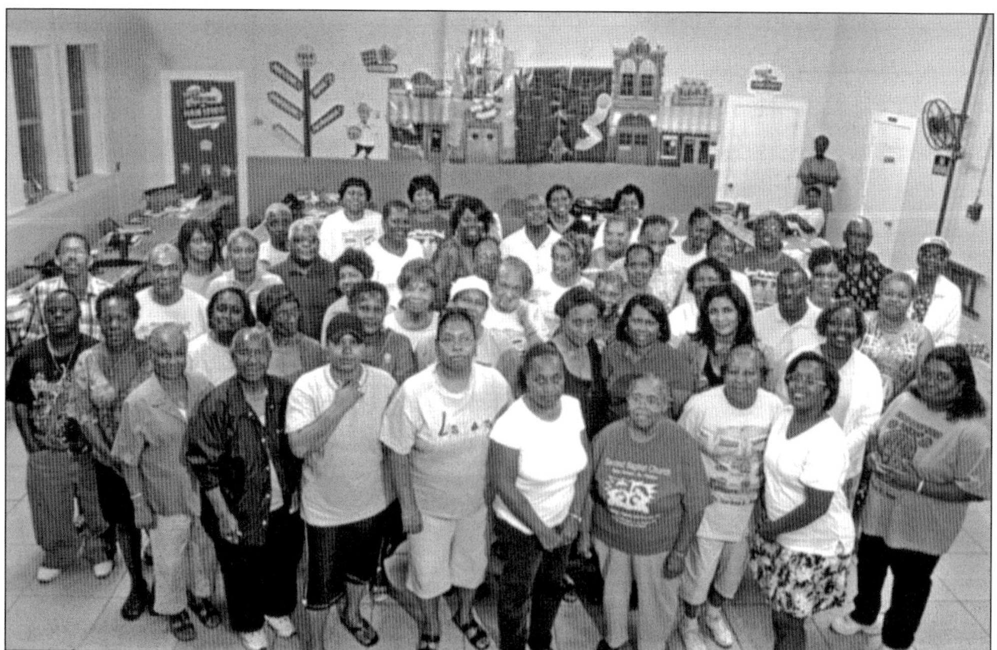

Leaders of Second Baptist Church are gathered together in this photograph, in what is now referred to as the "Old Rosenwald" school building. Members of the church and community gather in the building annually for Vacation Bible School services. (Courtesy of Ira Green.)

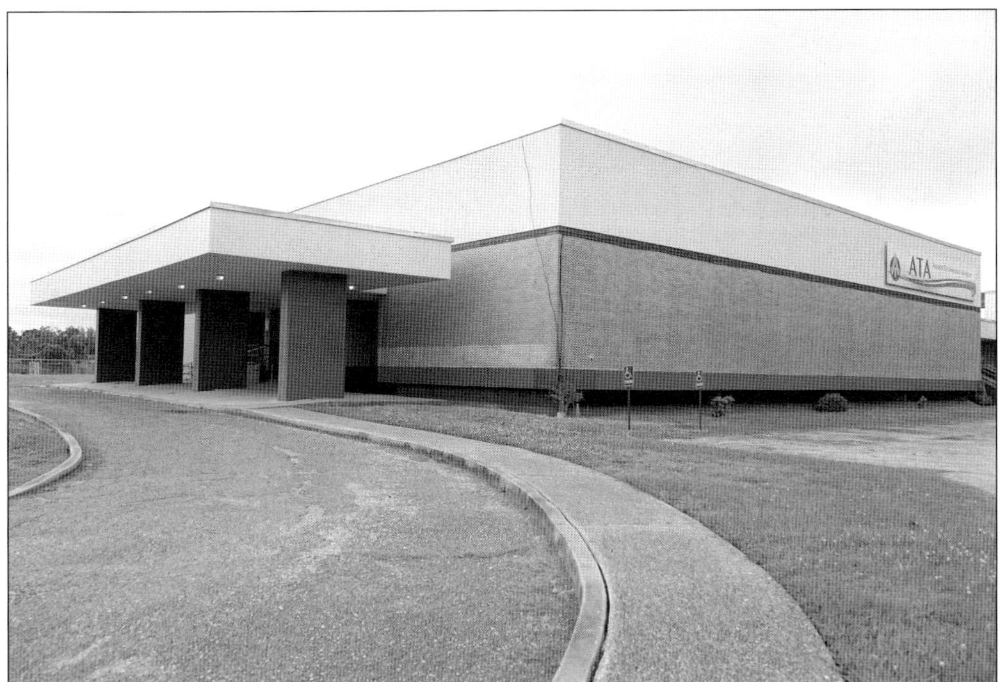

Located at 6501 Berkeley Drive, this building was once the new and improved space that housed Julius Rosenwald Accelerated School. This school was the only elementary school in the area that served the children of the Cut-Off community. In 2007, the school closed, and the structure was later reopened as Algiers Technology Academy. The Algiers Charter Association closed the doors of Algiers Technology Academy in 2017. (Courtesy of Frederick Weil.)

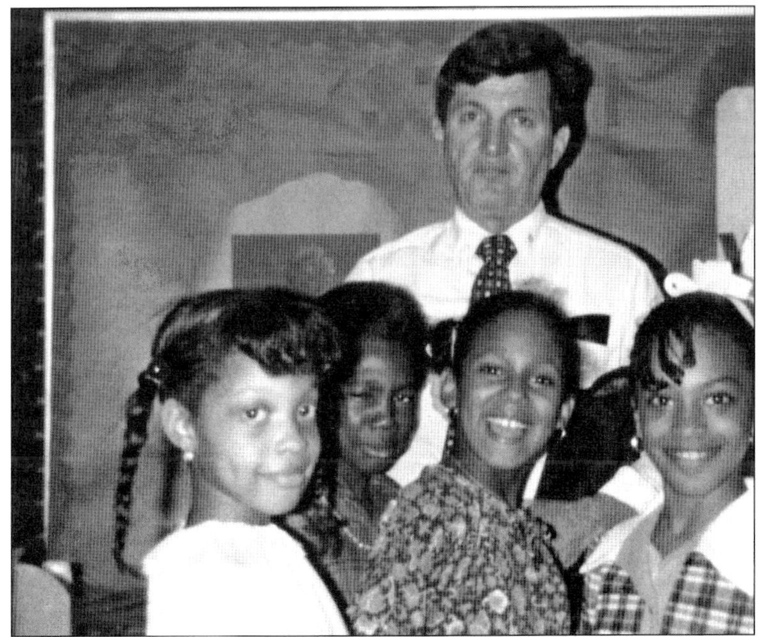

These children pose with an unidentified teacher in this 1980s image taken at Rosenwald Accelerated School. Despite the demographics of the surrounding community, many of the educators in the school were not from the immediate area. (Courtesy of Marylee McDonald.)

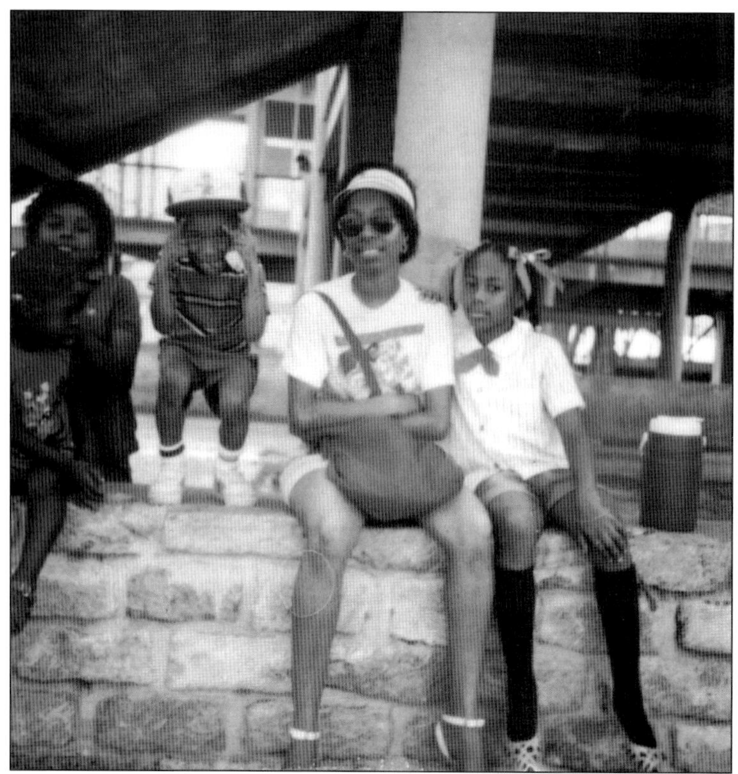

The 1980s was the first time that a Girl Scout troop entered the Cut-Off community. Schelander Phoenix, who is pictured here, was approached by an unidentified woman outside of the neighborhood who expressed an interest in seeing African American children participate in programs and activities that would broaden their horizons. Phoenix then decided to lead the Brownie troop. (Courtesy of Marylee McDonald.)

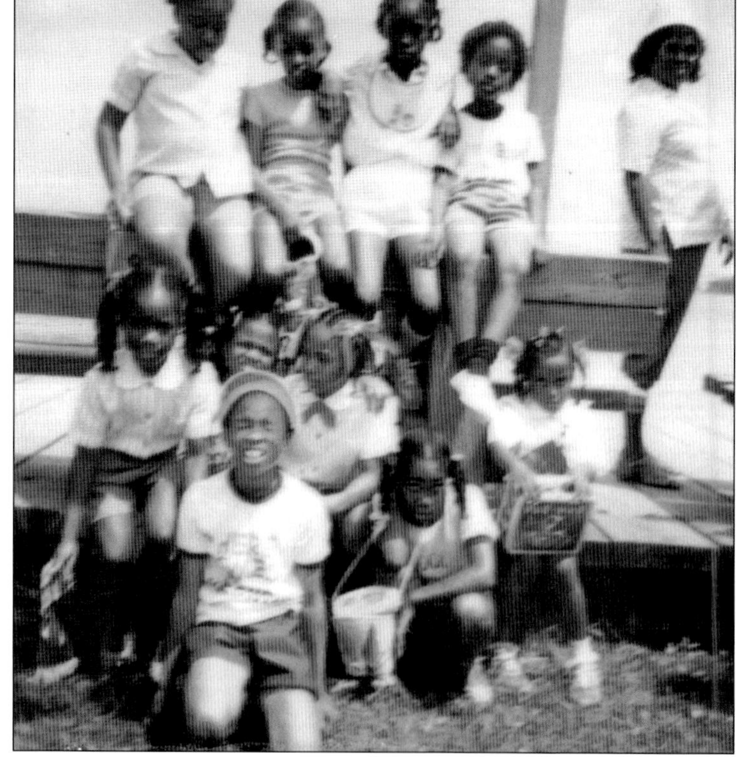

This Brownie troop was made up of second and third graders and overseen by Schelander and Ruth Phoenix. Pictured are, (first row) Krishuan Phoenix; and, from left to right, (second row) Trechelle Brickley, Crystal Lewis, LaToya Lovely, Keitha Nicholas, and Tondra Bowie; (third row) LaDonna Covington, Yashica Wilson, and Ruth Phoenix. (Courtesy of Marylee McDonald.)

Elsie Johnson-Rose was born to the union of Mary Johnson and Austin Johnson Sr. Educated in the Orleans Parish public schools, Johnson-Rose obtained a bachelor's degree from Southern University in Baton Rouge in education and a master's in education and administration from Nicholls State University. Elsie worked for more than 33 years in the Jefferson Parish public schools and went on to serve as president of the Algiers Charter School Association. (Courtesy of Robin Crawford.)

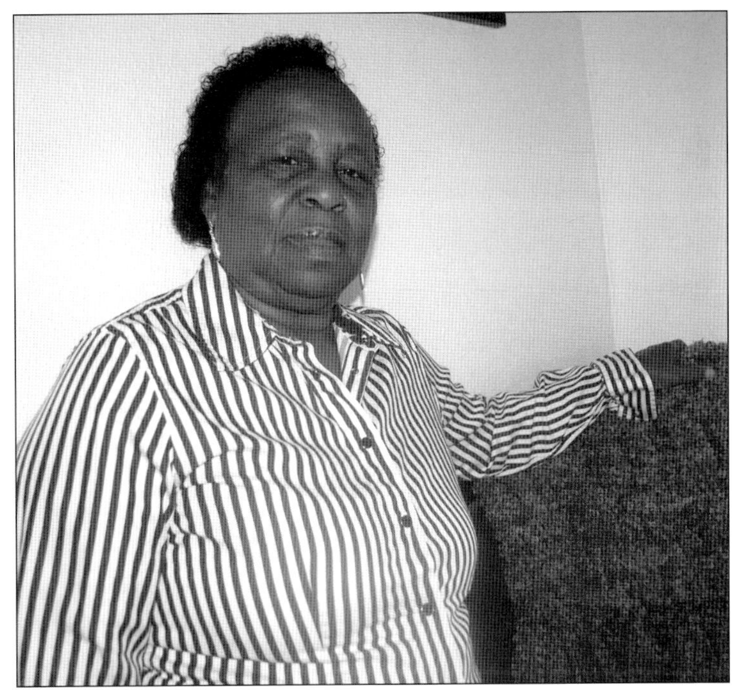

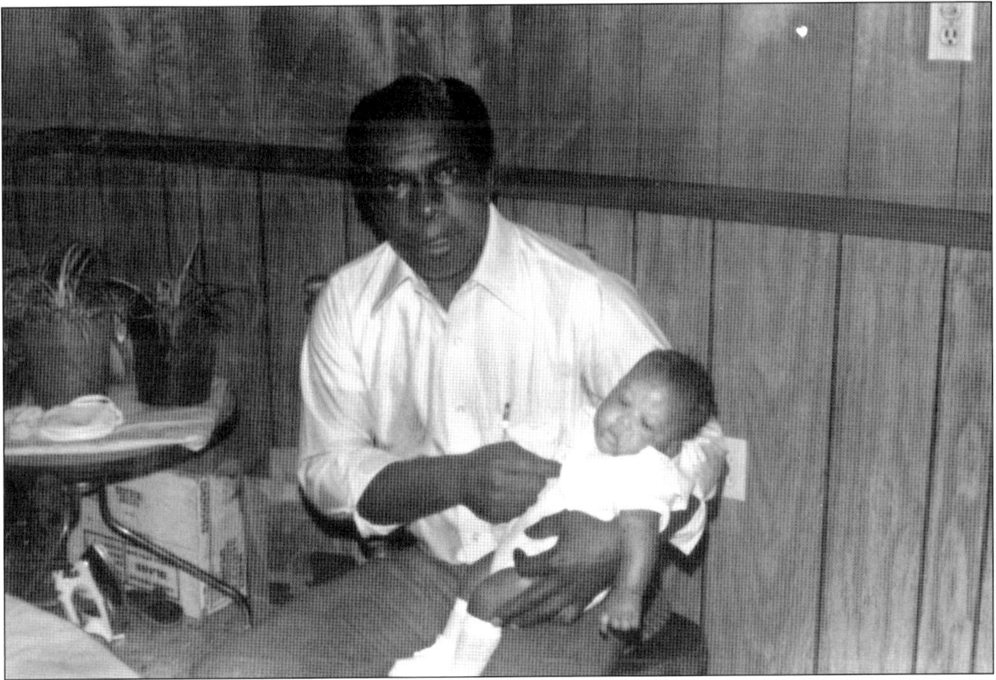

Charles "Morris" Green, was born to Rev. Dr. Earl and Lillian Gastinell-Green. After graduating from L.B. Landry High School, he enlisted in the US Army. After serving in the Army, he attended Xavier University, where he studied administration of education in 1960. He then received a job in the Orleans Parish public schools and taught at Edna Karr Jr. High for many years. He desired to see children from all walks of life receive adequate educations and taught for over 24 years in attempt to reach that goal. (Courtesy of Veronica St. Cyr.)

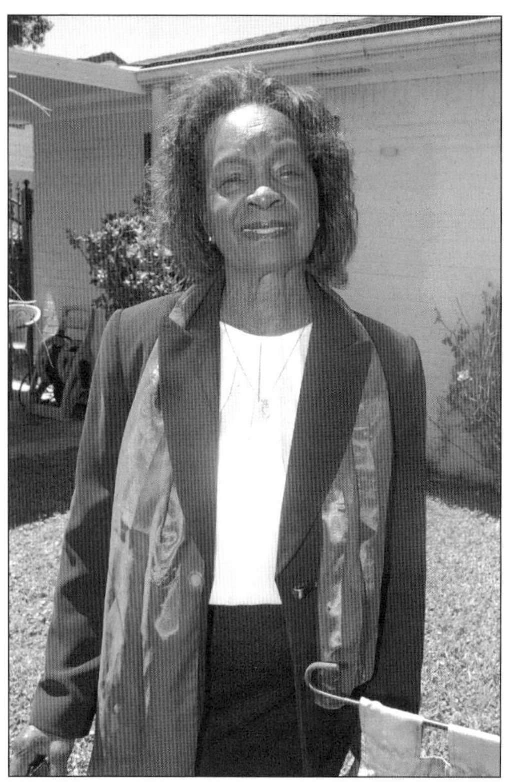

Geraldine Green-Williams was also born to Rev. Dr. Earl and Lillian Gastinell-Green. She graduated in 1956 from L.B. Landry High School. Afterward, she attended Dillard University and Nicholls State University, where she majored in administration and education, respectively. She earned a bachelor of arts and a master's degree and began her teaching career in 1960. She retired in 1990. She was employed with the Orleans Parish public schools, teaching at various schools throughout her life. (Courtesy of Robin Crawford.)

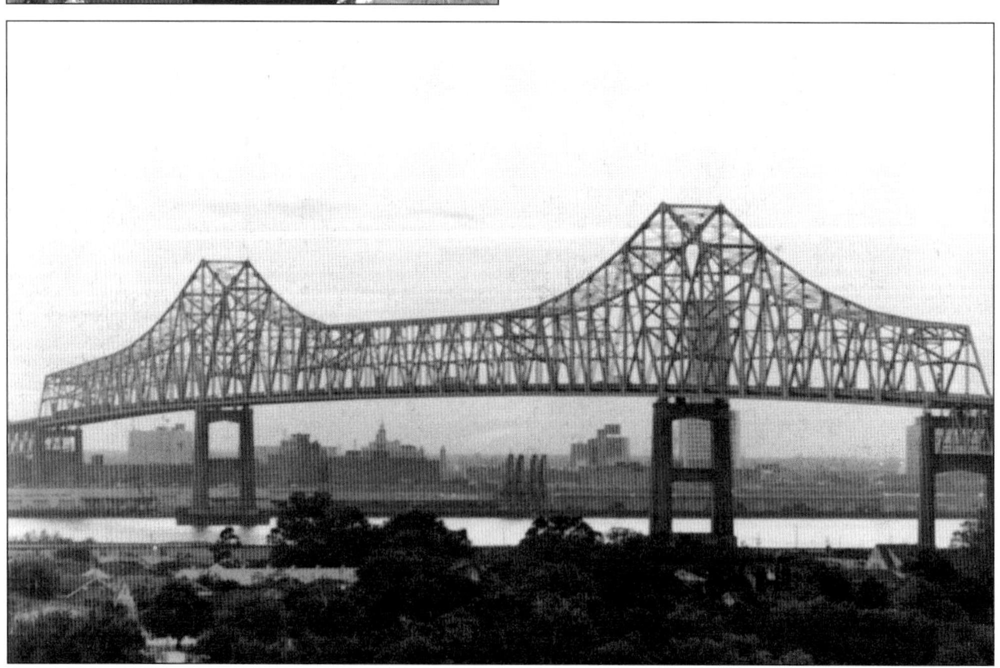

This photograph of the Crescent City Connection was taken in the 1960s, a few years after its construction. This bridge had been opened on a limited basis since April 15, 1958, and was officially dedicated and opened for public access on October 18, 1958. This bridge connects New Orleans's East Bank to the Algiers community. (Courtesy of Veronica St. Cyr.)

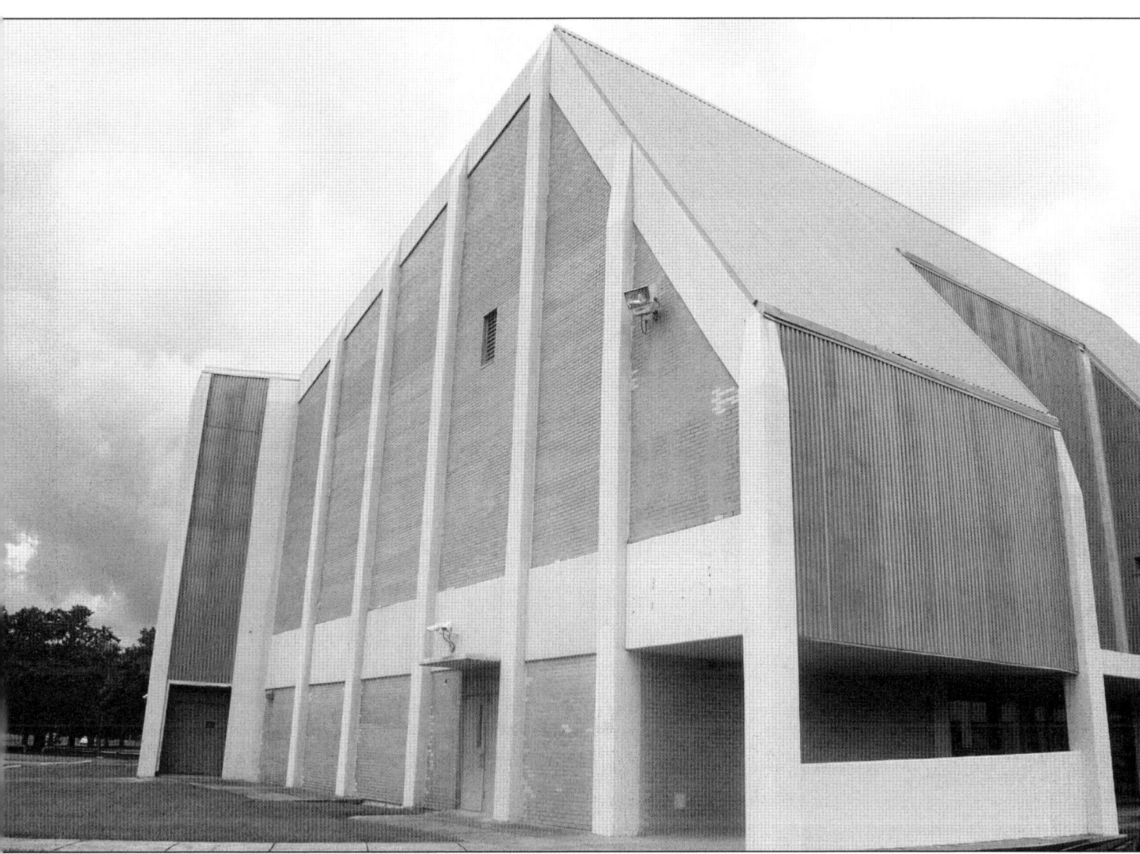

O. Perry Walker High School was originally housed at 2832 General Meyer Avenue in New Orleans, Louisiana. Named after a longtime educator in Orleans Parish, Oliver Perry Walker, this school opened its doors in 1970. Walker was intended to cater exclusively to a white student population. The school was integrated, however, within the first year of its opening, and the demographics of the student body quickly changed. (Courtesy of Robin Crawford.)

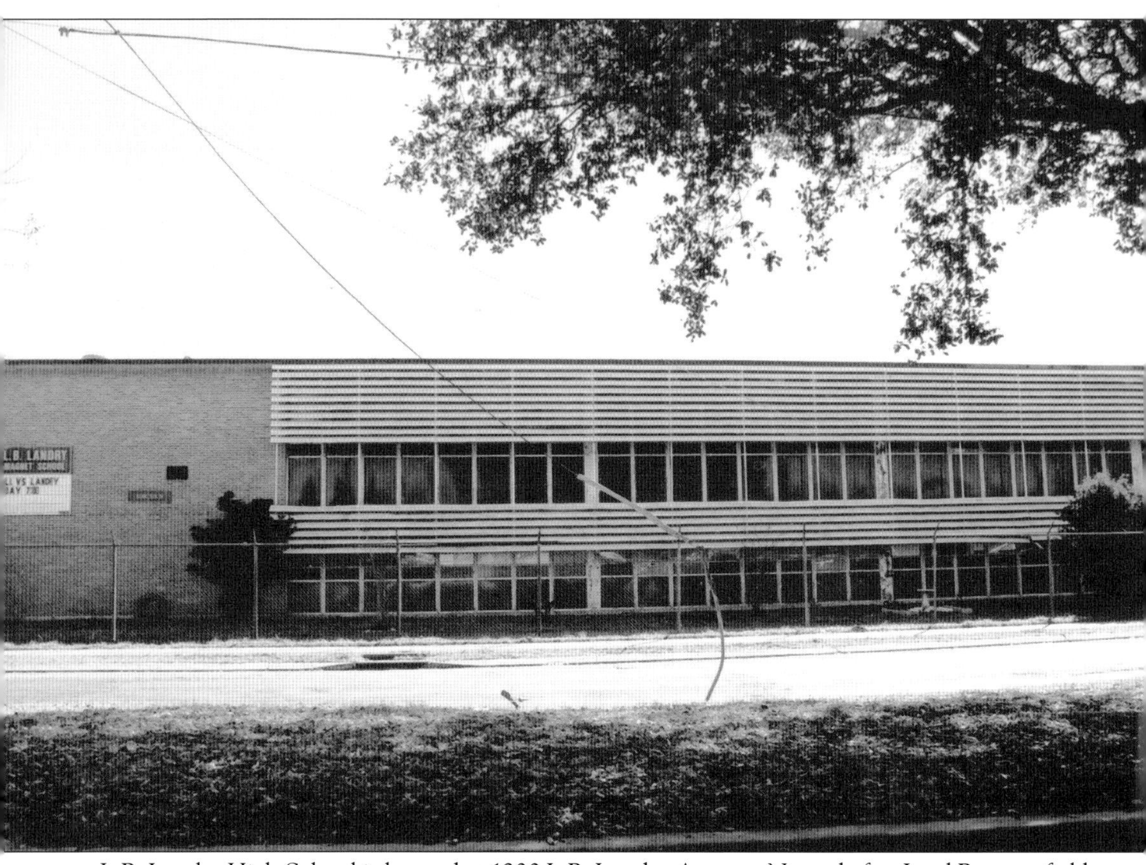

L.B. Landry High School is located at 1200 L.B. Landry Avenue. Named after Lord Beaconsfield Landry, an African American activist, physician, and vocalist, the school opened its doors in 1938 as an elementary school. In 1942, it became a high school that enrolled African Americans from diverse socioeconomic backgrounds. L.B. Landry High School serviced much of Algiers, though many from the Lower Coast of Algiers initially had trouble taking advantage of this opportunity. The lack of transportation and long distance kept many students from enrolling in the school, though many went on to graduate from the institution in later years. Today, Landry-Walker College and Preparatory High School houses students from all over the city of New Orleans. (Courtesy of Robin Crawford.)

Charlie Benn Jr. was among the group of students that helped to integrate O. Perry Walker during the 1970–1971 academic year. Benn was the first black athlete to be introduced to any sports team on the high school campus. He was the only African American on the football team and played as both a defensive end and an outside linebacker. (Courtesy of Charlie Benn Jr.)

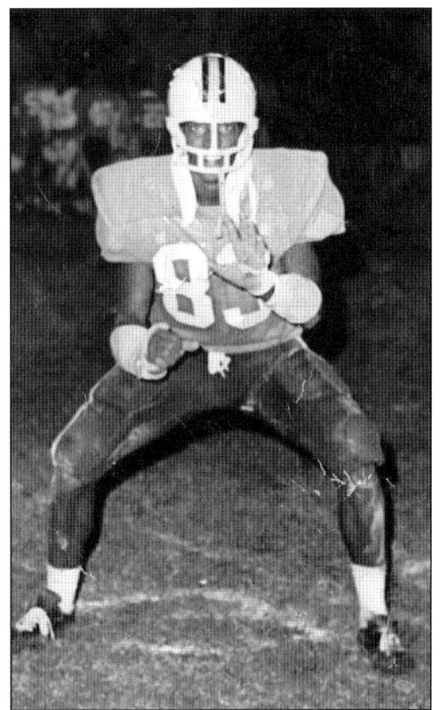

This 1970s photograph shows the newly integrated football team of Oliver Perry Walker High School. Charlie Benn Jr. is highlighted in this image as the only African American student on the team. (Courtesy of Charlie Benn Jr.)

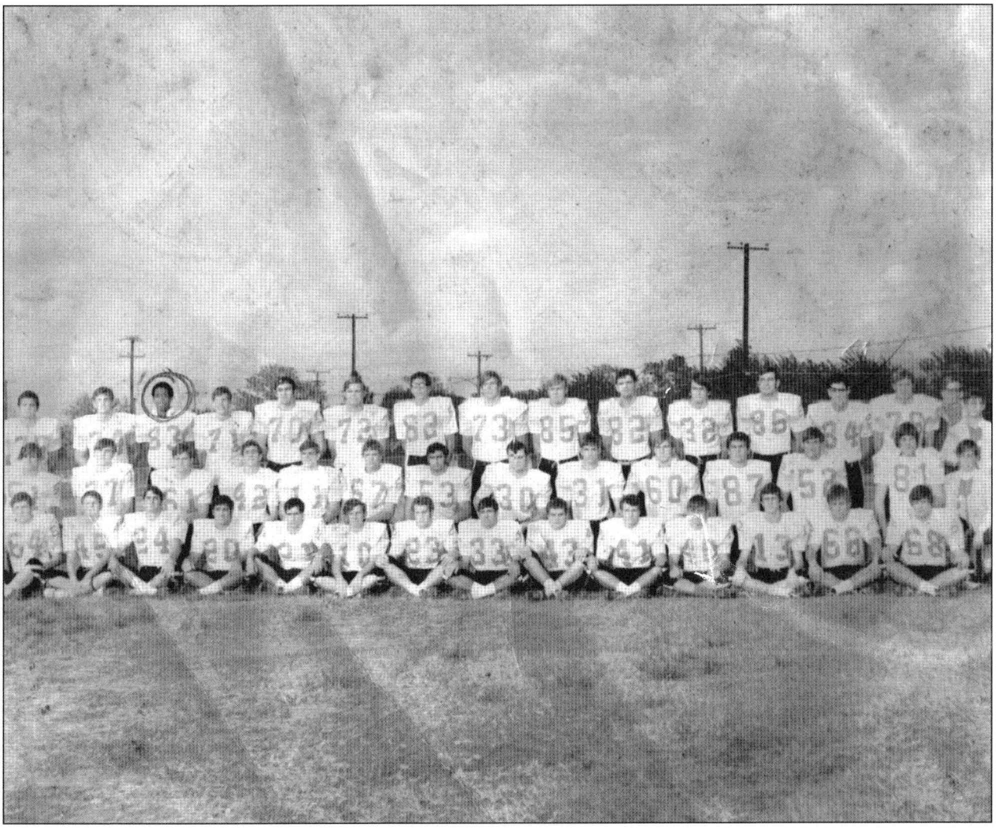

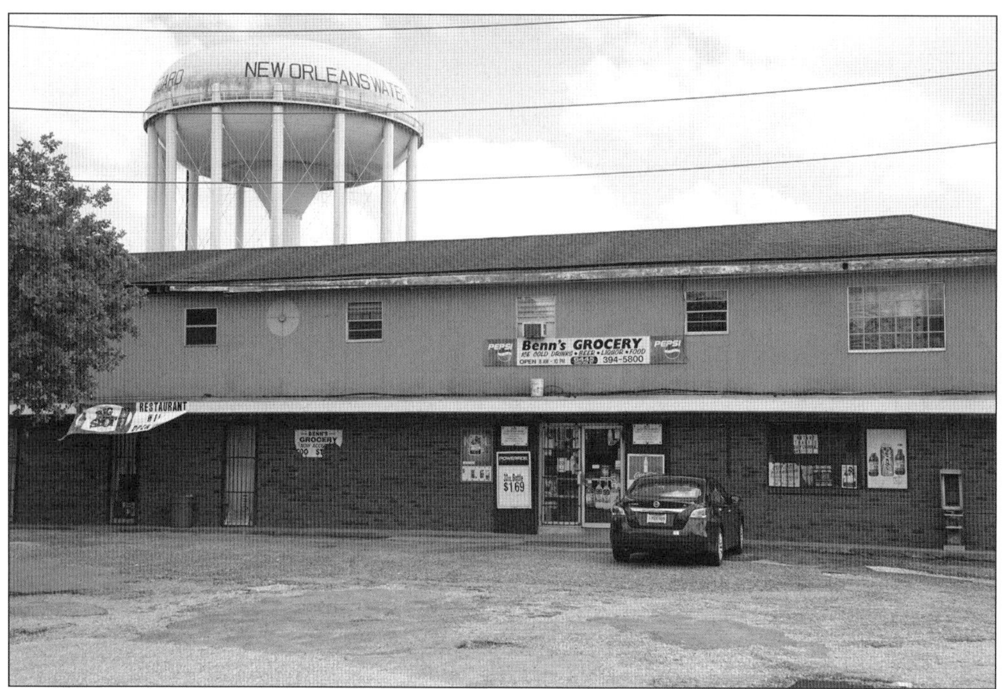

Benn's Grocery is located at 6445 Isadore Street in the Lower Coast of Algiers. Benn's Grocery was the first grocery store to ever stand in the Cut-Off community. This business began in 1886 and still stands in its original place today. (Courtesy of Frederick Weil.)

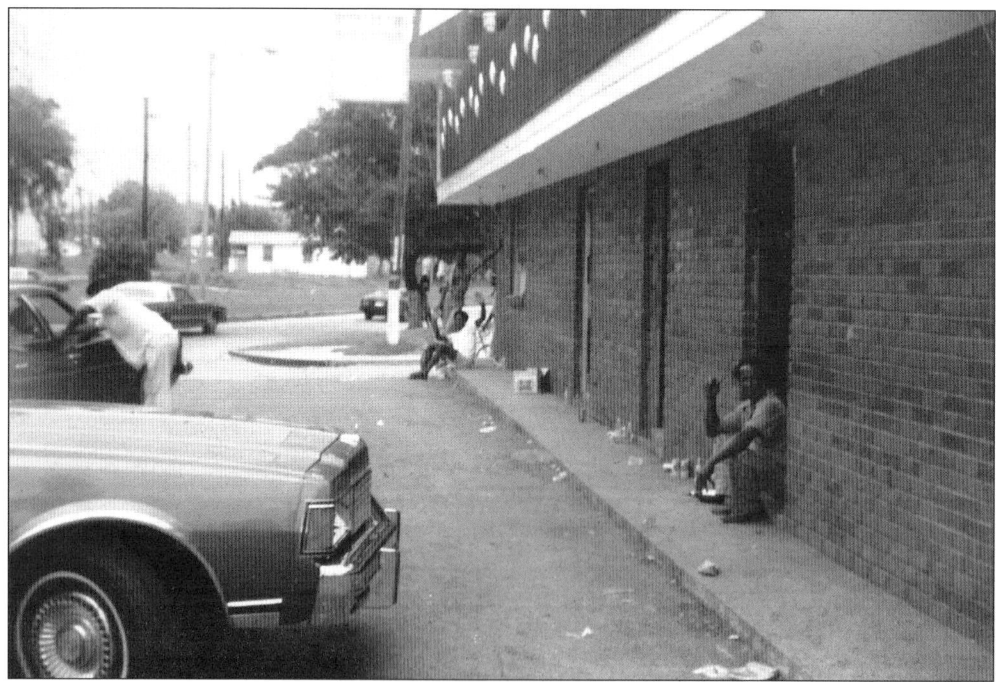

Benn's Grocery is a split-level complex. Over the years, the top level of the store has been used for many different purposes. The bottom level has always been used as the storefront. (Courtesy of Charlie Benn Jr.)

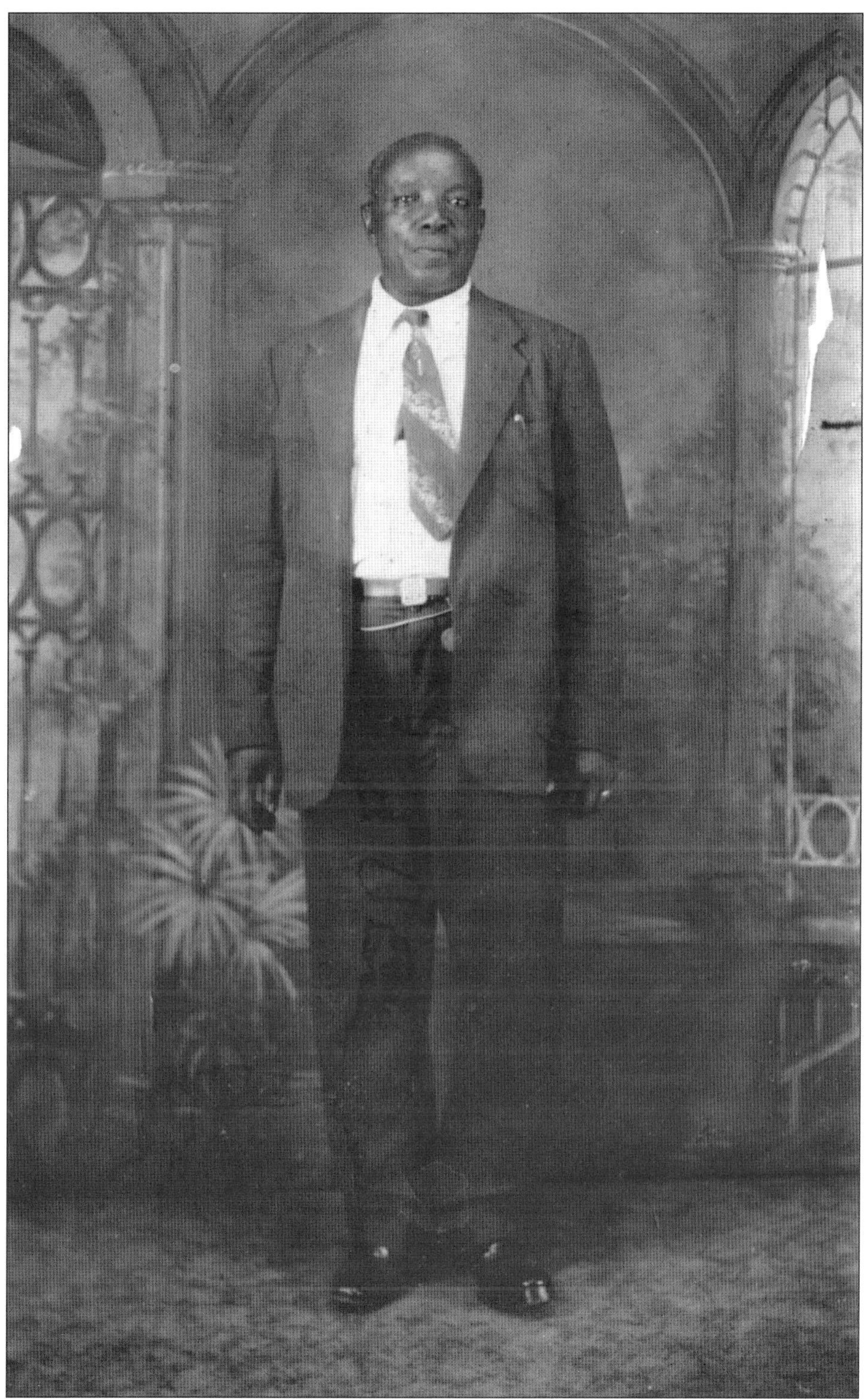

Isaac Been Sr. was born on May 1, 1889. He was the second proprietor of Benn's Grocery. Prior to his proprietorship, the store was run by his eldest sister. (Courtesy of Charlie Benn Jr.)

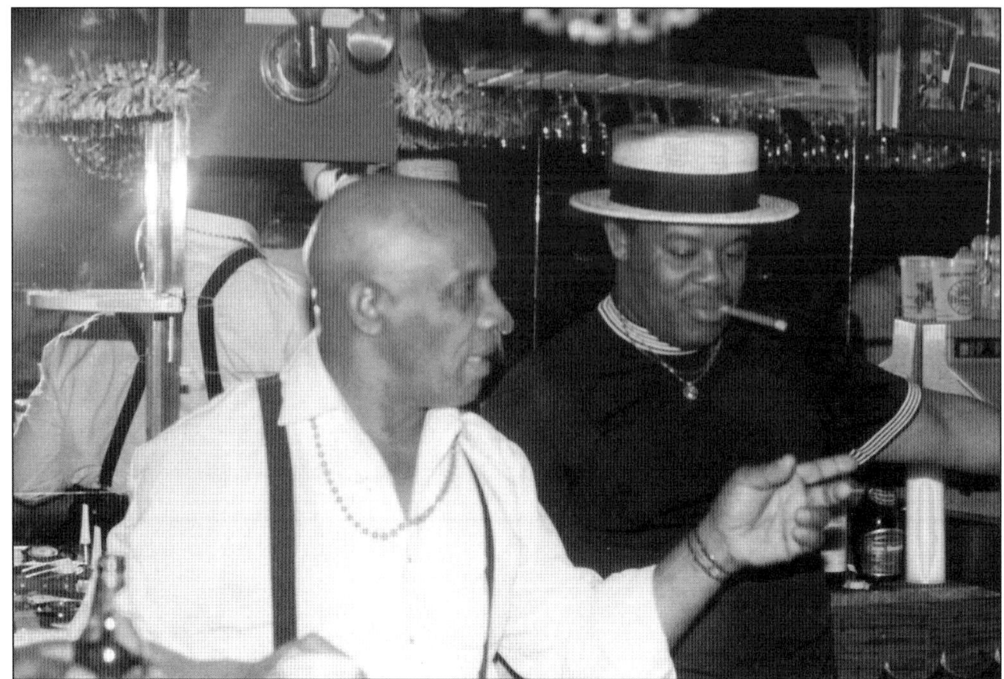

Isaac Benn Jr. served in the US Army during World War II, where he received numerous commendations. After completing his duty in the Army, he worked as a seaman and a carpenter. Years later, he became an entrepreneur. Following in the footsteps of his father, Isaac Benn Sr., he opened Isaac's Bar and Lounge, which was located on top level of Benn's Grocery. Isaac was the sole proprietor of the lounge, which he owned in the late 1970s. He is pictured in his establishment with Kermit Benn. Isaac Jr. brought much life to the community. He passed from this life on July 11, 2017, at the age of 95. (Courtesy of Charlie Benn Jr.)

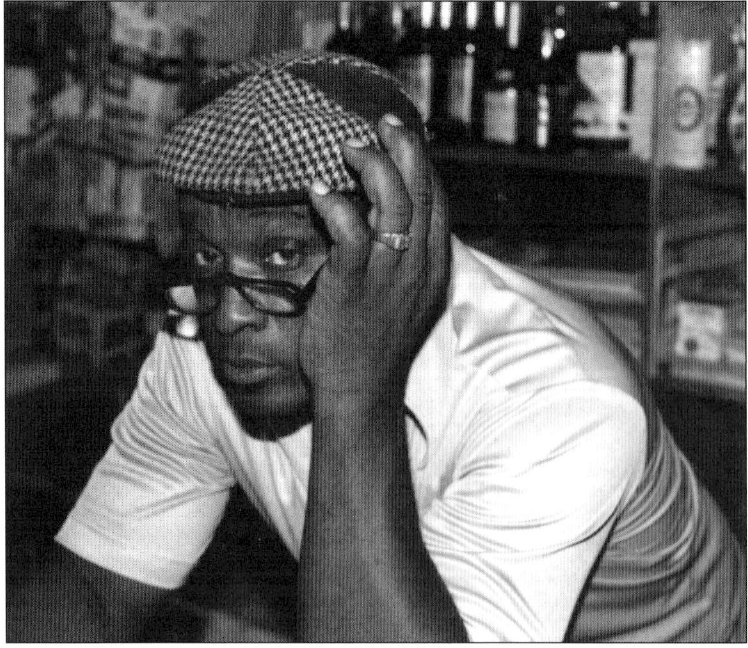

Charlie Been Sr. sits behind the counter of Benn's Grocery in this photograph taken in the 1980s. Charlie was a seaman with a sixth-grade education who saw to it that each of his children was college-educated. After returning from sea, Charlie and his brother Kermit Benn began comanaging Benn's Grocery in the 1960s. Charlie continued helping with the family business for over 40 years. (Courtesy of Charlie Benn Jr.)

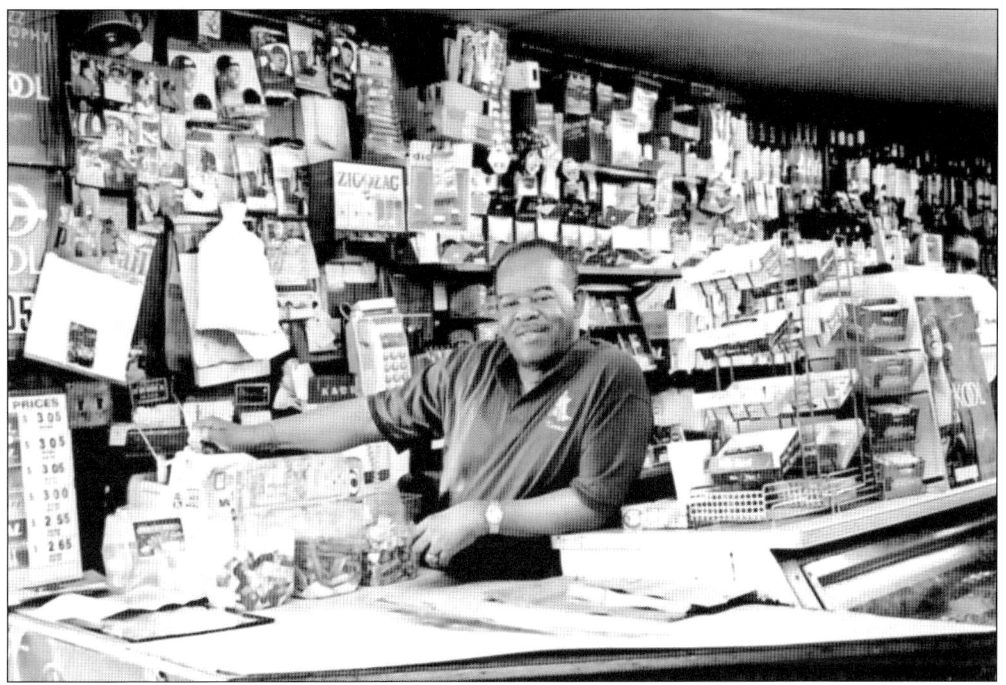

Kermit Benn, or "Conay," as he was affectionately known to the community, took ownership of Benn's Grocery in the 1960s after the passing of his father, Isaac Benn Jr. (Courtesy of Robin Crawford.)

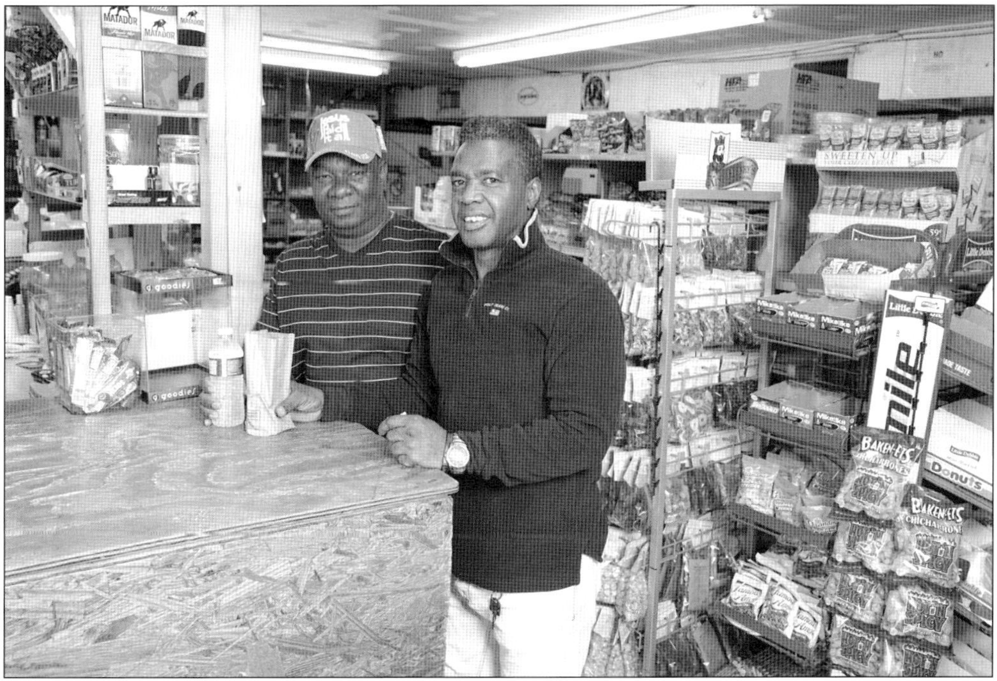

Taken in 2017 at Benn's Grocery, this photograph shows Renny Riley (left), a current store manager, alongside an unidentified customer. (Courtesy of Frederick Weil.)

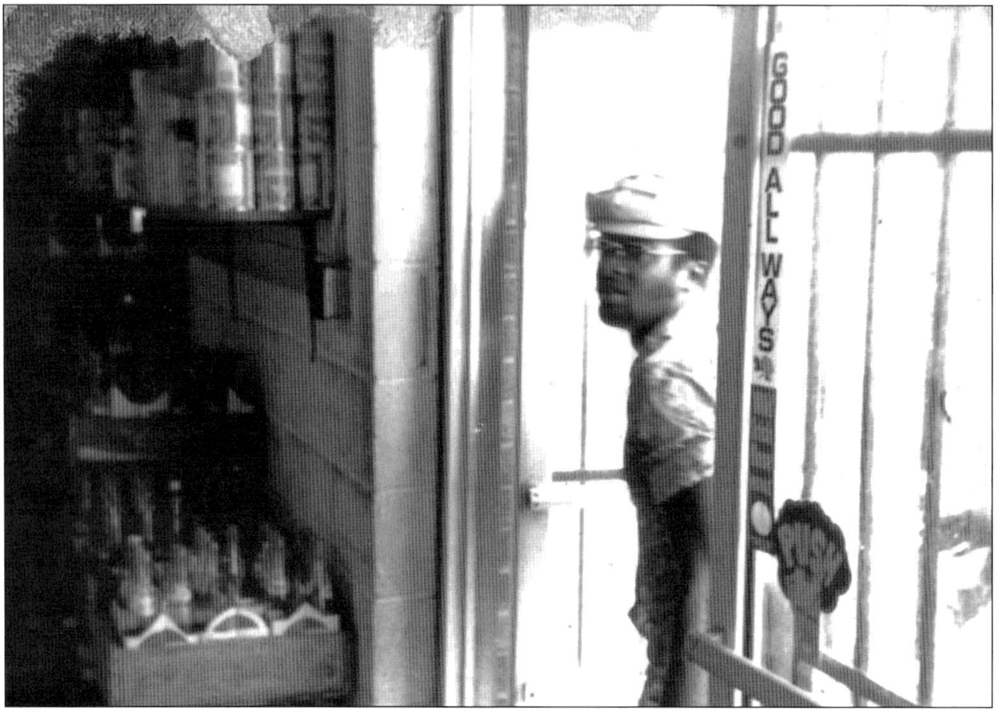

Lionel McDonald Sr. is pictured entering Benn's Grocery store in the 1950s. The original cinder-block walls and the glass bottled drinks of the time can be found in the background of the image. (Courtesy of Marylee McDonald.)

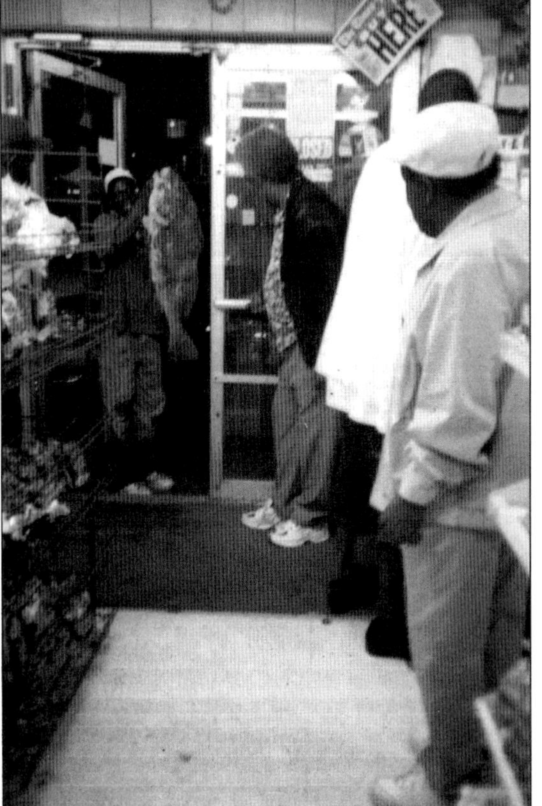

This photograph captures members of the community celebrating a large catch in Benn's Grocery. Benn's has not only provided the physical needs of the people in the community but has also served a social space for many years. (Courtesy of Charlie Benn Jr.)

This image taken in the 1990s shows a delivery being carted away from Benn's Grocery. Throughout the history of Benn's Grocery, it has not been uncommon to find group economics being practiced with other African American business owners. At some points in history, this was done out of necessity; other times, it was done out of determination. (Courtesy of Charlie Benn Jr.)

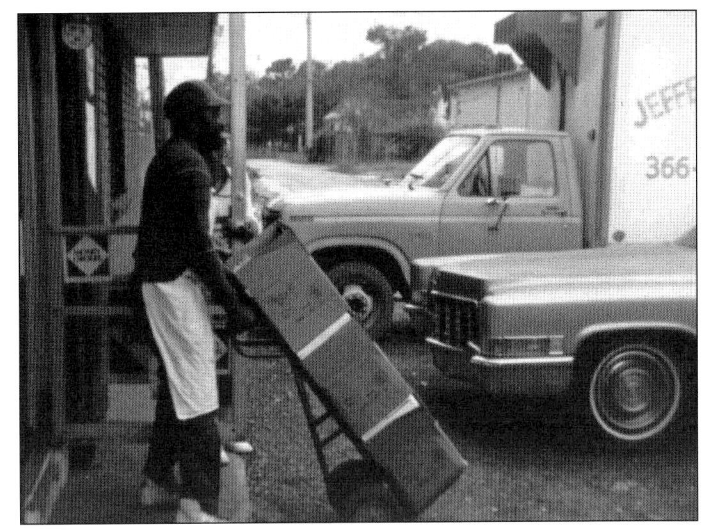

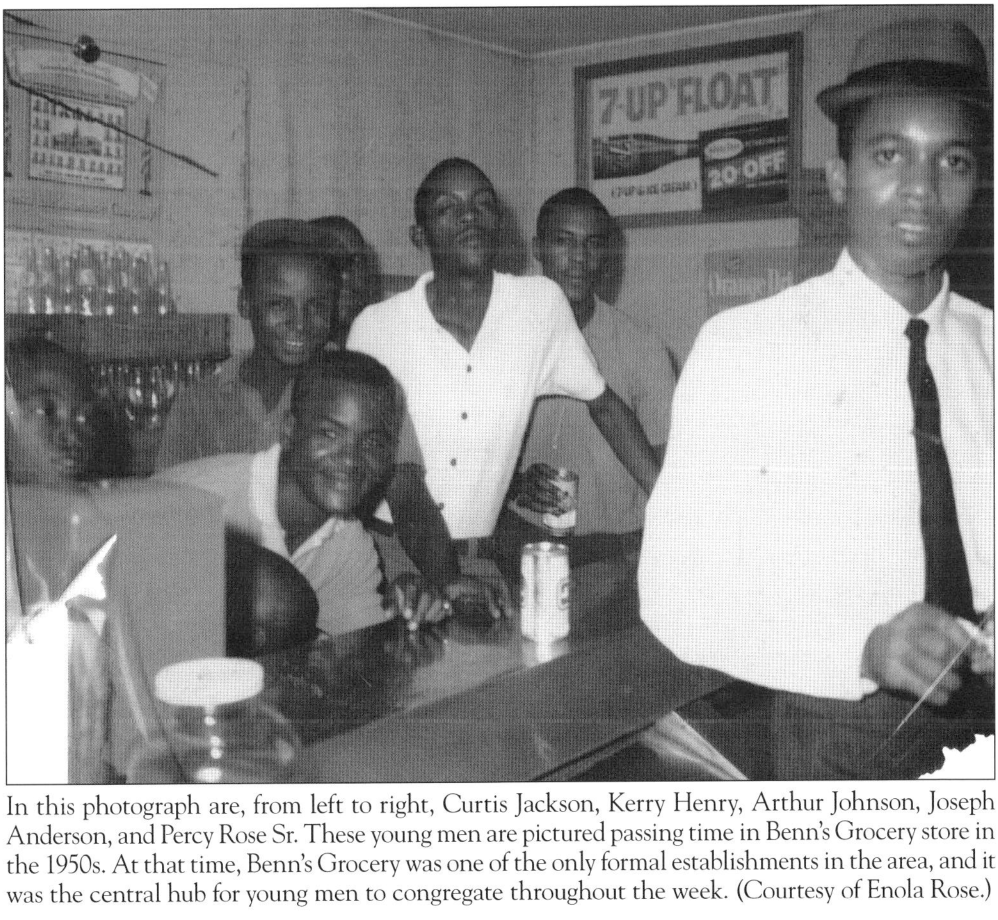

In this photograph are, from left to right, Curtis Jackson, Kerry Henry, Arthur Johnson, Joseph Anderson, and Percy Rose Sr. These young men are pictured passing time in Benn's Grocery store in the 1950s. At that time, Benn's Grocery was one of the only formal establishments in the area, and it was the central hub for young men to congregate throughout the week. (Courtesy of Enola Rose.)

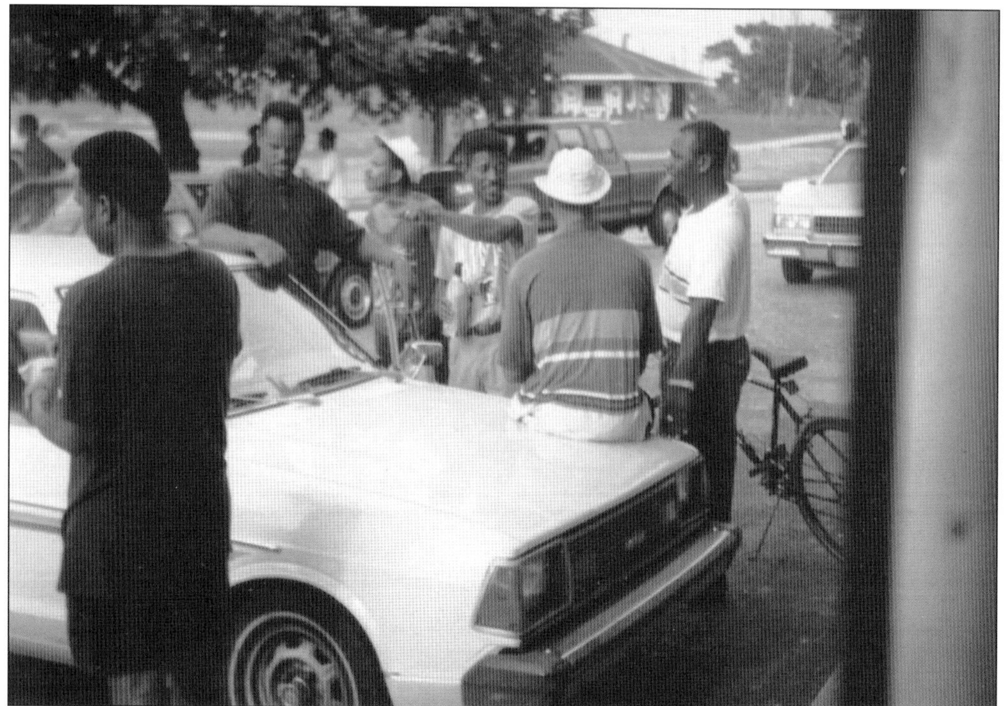

Benn's Grocery has served as the hangout for men in the community for decades. Groups of men gather throughout the week, and especially on weekends, to talk and commune. Men can be found gathered at the front of the store, as pictured above. They also partake in games of horseshoes or dominoes in the lot at the rear in the store, as pictured below. While many outside of the community may find it difficult to appreciate such large gatherings, those who are indigenous to this neighborhood understand it to be a communion that has seen many in the area through both the best and the worst of times. (Above, courtesy of Charlie Benn Jr.; below, courtesy of Marylee McDonald.)

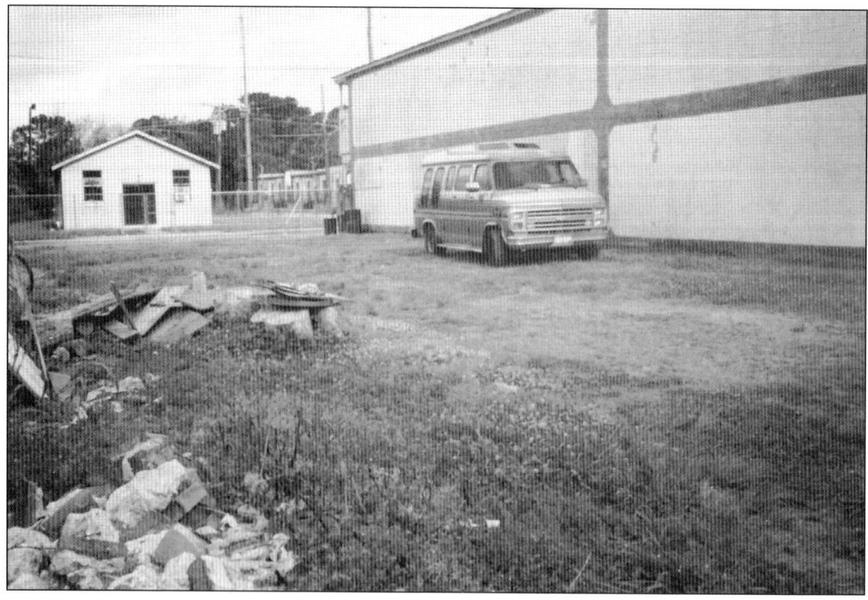

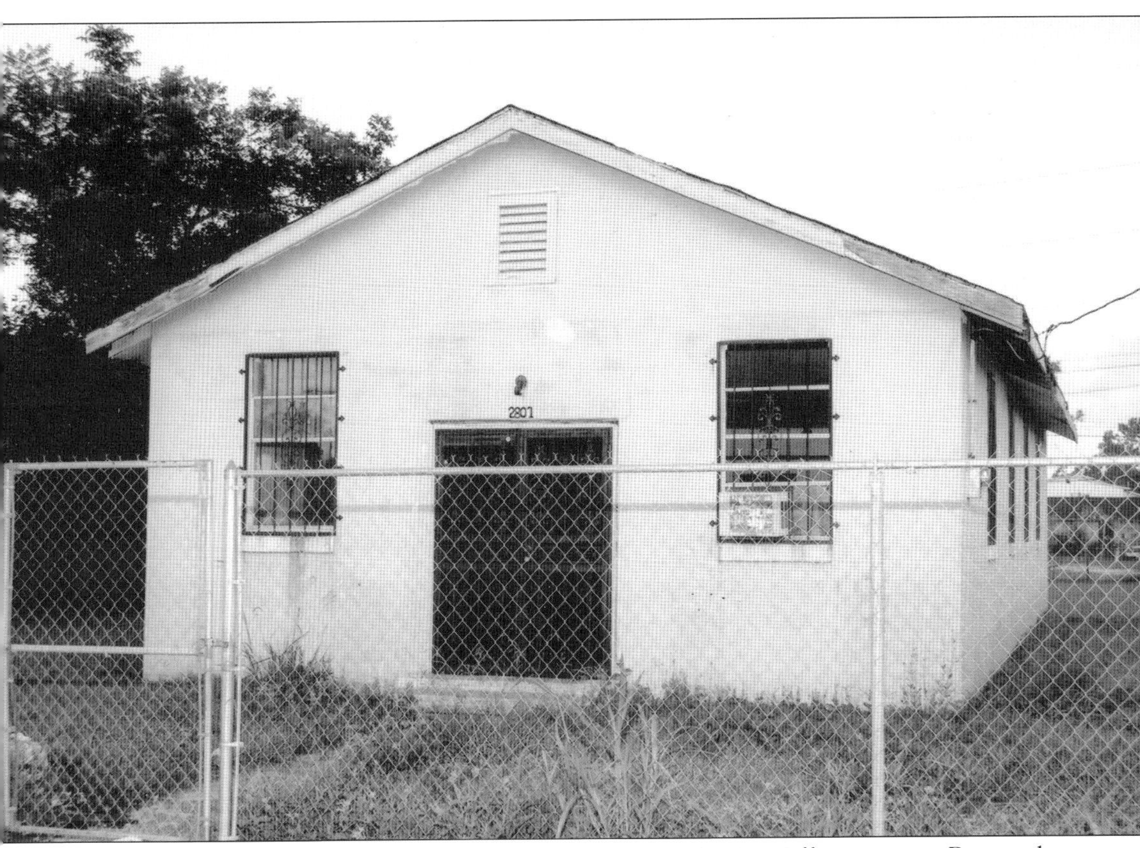

The Eureka Hall is one of the most notable historic sites in the Cut-Off community. During the 1930s and 1940s, the hall served as a movie theater. At the time, the cost to watch a movie was 15¢. Each weekend, Isaiah Williams or John Phoenix would walk through the neighborhood and yell which movie would be playing. These two men would alternate running the movie projector during the show, which traditionally played Hopalong Cassidy films. The hall closed for about a decade, and relaunched in the 1950s as a meeting space for benevolent societies. These "societies," which included Eureka, Nazarene, and Friends of Charity, would gather to collect monthly dues, used to pay for medical costs and burials. The site was later demolished and the land was purchased by Second Baptist Church. (Courtesy of Robin Crawford.)

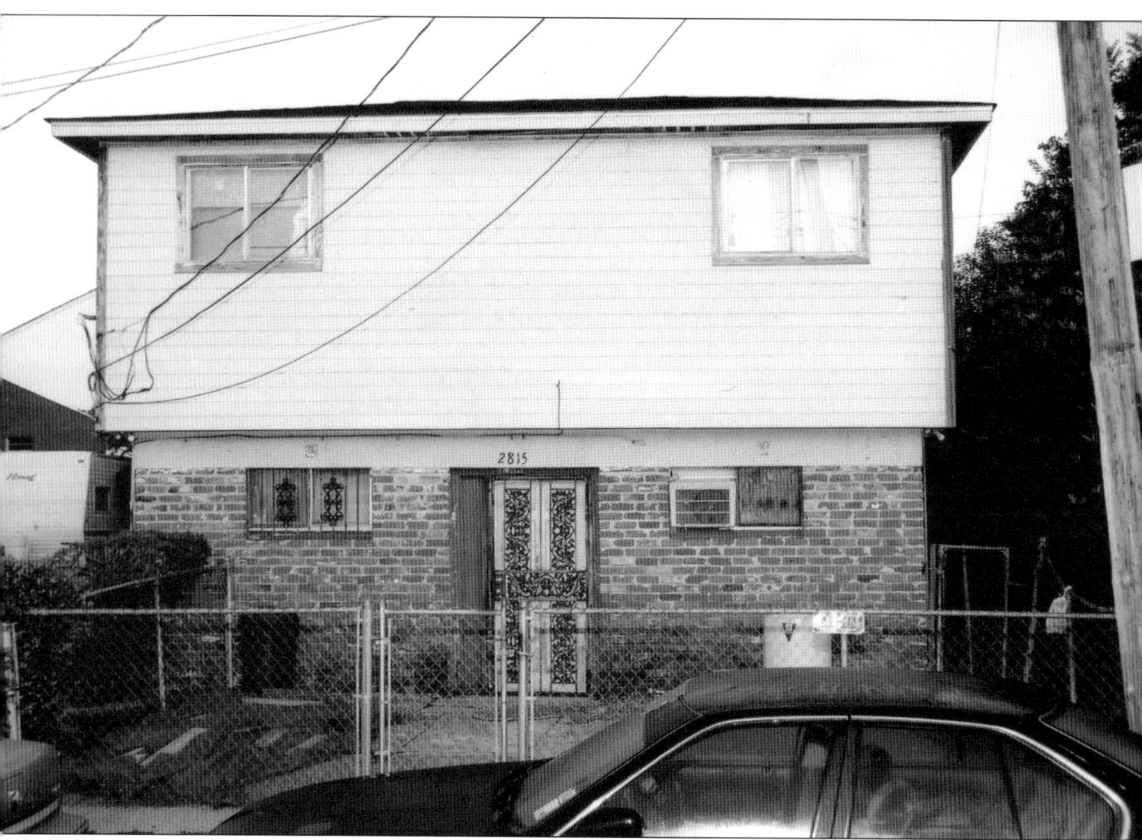

Hazel's Sweet Shop was a neighborhood hangout located on Boyd Street, where community members would gather on weekends to dance and play during the 1960s. This candy shop was also a juke joint that attracted children and adults alike. Sundays were particularly popular, as neighbors would gather to play trending music on the jukebox and purchase giant Lance cookies, which were a customer favorite. (Courtesy of Robin Crawford.)

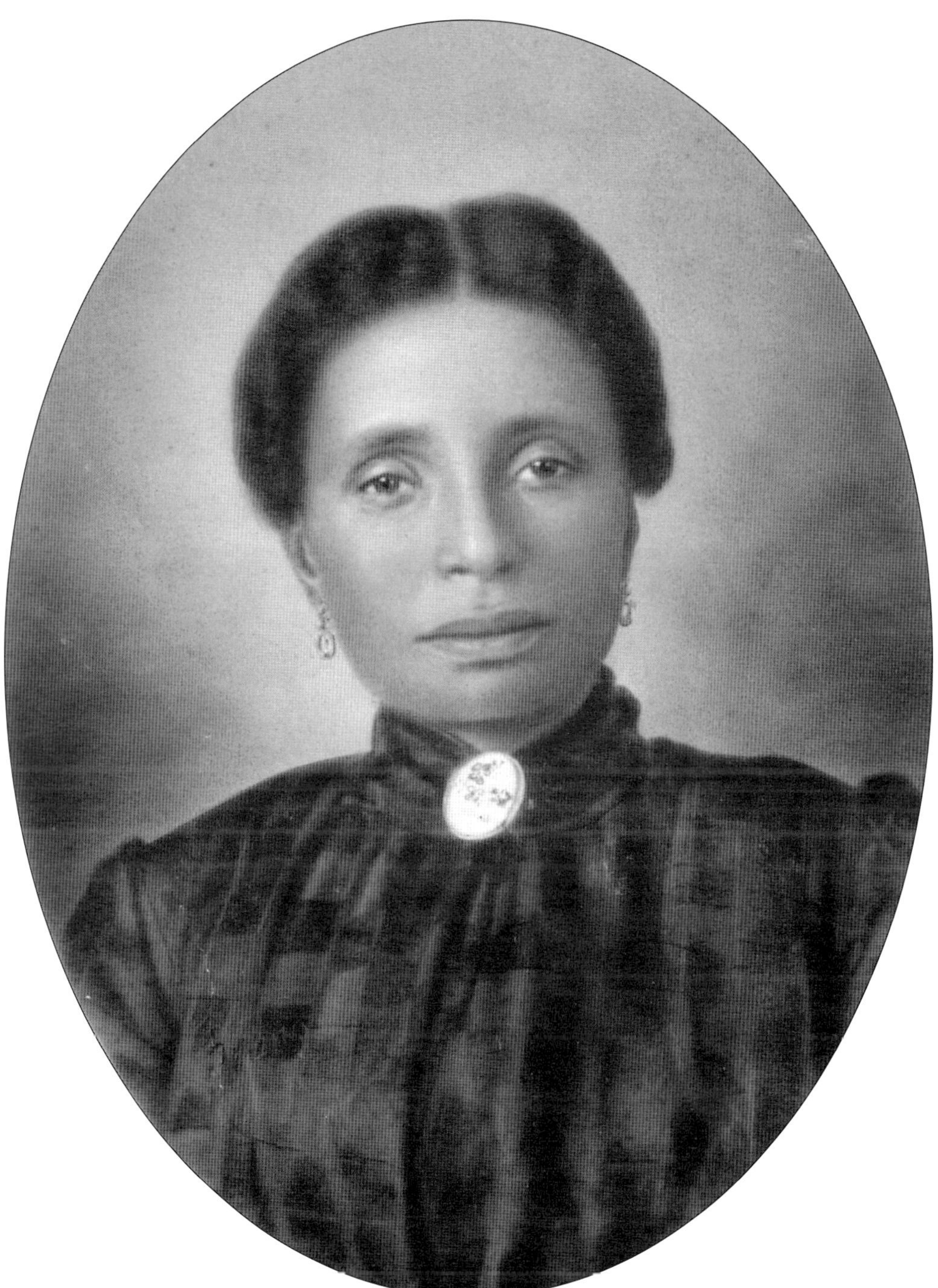

Philomene Landolph (Williams) Boyd was born April 1, 1866. She and her husband, John Boyd, owned a small grocery store in the Lower Coast of Algiers. The community would go to their store to purchase items needed for their homes. The store was established sometime in the early 1900s and remained open until the 1950s. Prior to the installation of pipes for running water in the area, Philomene also owned a cistern from which many in the community were able to draw clean drinking water. (Courtesy of Jerome Bush.)

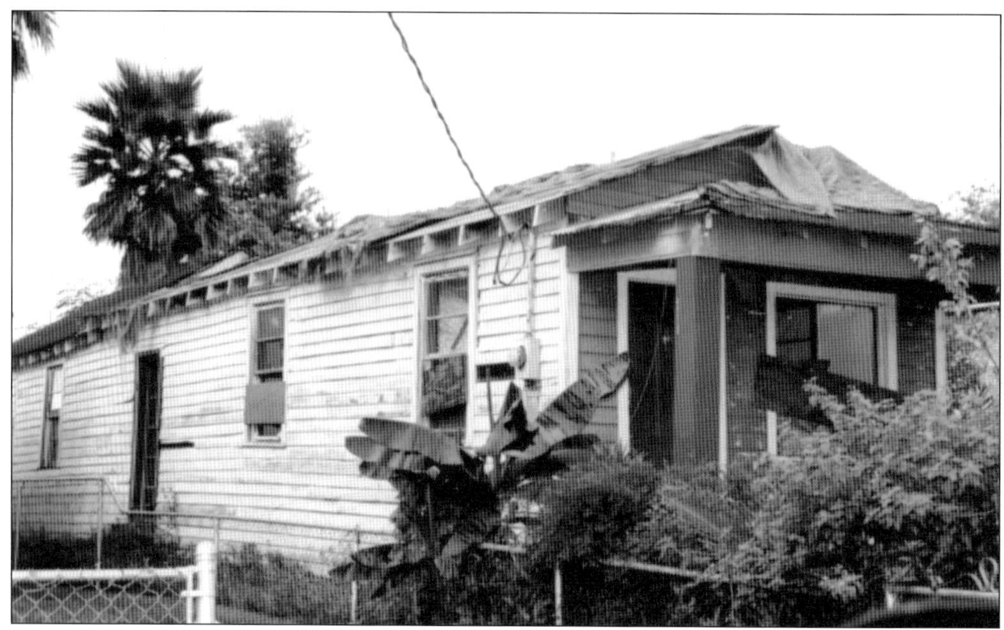

The Lower Coast of Algiers Community Development Center originally began at 6419 Ivory Street. It was first organized on April 13, 1973, at the home of Irma LaCroix-Taylor. The home was torn down after Hurricane Katrina in 2005. The founding members were Irma L. Taylor, Alberta J. Franklin, Alberta R. Gant, Edna Martin and Elnora M. Brasley, Lillian C. Perrymon, Amelia W. Price, and Evelyn Gastinell. (Courtesy of Robin Crawford.)

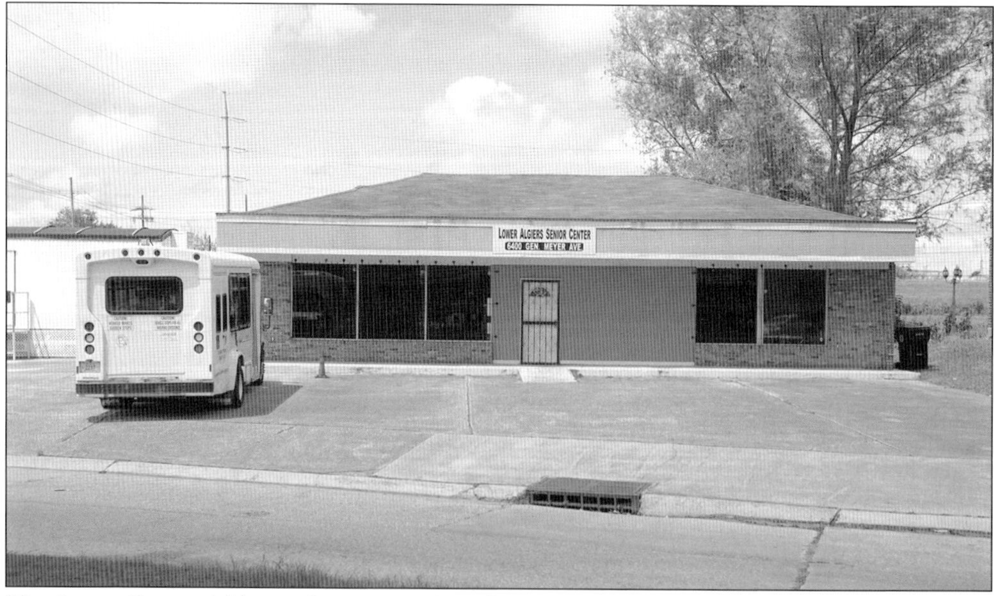

The Lower Coast of Algiers Community Development Center is now located at 6400 General Meyer Avenue. It was chartered on June 10, 1975, with the following founding committee members: Ellen Nevil, Sedonia Wilson and Sophia Charles, Edna Martin, Armentine Jefferson, Alberta Taylor, Herbert Sullen Sr., Ernest Pettigrew, Emile Kelly, Donald King, Roy Jackson, Earl Amedee, Sharon Swayne, Veronica Lee, Milton Rose, Evelyn Lewis, Pricilla Lee, Jean Marie Gary, Al Sergeant, and Carlton Pecou. (Courtesy of Frederick Weil.)

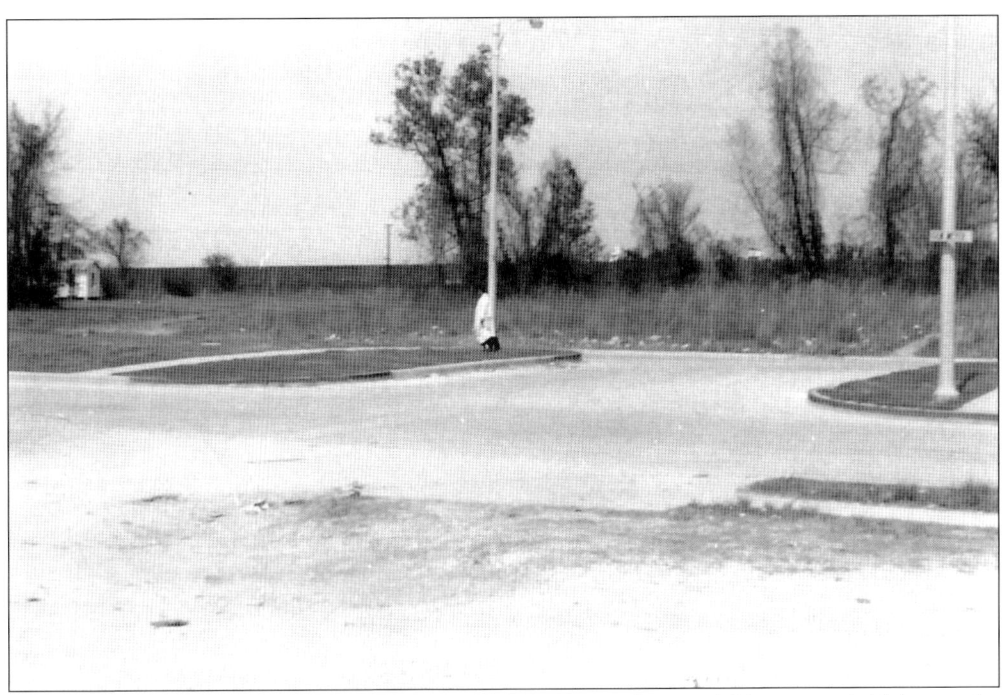

To those unfamiliar with the area, this image may appear to depict a lifeless open field, but to the residents of the Cut-Off, this field, known as "the green," was the place to be on Sunday afternoons. This land was home to baseball games and gatherings that brought the entire community into one space. (Courtesy of Charlie Benn Jr.)

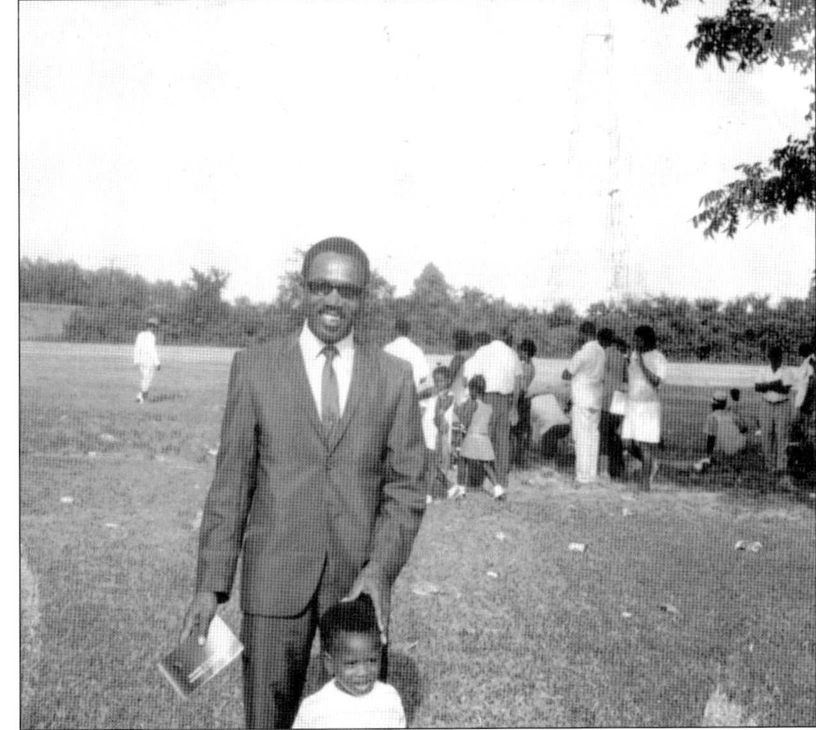

Percy Rose Sr. is pictured with his grandson Eddie Rose Jr. on "the green" in the 1960s. The two are dressed in their Sunday best and pose in front of a crowd that is likely anticipating a game scheduled to be played by the Cut-Off Sports team. (Courtesy of Enola Rose.)

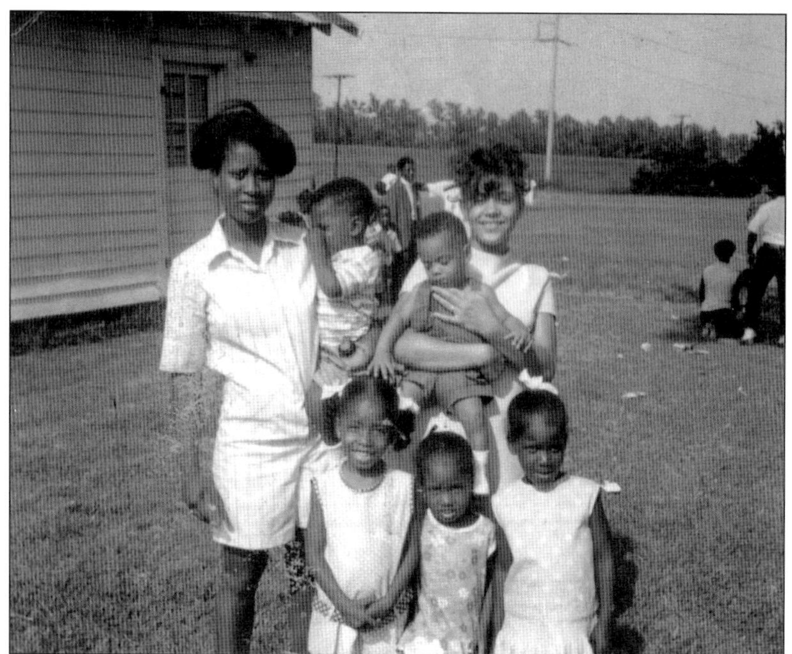

The photograph was taken on "the green" in front of the home of Lewis and Dianne Smith. June Price (right) holds her son Donald and Enola Rose (left) holds her son Eddie Jr., behind her nieces Dena (left), Tammy (center), and Tracy Manuel as they pause from an enjoyable Sunday evening watching sports. (Courtesy of Enola Rose.)

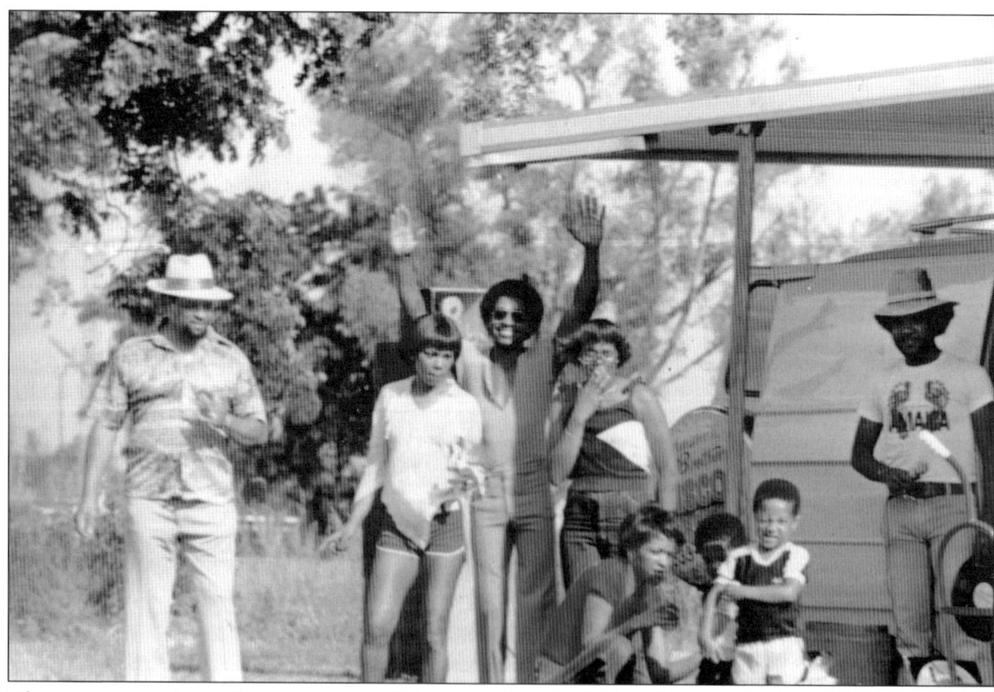

This group is gathered for an outing at "the green" in the 1970s. Despite the fact that the tradition began as early as the 1930s, it remained a staple until the New Orleans Recreation Department saw fit to build a recreation center. (Courtesy of Marylee McDonald.)

In the 1930s Alexander "Shack" Washington Jr., Louis Davis Sr., Dood Johnson Sr., Octave Franklin, Freddie Ross, and a few other men took part in making Sundays a day for baseball. After a few years, the next generation took over and formalized the team, calling themselves Cut-Off Sports. Members of the Cut-Off Sports team are pictured in this 1960s photograph. The Cut-Off Sports team became so popular and successful that it began to travel outside of the community to play other teams. Between the years of 1973 and1974, players rebranded the team the Big Red Machine. (Both, courtesy of Bevelyn Manuel.)

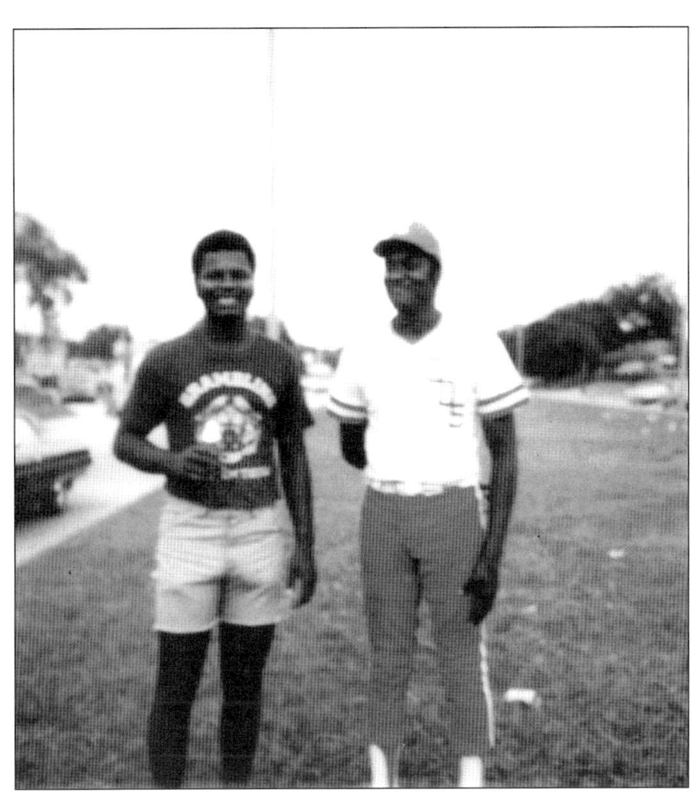

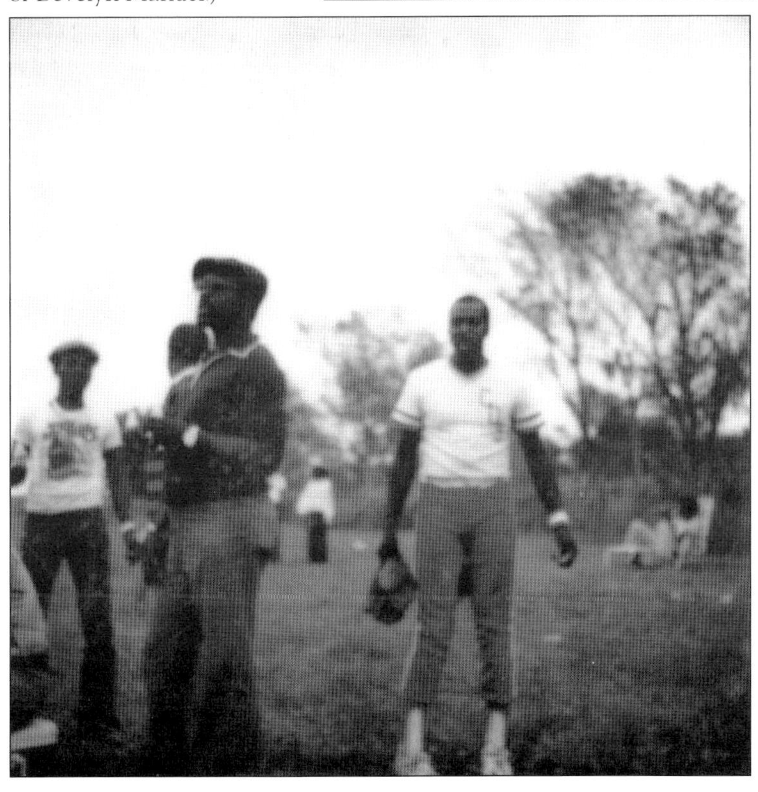

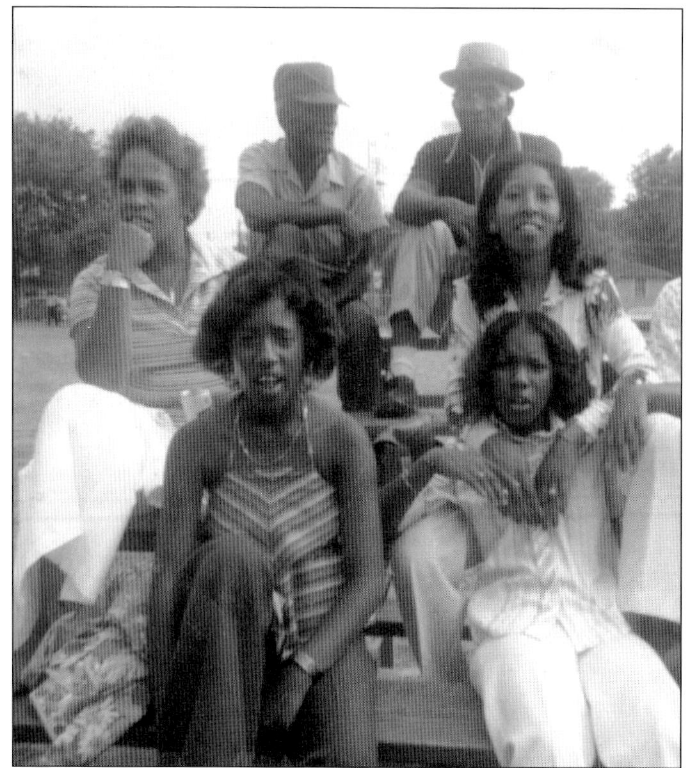

Kim Sullen and Tammy Manuel (first row, left to right) and Doris Sullen and Bevelyn Manuel (second row, left to right) are pictured with two unidentified men in the 1970s seated in stands on "the green" in anticipation of a game to be played by the Big Red Machine. (Courtesy of Bevelyn Manuel.)

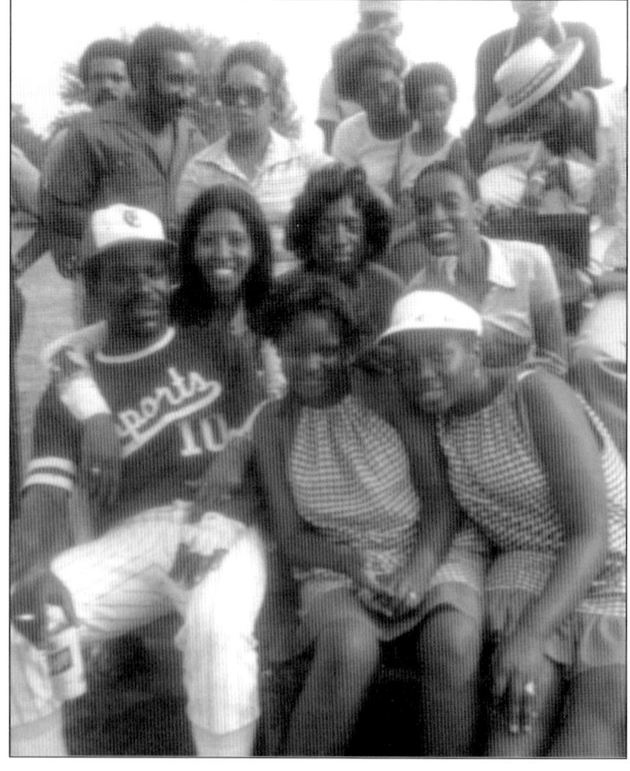

The Big Red Machine was coached by Curtis Benn and included Curvin "Moe" Augustine (on the left, wearing no. 10), Celo "Toby" St. Cyr, Warren "Dusty" Washington, Herman Bentley, Roy Jackson, Donald King, Calvin King, Huey Madison Sr., Irvin Washington, Kermit Jackson, Raymond, Fred "Toby" Banks, Leonard Green, Neal Charles, Kent "Polly" Ross, Excel Petty, Jeffrey Benn, Ike and Thomas Williams, Jackie Riley, Herman King, Isaiah "Big Boy" Carter, and Alexander "Shack" Washington, who returned as the umpire. Also identified in this photograph are Bevelyn Manuel, Kim Sullen, and Saundra Sullen (second row, left to right). (Courtesy of Bevelyn Manuel.)

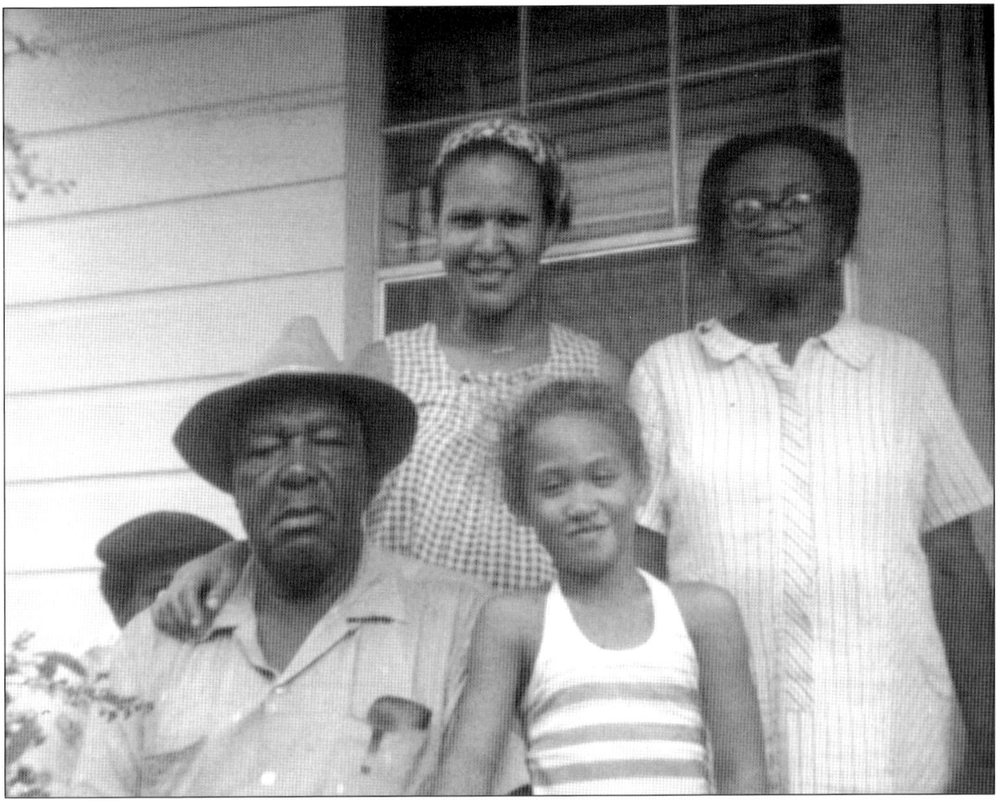

Alexander "Mr. Bay" Washington Sr. was born to Warner and Isabella Washington in 1899. Mr. Bay, pictured with family and friends in this photograph taken in the 1970s, was a dedicated worker and entrepreneur who provided goods to his neighbors. He owned a store on Boyd Street and sold produce and fresh game in the area. Aside from this, he was also active in the church as a Sunday school teacher and deacon, where he is remembered for instilling in children that "God is Spirit." Mr. Bay passed away in July 1980. (Courtesy of Augustine Washington.)

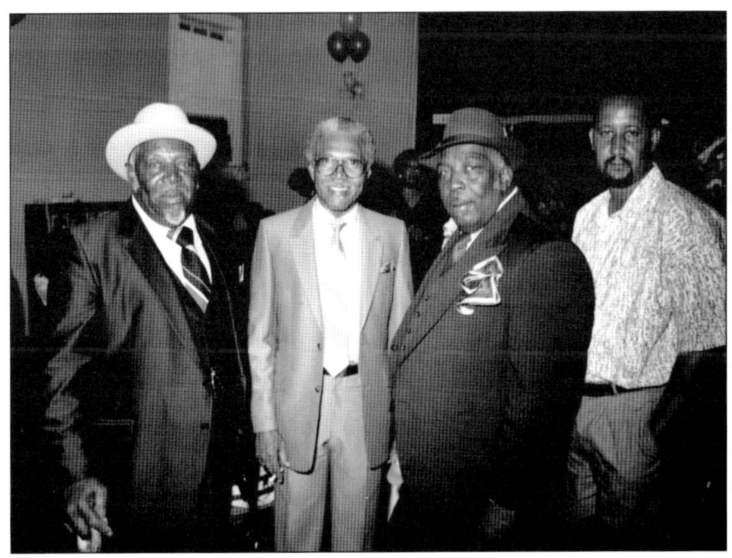

Alexander "Shack" Washington Jr. was born in 1921 and passed way in 2004. Shack continued in the footsteps of his father, managing the grocery store on Boyd Street during the 1950s and 1960s. In addition to this, he helped start the Big Red Machine team and served as its umpire. (Courtesy of Augustine Washington.)

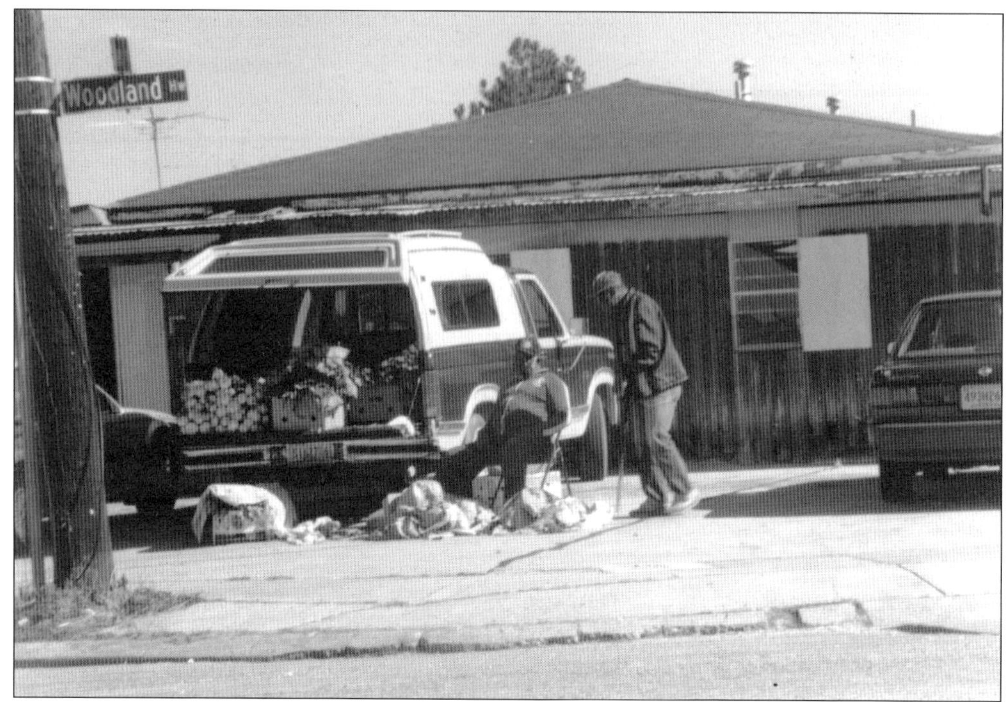

For many years, African Americans in the community worked with Italians in the area to continue farming fresh produce. The Italians owned much of the land but would allow African Americans in the Cut-Off to farm near the end of a plot near the canal, an area now known as Holly Park. Until the 1990s, it was not uncommon to find community members on the side of the road selling fresh foods from this garden and their personal gardens. (Courtesy of Veronica St. Cyr.)

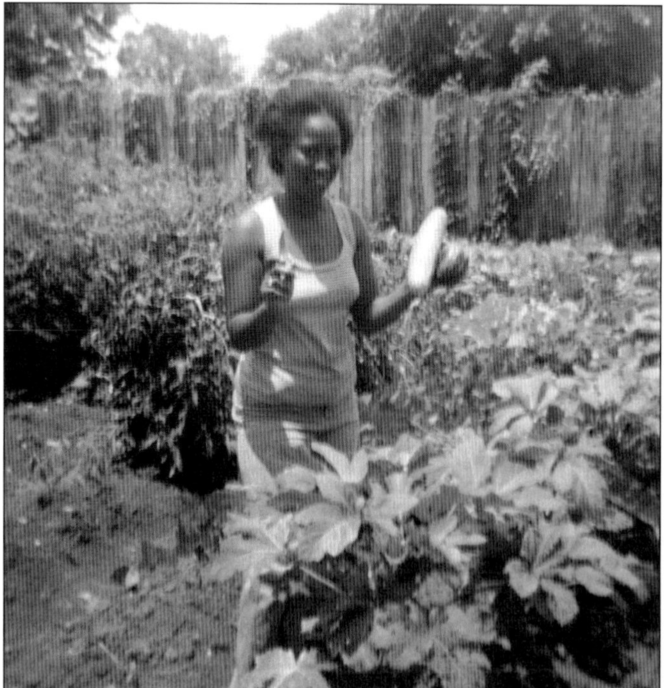

Enola Rose is pictured holding vegetables that were freshly picked from a garden in the community. The Cut-Off community once prided itself on being self-sufficient and things like gardening were often the means that allowed such independence. (Courtesy of Enola Rose.)

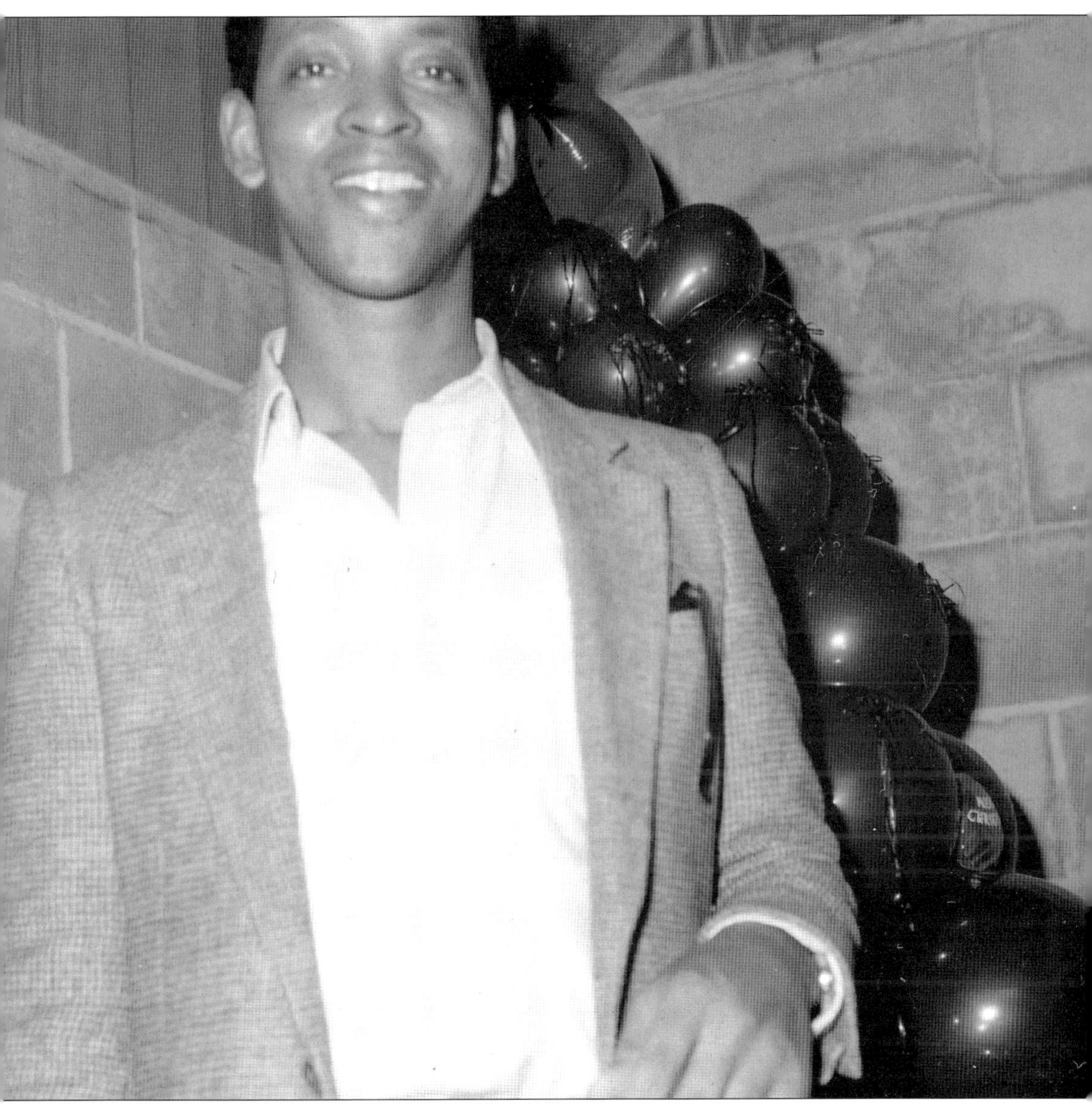

Charlie Benn Jr. was born in the Lower Coast of Algiers in 1952. From a very young age, Benn had an entrepreneurial spirit. In 1965, he was one of a few students who integrated Edna Karr School in the Algiers area. Despite the cruelty experienced, Benn went on to integrate Behrman School and later O.P. Walker High School in 1970–1971. The hostility that Benn often experienced in the society at the time motivated him to create parallel institutions for his community. His ventures began in 1976 when he became a photographer, which lasted until his equipment was stolen from his home in 1991. In 1980, he also began to invest in properties and remains a landlord today. (Courtesy of Charlie Benn Jr.)

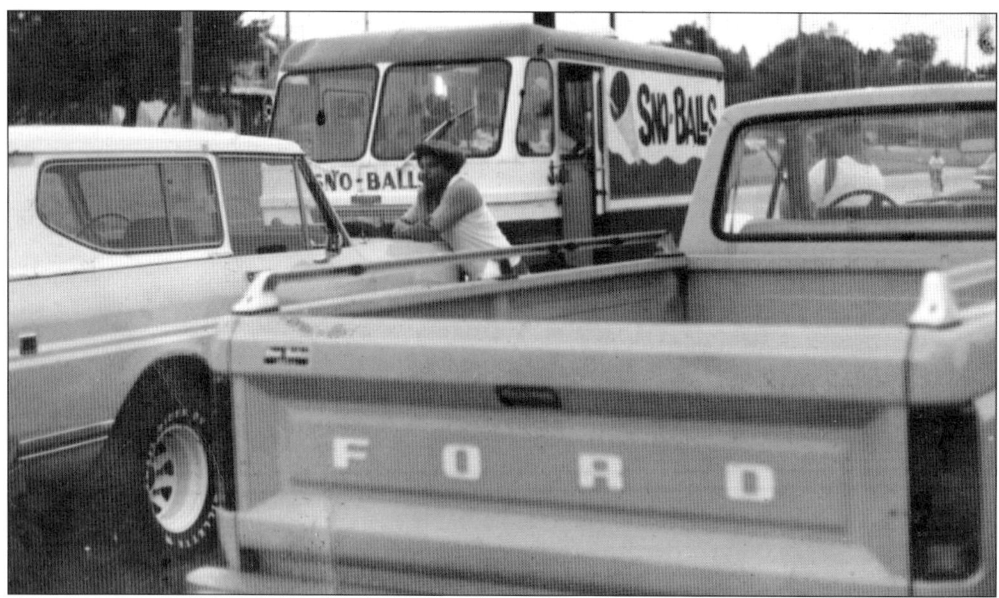

Snowball stands are very popular in the New Orleans area. Charlie Benn Jr. embarked on a path of entrepreneurship as a result of being reluctantly served due to the color of his skin. It was one particular incident that Benn recalled at a popular snowball stand as a child that gave him a burning desire to serve children of his community. Pictured here is the Sno-Ball truck that he owned in the 1970s. (Courtesy of Charlie Benn Jr.)

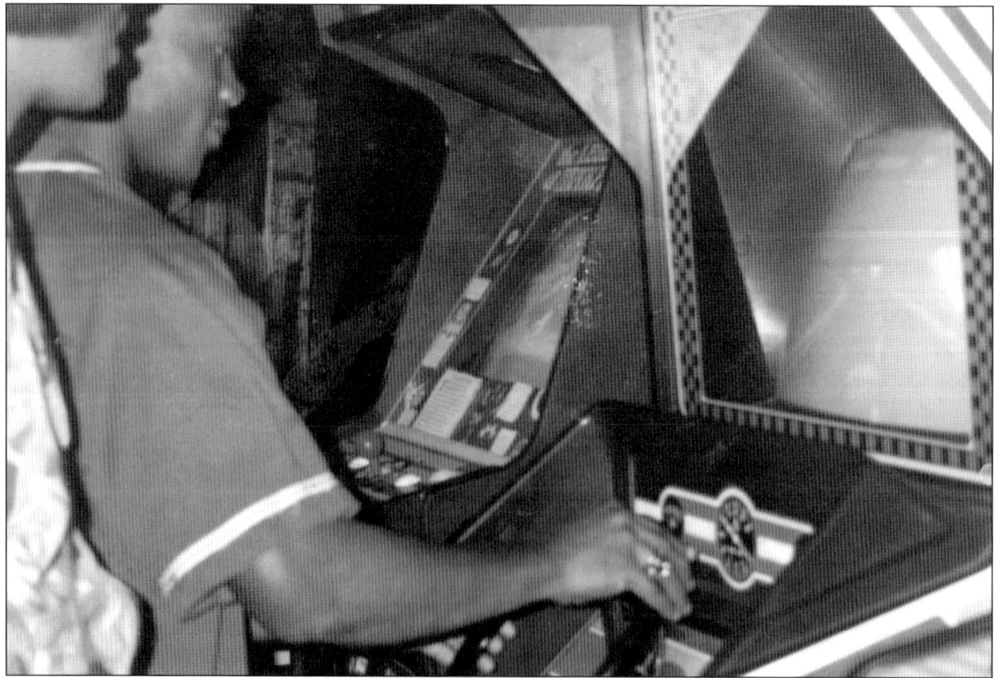
Coach Frank Wilson III is pictured playing a video game in Charlie Benn Jr.'s gaming center. At the time of the photograph, Benn's and Oakwood Mall were the only known places to have these gaming systems. In 1990, the video arcade room and snowball stand merged. Benn's was converted to the Frostop in 1995. (Courtesy of Gail Langford.)

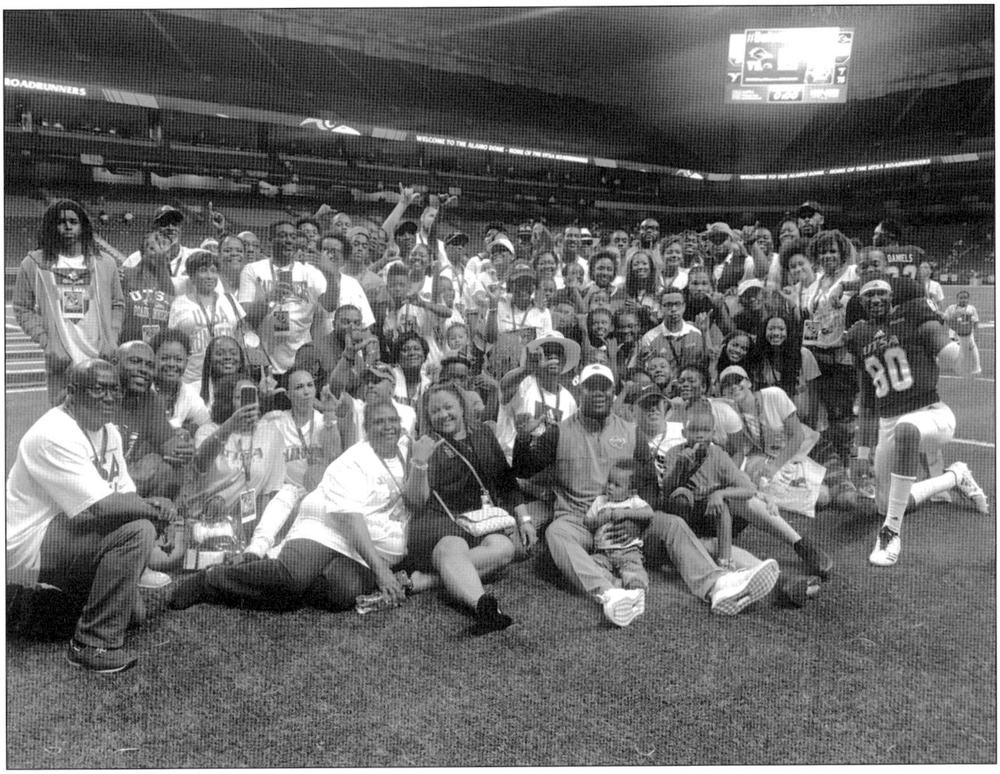

Coach Frank Wilson III is pictured with many members of the Lower Coast of Algiers community. He has won over the hearts of many in the community as he has inspired and opened doors for numerous natives to advance in society. Coach Wilson currently serves as the head football coach at the University of Texas at San Antonio. (Courtesy of Dari Green.)

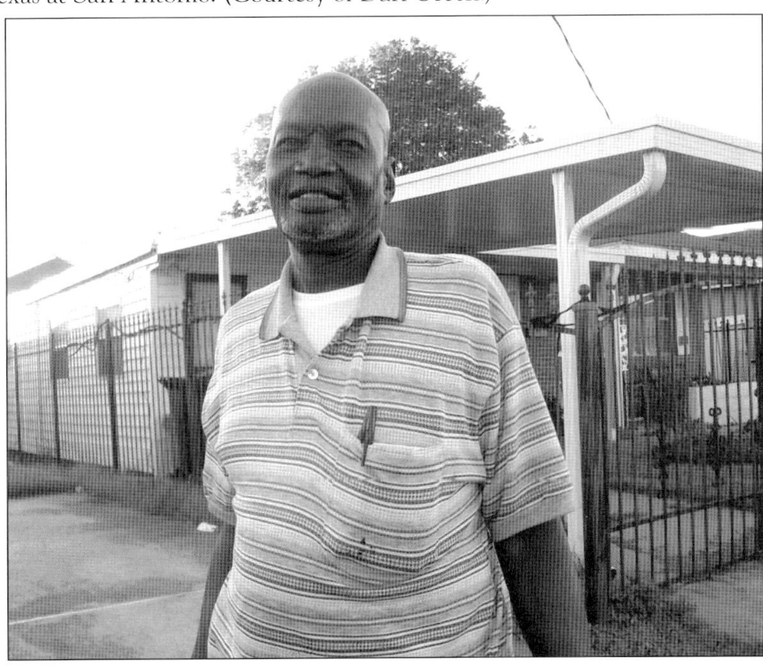

Raymond "Yankee" Gabriel was an entrepreneur in the area who owned a bar of his own. Yankee is pictured at Benn's Grocery, but two miles down the road, in what is often referred to as "the boondocks," Yankee and his father had their own place of business, Yankee's Bar. (Courtesy of Charlie Benn Jr.)

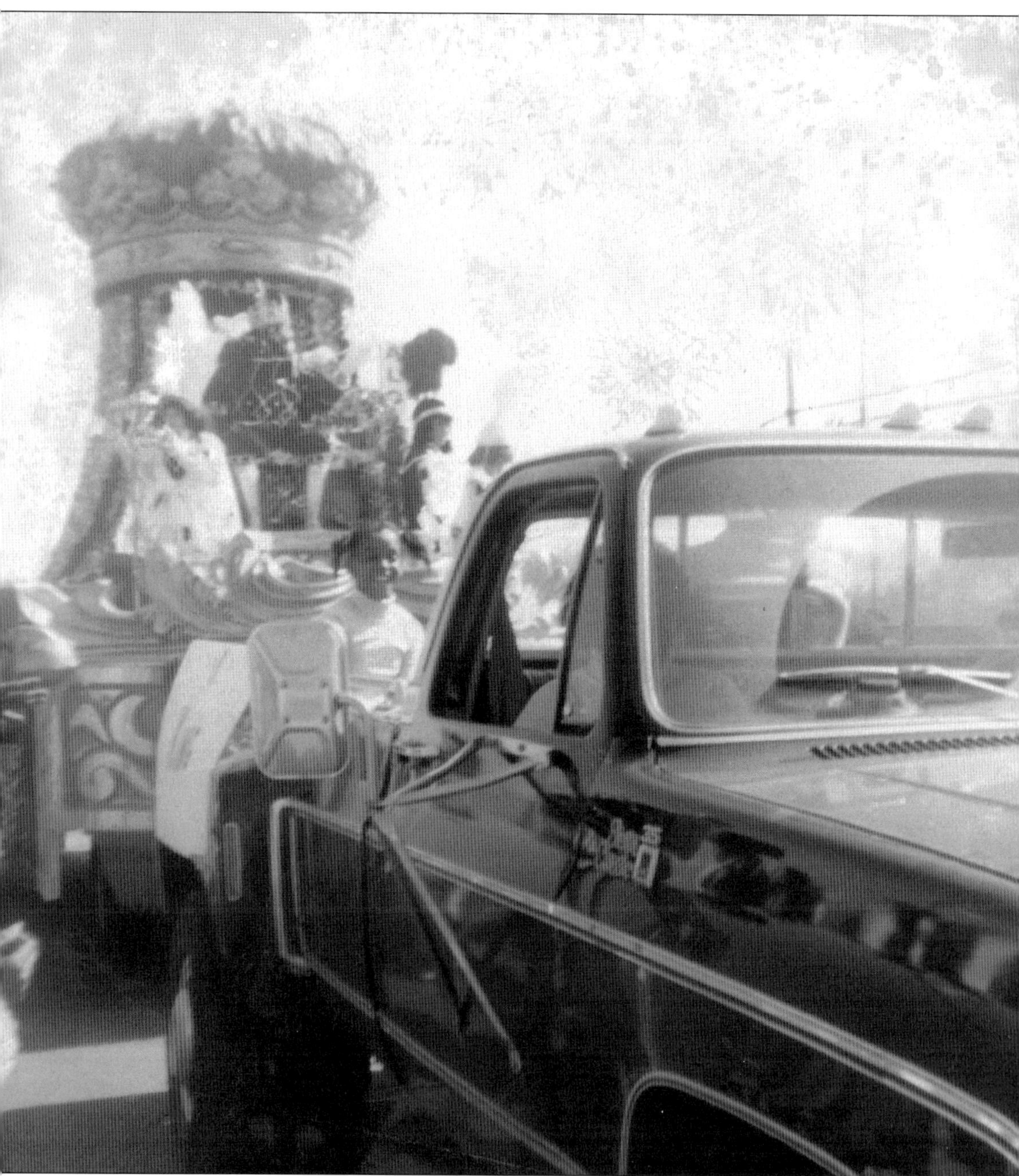

This photograph was taken during a NOMTOC (New Orleans's Most Talked of Club) parade in the 1970s. The only exclusively black parade in the Westbank, the NOMTOC parade currently begins its route at Holiday Drive and Fiesta Street. The Cut-Off had a parade of its own years before, but it ended after a couple of decades. (Courtesy of Bevelyn Manuel.)

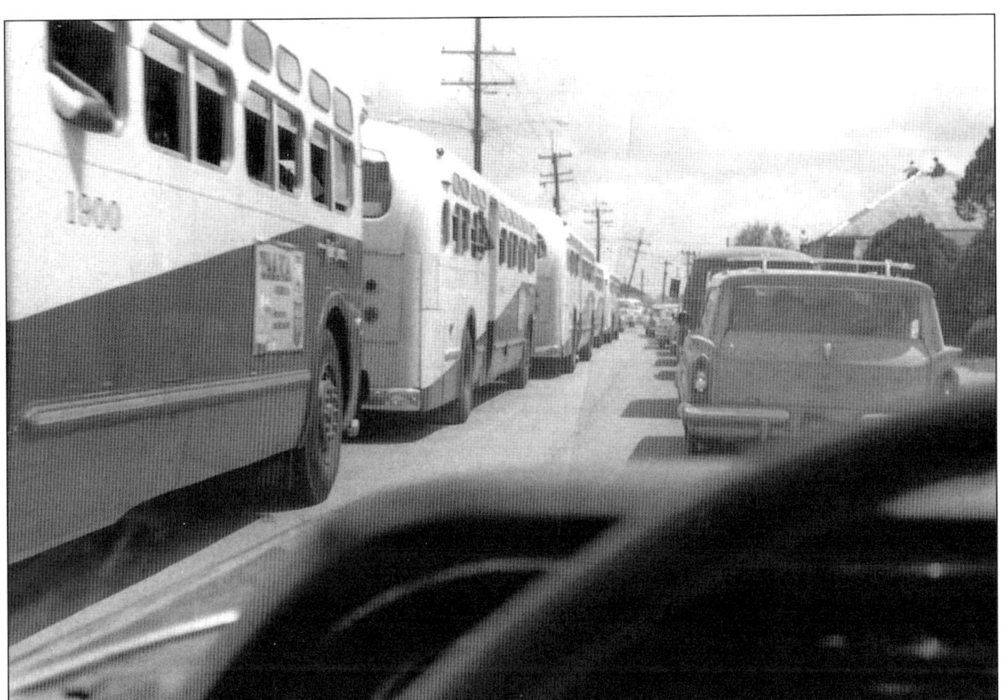

This photograph was taken in 1965 during the fright of Hurricane Betsy. The people of the Cut-Off community were being bused out in standstill traffic in an attempt to escape the expected damage from the storm. (Courtesy of Charlie Benn Jr.)

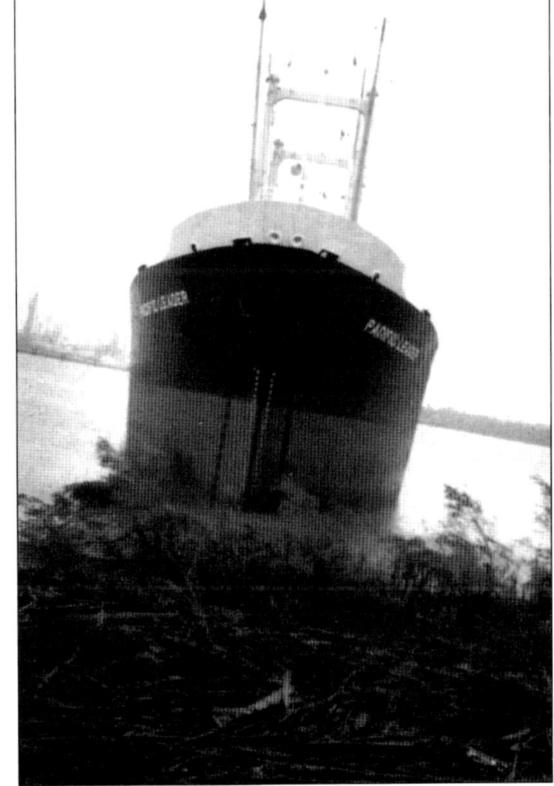

This photograph was taken from the levee near the Cut-Off community after Hurricane Betsy. The storm forced this vessel onto the coast with its brute-force winds. Betsy was one of the worst storms in New Orleans's history, but the Lower Coast of Algiers survived its damage (Courtesy of Charlie Benn Jr.)

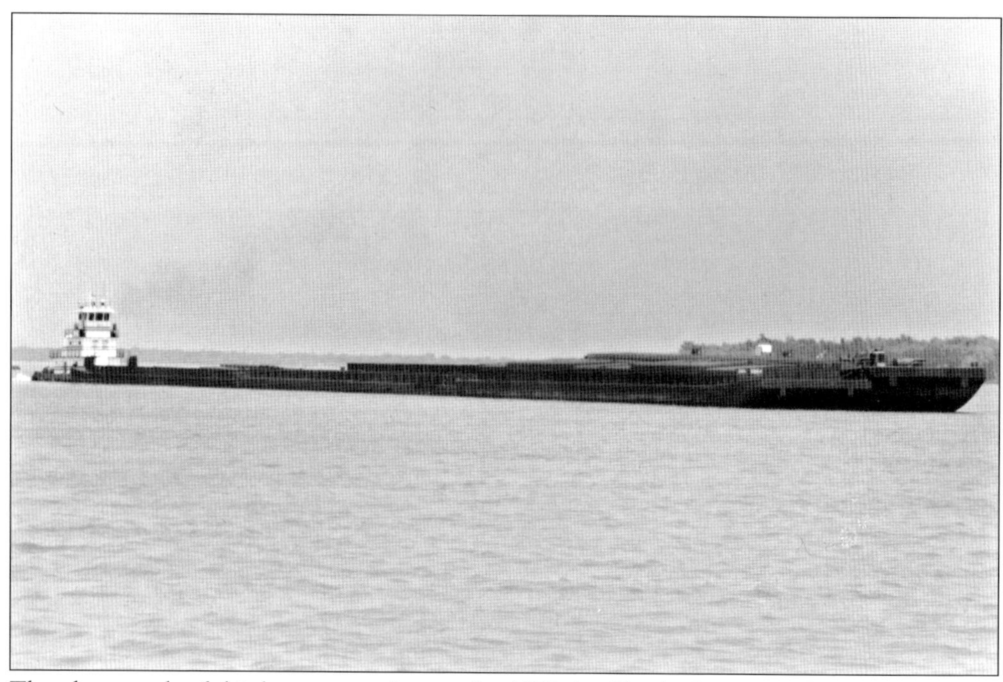

The photograph of this barge was taken in the 1970s by Charlie Benn Jr. The Lower Coast of Algiers is nestled along the Mississippi, separated only by a man-made levee. It is not uncommon to see massive vessels and shipments move up and down the river at any given time of day. (Courtesy of Charlie Benn Jr.)

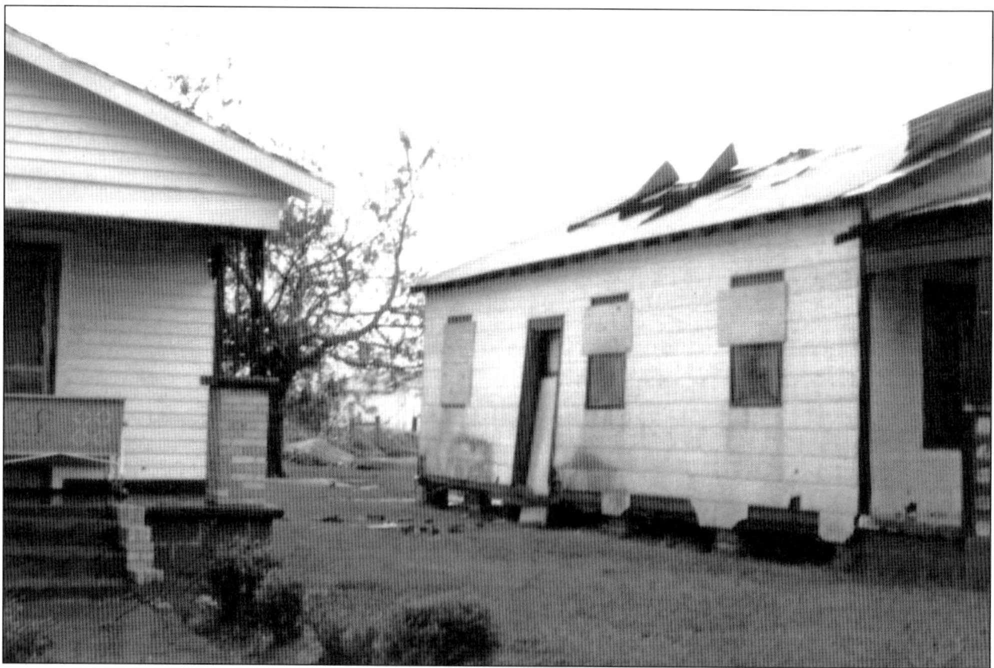

Captured in this image is a traditional home located in the Cut-Off community. This house, along with many others in the area, received extensive amounts of damage during Hurricane Betsy in 1965. (Courtesy of Charlie Benn Jr.)

The family home of Antoinette L. Jacobs was located on Boyd Street. Antoinette's three children—Mary, Martha, and Boyd Jacobs—were all raised in this house, as were 10 of her grandchildren. Antoinette lived to be 106 years of age and was self-sufficient until she was a century old. For an extended period of her life, in a small lot beside the home were small animals, including chickens and ducks, as well as fruits and vegetables that the family relied on for survival. (Both, courtesy of Leroy "Royal" Phoenix.)

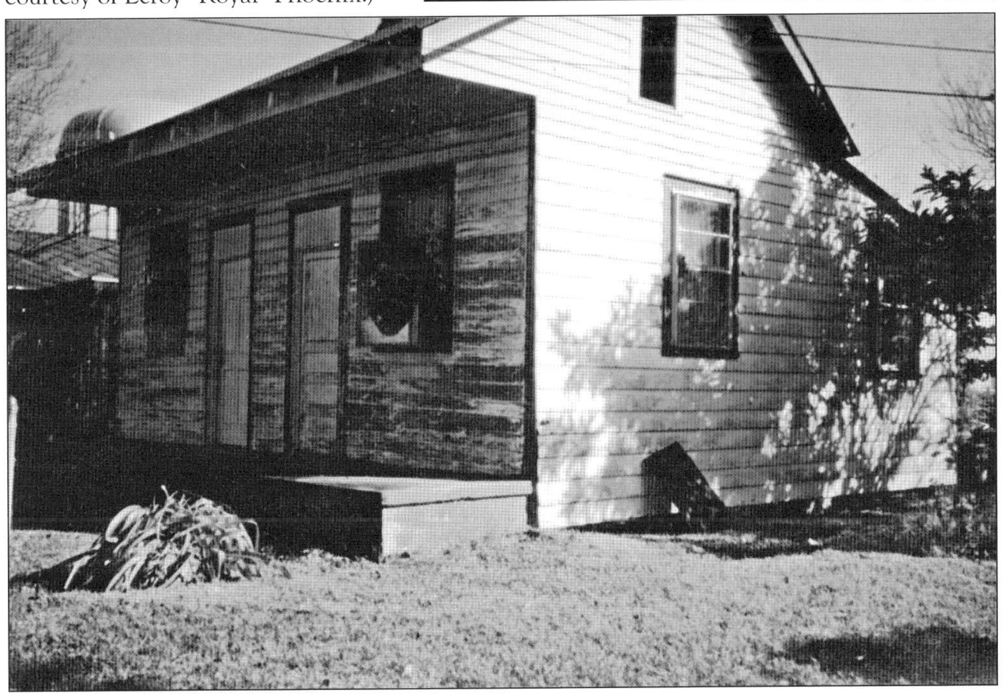

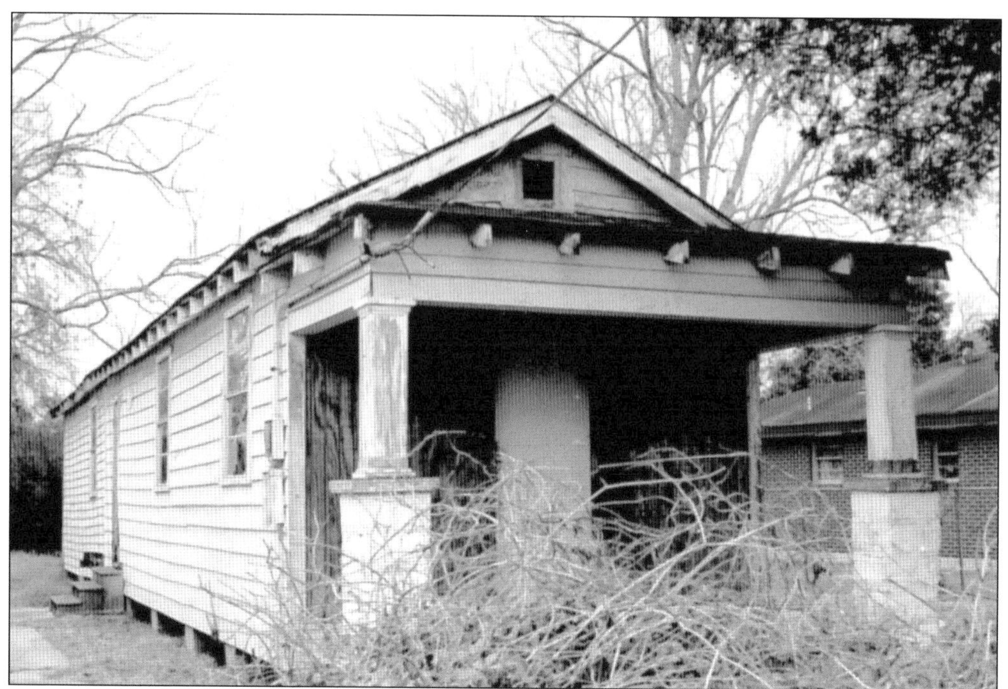

The family home of Lawrence and Orelia "Mama Felo" Johnson, this residence was located on Boyd Street. The home remained standing for many years but has now been demolished. The property is now owned by their great-grandson Dood Johnson III. (Courtesy of Robin Crawford.)

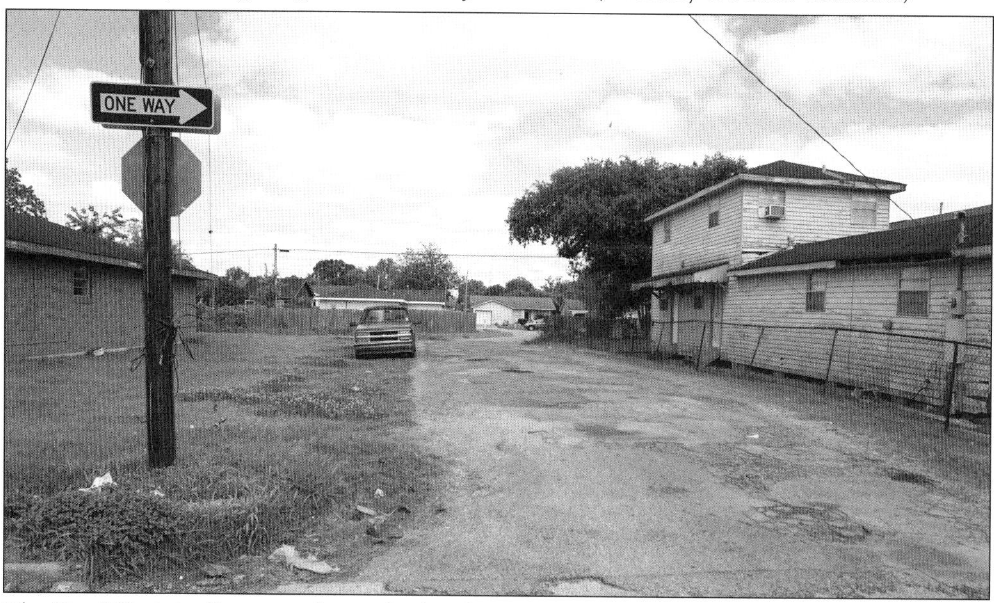

The Cut-Off originally was made up of only a few streets: Carver Street, Common Road, Casmiere Street, and Belgrade Street. Eventually, the community began to grow. Streets were added and some street names were changed in honor of iconic figures in the community. The village soon incorporated streets like Cut-Off Road, Common Street, Carver Street, Casmiere Street, Zion Street, Ernest Street, Belgrade Street, Ivory Street, and Isadore Street. This image shows a road that was added much later to extend the community. (Courtesy of Frederick Weil.)

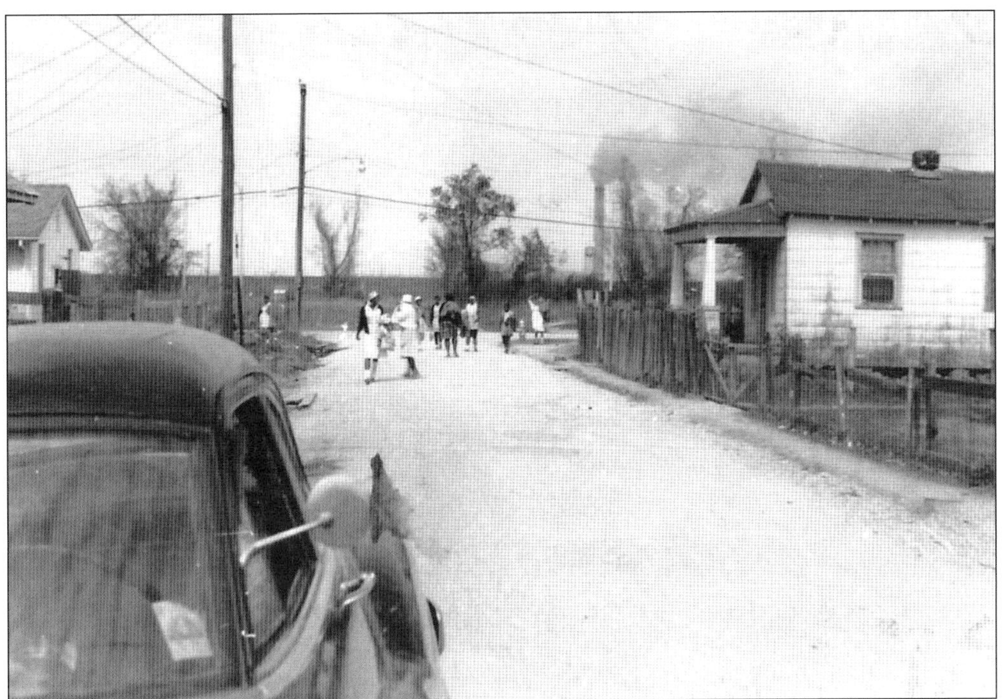

This 1950s image shows members of the community walking down unpaved streets to their homes. Further in the background is the Chalmette Refinery, which sits on the opposite bank of the Mississippi River. Pollution and unpaved streets were among items on a very long list of social ills that plagued the community at the time. (Courtesy of Charlie Benn Jr.)

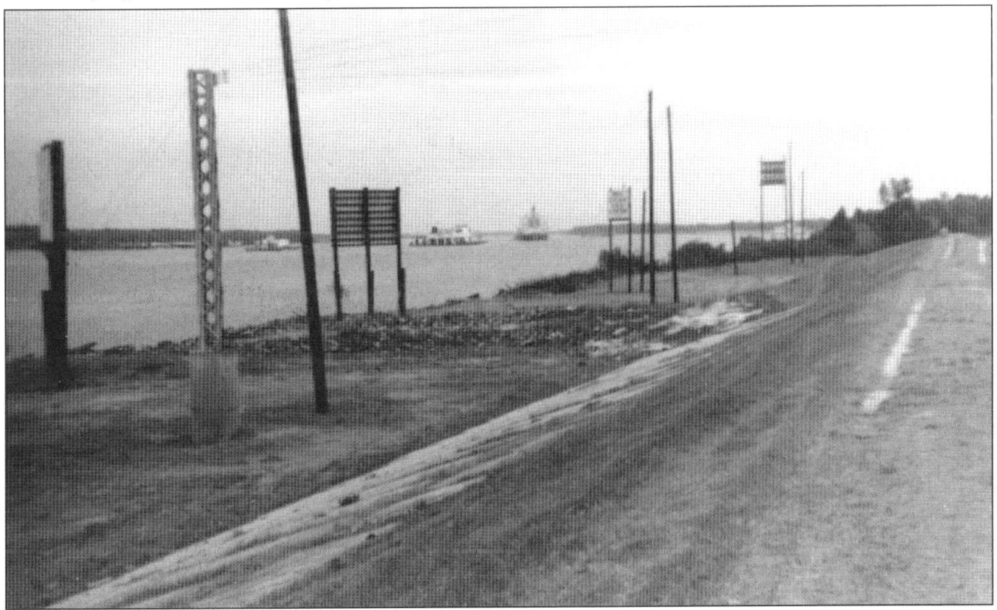

This photograph shows the levee that can be found running for miles and miles along River Road beside the Mississippi River. This levee was built to prevent flooding in the community and quickens the water flow to allow commercial products to move into the city. This image captures a ferry and several other vessels moving along the river. (Courtesy of Charlie Benn Jr.)

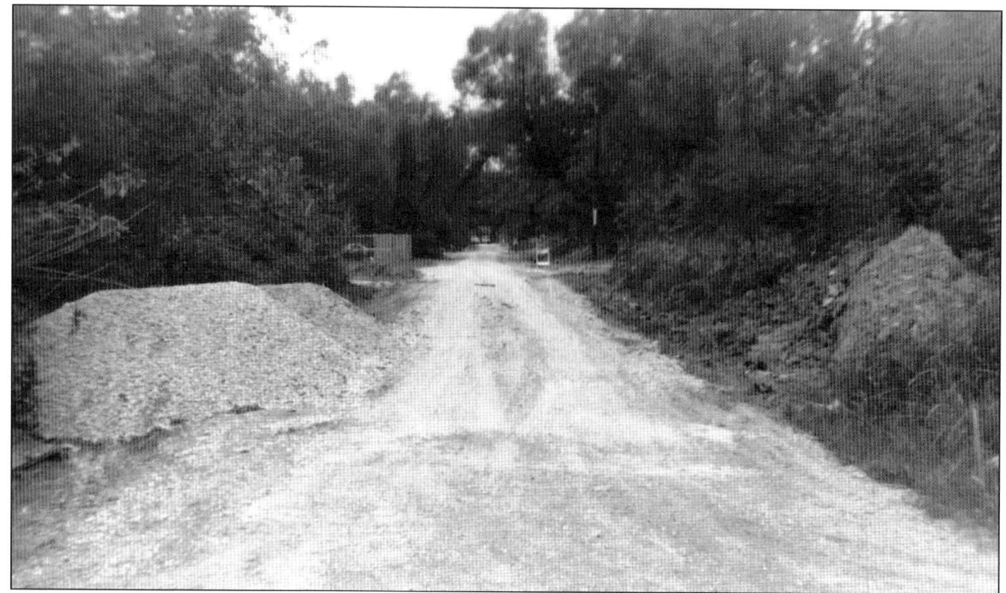

The Lower Coast of Algiers was historically distinguished from the other parts of town by the farms and dairies that eventually replaced land that was once devoted to sugarcane and cotton plantations. The Lower Coast of Algiers was noted for its fertile soil. Beyond these areas, however, some tracts would extend to forests and swamps. These areas were often referred to as "the boondocks." (Courtesy of Charlie Benn Jr.)

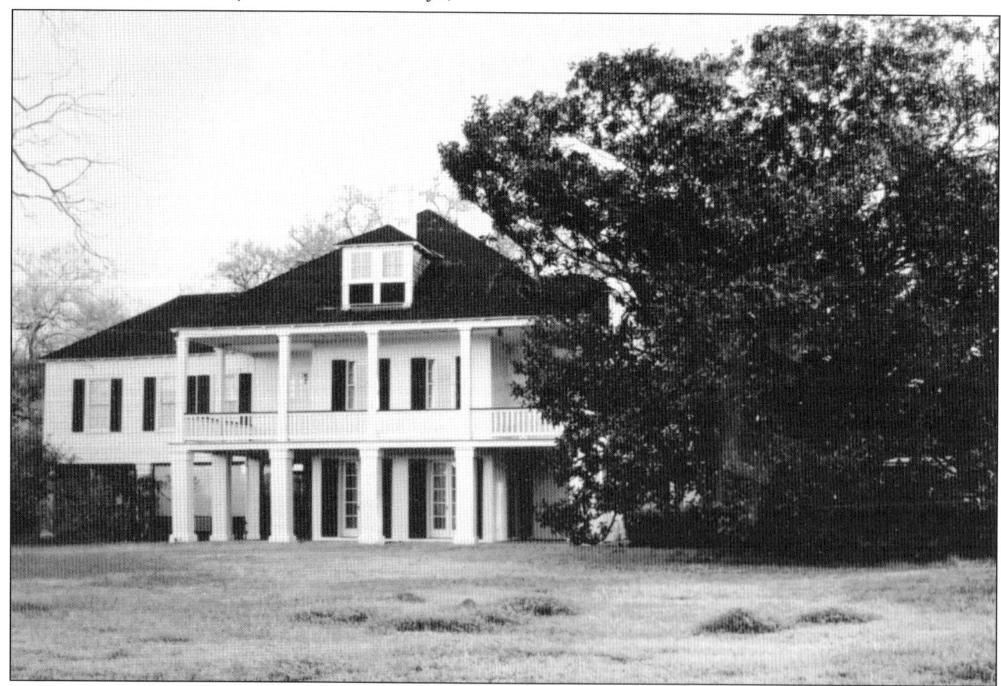

Agriculture played an important role in the Algiers economy throughout most of its history. As late as 1906, the Aurora, Stanton, and Norman plantations were still producing 5.3 million pounds of sugar between them. Pictured here is the Norman plantation, from which many of the original settlers of the area migrated. (Courtesy of Charlie Benn Jr.)

Coming a very long way from outhouses, basin tubs, and gravel roads, the Cut-Off community has made great strides toward equity: from its self-sufficient origins in which community members relied exclusively on one another for basic necessities, to the acquiescence of the city to provide street lighting, natural gas, and running water to the area; the cisterns and septic tanks that dominated society are now just a memory. Still, there is much to be desired. People who see this water tower in person know they have made it to the Lower Coast of Algiers. (Both, courtesy of Charlie Benn Jr.)

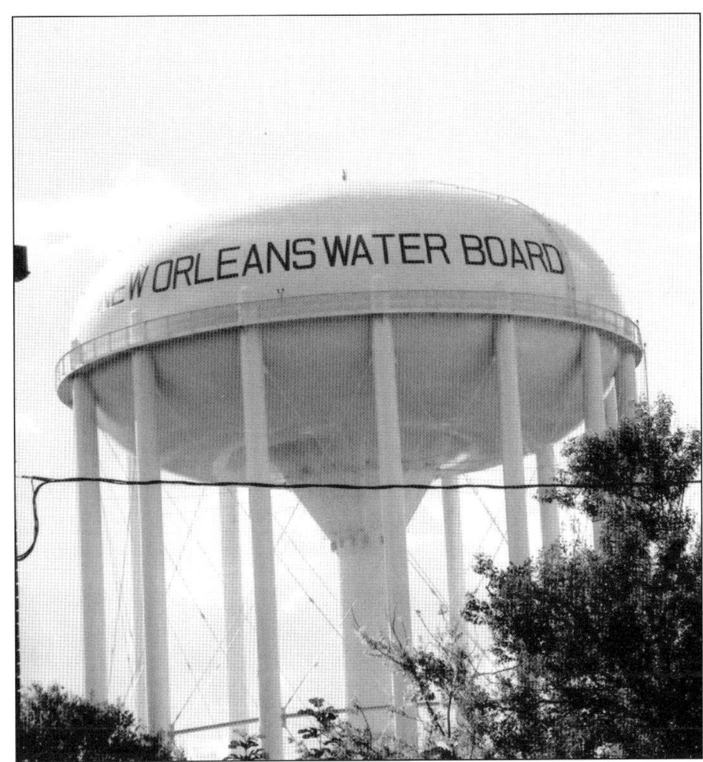

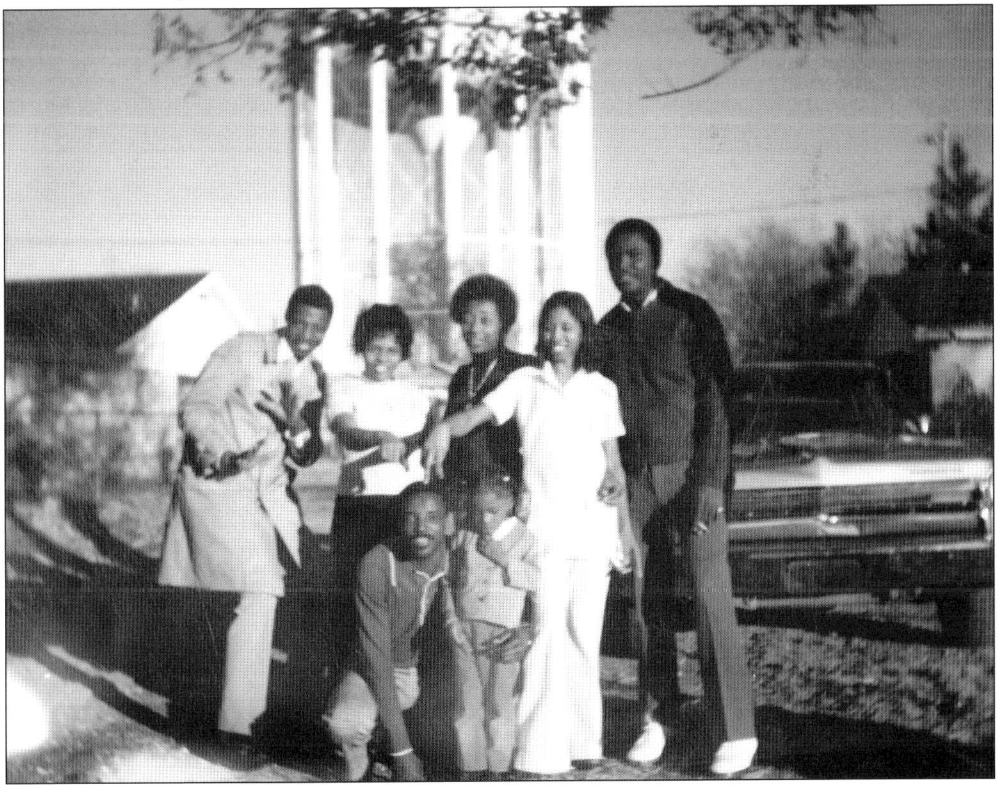